Family and Work in Rural Societies

FAMILY AND WORK IN RURAL SOCIETIES

Perspectives on non-wage labour

Edited by Norman Long

Tavistock Publications
London and New York

First published in 1984 by Tavistock Publications
11 New Fetter Lane, London EC4P 4EE

Published in the USA by
Tavistock Publications
in association with Methuen, Inc.
733 Third Avenue, New York, NY 10017

© 1984 Norman Long

Printed in Great Britain at the University Press,
Cambridge

British Library Cataloguing in Publication Data:
Family and work in rural societies.
1. Family farms—Social aspects
1. Long, Norman
338.6'42   HD1476.A3

ISBN 0-422-78480-X
ISBN 0-422-78490-7 Pbk

Library of Congress Cataloguing in Publication Data:
Main entry under title:
Family and work in rural societies
Bibliography: p.
Includes indexes.
1. Agricultural Wages—Case studies. 2. Agricultural
labourers—Case studies. 3. Peasantry—Case studies.
4. Rural families—Case studies. 5. Family farms— Case
studies. 6. Domestics—Case studies. I. Long, Norman.
HD4966.A29F35 1984   305'.9631   84-8759
ISBN 0-422-78480-X
ISBN 0-422-78490-7 (pbk.)

Contents

List of contributors

Norman Long Professor of Sociology of Development, Agricultural University, Wageningen.

Kathy R.G. Glavanis Lecturer in Social Anthropology, Birzeit University, West Bank.

Marit Melhuus Research Officer, Work Research Institute, Oslo.

Sarah Lund Skar Research Fellow, Department of Social Anthropology, University of Gothenburg.

Ray G. Abrahams Lecturer in Social Anthropology, University of Cambridge.

Tim Ingold Lecturer in Social Anthropology, University of Manchester.

Lucjan Kocik Lecturer in Rural Sociology, Uniwersytet Jagiellonski, Krakow.

Marie Johnson formerly Research Fellow, Department of Social Work Studies, University of Newcastle.

Alison M. Bowes Lecturer in Social Anthropology, University of Stirling.

Acknowledgements

The idea for this volume developed out of a Working Group on 'Non-wage remuneration and informal co-operation in rural society' which I organized for the XI Congress of the European Society for Rural Sociology held in Espoo, Finland, in August 1981. The general aim of the Working Group was to bring together scholars from different European countries to present findings on the role of non-wage labour in rural economies, focusing especially on the phenomenon of family farms and on peasant forms of social organization. Three theoretical issues were identified as central to the discussions: the question of the persistence of non-capitalist, small-scale agricultural enterprise within the framework of capitalist or market-oriented economies; the analysis of the changing roles of women within the context of the household division of labour; and the significance of inter-household and community-level patterns of co-operation and reciprocity. These aspects were to be examined from a broad comparative perspective, embracing not only European cases but also examples from the less industrialized countries.

The success of this venture is reflected in the publication of this volume. All but two of the case-study chapters were presented at Helsinki and later revised to take account of the comments made by members of the Working Group. The remaining two by Skar and Johnson were written especially for this book, although both had been involved in the idea of the Working Group from its conception. In fact Skar had participated in the Helsinki discussions and Johnson had sent an abstract of her contribution but was unfortunately unable to travel to Helsinki to attend the Congress.

One most rewarding aspect of the Helsinki meeting was that we were able to develop our discussions over a period of about three days which is most unusual for large international conferences. Each contributor was able therefore to present his or her ideas and have them fully discussed. This organizational format was conducive to the development of a lively exchange of views which formed the basis for this book. Our work was further assisted by the beautiful natural surroundings in which the Congress was held and by the excellent organizational support and hospitality we received from our Finnish hosts. We wish to thank them for all their help.

A special word of thanks must also be extended to Gavin Williams of St Peters College, Oxford, who read and commented extensively and so incisively on the manuscript. I and other contributors found his analytical and editorial advice most pertinent and stimulating, even though we were at times unable to resolve satisfactorily some of the points he raised.

The preparation of the manuscript for publication was carried out during the first two years of my new post at the Agricultural University in Wageningen, the Netherlands. Naturally, this was a very pressured time, especially as it entailed settling into a new environment and culture. However, fortunately I found myself in a most friendly and supportive working and living milieu. I am particularly appreciative of the assistance given by Nannie Brink, who has made every effort to keep me to deadlines and to help me create enough time to finish this volume. I also wish to express my gratitude to my wife, Ann, for the invaluable editorial work and personal support she has, as ever, given me.

Bennekom, April 1984   Norman Long

Introduction

Norman Long

This volume analyses forms of co-operation and the division of labour among rural producers in contrasting social contexts in both industrialized Europe and the less developed countries. A central theme concerns the character and significance of non-wage labour and the relationship between forms of paid and unpaid work in situations where local economic units are geared, directly or indirectly, to the market.

The 'survival' of non-wage forms and 'traditional' patterns of family and household organization in capitalist economies has been interpreted in various ways: as a transitional phenomenon that will eventually wither away as capitalist relations tighten their grip; as a structure with a logic of its own that resists the inroads of capitalist penetration; or as a system that is preserved by capitalism itself, but which selectively maintains certain non-capitalist elements because they are said to be either 'functional' or 'convenient' to its workings. A basic difficulty, of course, with this type of debate is that arguments are frequently posed in terms of either/or propositions in search of some universal validity. What we now know of agrarian transitions suggests that the issues involved are highly complex and require careful specification of the articulation of capitalist and non-capitalist forms placed within a broader analysis of the processes of economic and political incorporation (Goodman and Redclift 1981; Harriss 1982). The various contributions to this book underline the complexities involved in developing such an analysis.

The major emphasis in the volume is on examining labour processes within and between households and on showing how different local social structures and cultural frameworks underpin these varying organizational forms. While documenting the importance of wider structural factors, stress is placed upon the adaptive strategies developed by rural producers for solving their livelihood problems.

Several of the chapters express the view that the viability (or vulnerability) of production units and of the household economy depends upon the types of local, social and cultural resources available and how they are used.

Depending upon the circumstances, local structures and commitments may inhibit or undermine the continuity of farming or household units, or may provide the basis for a restructuring of economic life leading to satisfactory accommodation with the wider system. Non-capitalist relations of production can, therefore, only be 'functional' for capitalism, or meet the demands of the wider commercial economy, if their forms of labour organization, and the sets of social relationships and normative frameworks upon which they depend, can effectively meet their own internal reproductive needs. Peasant households or family farms are thus not simply reproduced by the workings of the wider structure but also depend upon the way existing cultural rules and social relationships affect access to and utilization of essential resources. These internal reproductive processes also influence people's work ethics and generate different types of social consciousness.

A central analytical challenge, then, is to explain the various adaptations that arise by showing how different dimensions intersect: for example, state development policies, the changing nature of the national economy and international commodity markets, the pattern of rural–urban relations, and the persisting (though possibly re-structured) local institutions and social processes.

Each contributor to this volume gives different attention and weighting to these factors. Two themes predominate: first, the role of non-wage labor and patterns of co-operation, and, second, the changing nature and social evaluation of women's work. The aim of this introductory chapter is to provide a general overview of the major issues raised and to show how the various contributions relate to these analytical problems.

THE SIGNIFICANCE OF NON-WAGE LABOUR
WITHIN CAPITALIST ECONOMIES

The persistence of non-capitalist relations of production within capitalist economies has long been recognized. However, there remain major theoretical difficulties in explaining this phenomenon. Marx (1867) himself concentrated his efforts on analysing the logic of industrial capitalism and failed to offer any adequate explanation for the continuance of non-capitalist labour relations in certain areas of the economy. Although, for example, he argued that reproduction of the working capacity of individuals was necessary in order that labour be made available to capitalist enterprise, he did not enter into an analysis of the household to show how unpaid domestic labour contributed to this process. Nor did he give attention to the continuing role played by simple commodity forms, which he treated as essentially 'transitory', merely preparing the path for the emergence of capitalist enterprise based on a strict separation of capital and labour. Luxemburg (1913) later developed the model of capitalist accumulation processes to take account of the exploitation of non-capitalist forms by the capitalist mode of production, but she saw this in terms of articulation with peripheral economies and not as an internal process.

Recent decades have witnessed a renewed theoretical interest in the role of non-wage labour in capitalist economies. This has occurred primarily with respect to two specific areas of research: the study of peasant and simple commodity forms of production,[1] and the study of unpaid domestic work and the sexual division of labour in the household. Let us briefly outline the discussions in these two fields.

The analysis of agrarian change

Research on the transformation of agrarian populations under the impact of wider economic forces has tended towards one of two contrasting interpretations.[2] The first view holds that, although the consequences of capitalist penetration may vary from society to society, there are nevertheless similar patterns in the ways in which agricultural and rural populations are affected. Hence it has been argued that the mechanization and commercialization of agriculture generates increased economic differentiation within the rural population, creating a relatively small entrepreneurial land-owning class and a growing agricultural proletariat or marginalized peasantry. Concomitant with this is a high rate of displacement of the rural population, as many individuals and families are forced to seek work outside agriculture, even if industry is unable to absorb fully this 'surplus' population. The classical works of Lenin (1899, on Russian agriculture) and Kautsky (1899, on Western European agrarian developments) raised important theoretical and methodological issues concerning this transformation process; and a number of researchers have explored the same problems in contemporary Third World contexts (see, for example, Bartra 1974; Arrighi and Saul 1973; Cliffe 1977; Archetti 1978; and Paré 1977).

A somewhat different interpretation stresses the need to understand certain persisting forms of peasant-type organization, such as the family farm, with its intensive use of non-wage household and extra-household labour (see Chayanov 1925; Nash 1968; Servolin 1972; Shanin 1973; and Vergopoulos 1978). This persistence is explained either in terms of the way in which capitalism selectively sustains certain forms of small-scale, peasant or simple commodity production, which cheapen the reproduction costs of labour for the capitalist sector (Meillassoux 1972, 1977; Wolpe 1972, 1975; De Janvry and Garramon 1977; Vergopoulos 1978; and Mann and Dickinson 1978), or in terms of a certain internal dynamic which generates social and cultural resistance to capitalism itself (Chayanov 1925; Foster 1965; Bradby 1982). A further attempt (Friedmann 1980) at explaining the predominance of simple commodity forms in modern agriculture emphasizes their competitive advantages over capitalist production:[3] there is no structural necessity for profit and therefore under intense competition it is possible, if necessary, to work harder and consume less in order to preserve the enterprise. If this is not feasible, then some members can seek wage work outside to supplement household income. Friedmann also emphasizes the important direct and indirect effects of state policy. Her example concerns the encouragement of settlement in North America of commercially-oriented, agricultural households through making available land, basic infrastructure, and credit (Friedmann 1978b: 582–86).

It is important to emphasize that both perspectives acknowledge the unevenness of change and the coexistence of different economic processes. They both work towards a refinement of conceptual categories so that one can specify more precisely the conditions under which depeasantization or proletarianization occur, or under which peasant or simple commodity forms of production continue to predominate. However, the conclusions they draw are rather different.

This is clearly seen, for example, when considering economic diversification at household level. The first perspective interprets diversification into agricultural and non-agricultural activities as evidence for a process of peasant decomposition whereby a growing proportion of the rural population is expelled from the countryside as the land base is unable to sustain or reproduce the household economy. In this situation, an increasing number of members of households, and indeed entire households, are forced to seek wage work outside agriculture. Thus, at a certain stage in the transition process, household economies may be expected to exhibit highly diversified and fluctuating combinations of economic activity. The second perspective treats diversification as an adaptive strategy contributing to the persistence and viability of small-scale agricultural production. For example, Archetti and Stølen (1975) have shown how diversification of crop production is fundamental to the successful operation of family farms in Argentina, and Long and Roberts (1978a: 297–328) have argued, for the Mantaro Valley of Peru, that the survival of the peasant household has depended upon the creation of new forms of work in the mining, commercial, and urban sectors of the regional economy.

A fundamental difference between these two types of interpretation is the way in which land enters into the equation. For those who propound the 'decomposition' argument, stress is placed on the vulnerability and productive insufficiency of smallholder agriculture, which leads in the long term to a mass exodus from the countryside. This view focuses upon the precariousness of economic life for the bulk of the rural population and regards off-farm wage employment as a critical factor for the transformation of the peasant economy. Hence, it is common to find small plot-holding families described as a 'disguised', 'concealed', or 'semi' proletariat (see Paré 1977; Mintz 1974; Banaji 1977 and Roseberry 1978), thus asserting the priority of relationships involving wage labour over other social relations of production.

In contrast, the second approach concerns itself more with an analysis of the nature and continuity of peasant or simple commodity forms of organization and treats access to land as a central element. This perspective, while acknowledging the tendency towards increasing diversification into non-agricultural activities, emphasizes the primary role that agricultural production plays. Non-agricultural work is viewed as essentially supplementing the farm income, and therefore ancillary to the farming component, around which the life experiences and social commitments of the members of the household are, for the most part, formed (see Galeski 1972). This latter point is particularly important since it has sometimes been suggested that it is this independent control and attachment to land and to farming as a primary occupation that produces resistance to the introduction of certain state-initiated development schemes (e.g. integrated rural development and rural industrialization programmes). It has also been argued that, because of the central part played by the family farm, there is a reluctance of household members to commit themselves fully to external types of relationship, for example, as participants in an industrial labour force (see, e.g. Laite 1981; DeWind 1977; Roberts 1978).

Both approaches identify and attempt to explain important processes of change and continuity among agrarian populations. The depeasantization/proletarianization argument raises important issues concerning the formation of class structures that are integral to the process of capitalist expansion and accumulation in agrarian economies, and attempts to isolate the historical forces that have generated particular processes of socio-economic differentiation. On the other hand, peasantization studies have made important contributions towards delimiting more precisely the internal dynamics of the small-scale sector, and towards the analysis of the household as a unit of production and consumption. This has involved considering such dimensions as the division of labour within the household in relation to family size and stage in the life cycle; and the definition of the types of cognitive orientation and economic rationality characteristic of smallholders, including what has been described as the tendency to 'over-exploit' their own labour (Chayanov 1925; Franklin 1969; Harrison 1977). However, this approach tends to present too homogeneous a picture of the peasantry and to explain changes in the composition and economic organization of the household mainly in terms of internal demographic and social processes, thus neglecting the impact of forces external to the household unit itself. This perspective can also be criticized for unduly separating the small-scale sector from the broader changes occurring in agriculture and in the national economy (Bartra 1974). It likewise under-emphasizes the part played by non-agricultural activities (e.g. trade, transport, craftwork, and the services), migration to urban areas, and involvement in wage labour for the 'survival' of the peasant household or family farm. A central feature of this approach is that it treats the farm as the core element structuring economic decisions and household organization.

My brief review of these contrasting approaches is necessarily schematic. However, it points to the need to take a much closer look at the relationship to land, and at the relative weight which non-agricultural activities, including wage labour, have within various types of households and within different social strata of the rural population. In order to do this, one must start with the premise that rural society is differentiated in terms of economic opportunity, size, and social composition of households, and access to land, labour and other resources. One then needs to explore the part played by land in the operation of types of household economy.[4] From this point of view, access to land will not only figure differently for households of different size and economic orientation but will also mean something different to the individual members themselves. Indeed, the precise combinations of diverse income-generating activities require detailed investigation in order to determine which activities constitute the central elements in the running of the household economy.[5] One would expect to find a wide range of possible patterns – from a situation where the household plot constitutes the major source of income for the family to one where land becomes subordinate as a source of income in relation to various non-agricultural activities. Furthermore, these two situations may be identical in terms of the size and quality of their land bases and in terms of the demographic and labour composition of the households, yet nevertheless represent different livelihood solutions, as shown by the different combinations of non-agricultural activities engaged in, and with respect to the social commitments, relationships, and ideological orientations of the members of the households concerned.

This type of analysis requires close examination of cropping systems, the degree of intensification of agriculture, the availability of various types of labour, and the possibilities for earning income from the sale of crops. It may also be important to consider the relationship that smallholder agriculturalists have with larger-scale, more commercialized agricultural enterprise in the region, as well as their integration or subordination to systems of credit, marketing, and technical inputs (see, e.g. Scott 1976; Taussig 1978; Davis 1980). Moreover, as I have already emphasized, land utilization is affected by the existence of other sources of employment and income open to the family, and by the career and social aspirations of its members. The identification of particular patterns, then, entails a careful analysis of the internal characteristics of the households in question, as well as an appreciation of the ways in which these and their individual members respond to and manage external resources and relationships. These are complex problems which are best explored through a systematic examination of the part played by agricultural production within the overall strategies of households who make up the different rural social strata.

The analysis of peasant farm/household dynamics requires close attention to patterns of inter-household co-operation. Chayanovian and similar household models of peasant economy have frequently stressed the independence of the household unit, thus minimizing the importance of links with other households and of patterns of co-operation or exchange at the wider village, locality, or regional levels. These inter-household exchanges are critical for the viability of household livelihood strategies and for the reproduction of this type of agrarian economy. However, co-operation is double-edged: it can serve to protect the peasant household from losing its relative independence in the face of market forces and increasing state control, whilst at the same time it may serve to promote the interests of the richer peasant class, which is usually better placed to manipulate exchange relationships, and in this way it may contribute to processes of socioeconomic differentiation. Furthermore, the state itself may play a part in strengthening the role of community and inter-household co-operation through the passing of legislation in favour of the interests of peasant communities or smallholder property owners. This, in turn, furthers processes of political incorporation.[6] The examination of inter-household co-operation, then, becomes a central issue in the analysis of capitalist expansion and state–peasant relations.

Whilst the contributions to this volume can in no way claim to meet this huge research agenda, each chapter explores various of these dimensions in relation to specific field data.

The social value of labour

The discussion of non-wage labour in peasant and simple commodity forms of production has recently been linked to the question of unpaid domestic work. Bennholdt-Thomsen (1981), for example, has argued that peasant labour and housework have in common the commitment to 'subsistence' activities aimed at the reproduction of human capacity and the maintenance of a labour force which, simultaneously or serially, works for capitalist enterprise or which, in the case of the peasant household, may also produce goods for sale in capitalist markets. Hence 'it would be wrong to consider the production of use-values as being outside the capitalist mode of production, even though at first sight it may not seem to be integrated into generalized exchange relations' (Bennholdt-Thomsen 1981: 19). It follows from this that it is incorrect to regard these types of non-wage labour as belonging to another 'domestic' or 'peasant' mode of production that articulates with the capitalist mode. Capital cannot operate without subsistence production since the goods and labour power it appropriates are based upon previous expenditure of labour which takes place within the household. The use-value of peasant production is converted, through marketing, into exchange-value; and the same principle holds for domestic labour when use-value is transformed into exchange-value at the moment when labour power is sold. Although there may be a considerable time-lag between the production of use-value and its realization as exchange-value, the chain of conversion nonetheless exists.[7] According to Bennholdt-Thomsen, this means that the domestic production of housewives (and probably that of peasants as well) is subordinated to capital and 'to capitalist valorization of their labour'.

This conversion process is concealed by the subjective evaluations placed upon household work by the housewife and other household members who do not normally think of the domestic labour process as producing commodity labour power. And, in the same way, the peasant producer does not calculate abstractly, or in advance, the exchange-value of his products, since in the first instance he is interested in use-value. Bennholdt-Thomsen argues that in capitalist society there exists a series of ideological mechanisms which function to mask the process by which use-value is produced and later converted into exchange-value: for example, the ideology of familial affection and the woman's commitment to the idea of working for the well-being of husband and children.

Bennholdt-Thomsen's discussion constitutes one of the clearest attempts to show how non-wage household labour contributes to capital accumulation through the provisioning of labour power for capitalist production. She emphasizes that there is a basic contradiction within all capitalist economies due to the separation of subsistence from capitalist production, but that the former is essentially necessary for the accumulation process. In many ways, her analysis is reminiscent of that of Bernstein (1977) who attempts to demonstrate how peasant labour in peripheral economies is subsumed within the wider capitalist system. Bernstein shows how the intensification of commodity relations among household producers through the sale of peasant produce and labour power makes such households more and more dependent upon capital for their reproduction; but that this does not necessarily destroy the household form of production. On the contrary, it seems to be in the interests of capital and the state to maintain peasant forms of production providing they can exercise some control over what is produced and can appropriate a significant proportion of the surplus, leaving the peasant with no more than a bare subsistence wage. Hence, according to Bernstein, many peasants can be regarded as 'wage-labour equivalents', since the logic of peasant forms of labour can only be understood in relation to how capital superimposes its own mechanisms of control.

A major implication of Bennholdt-Thomsen's analysis is that one can formulate a general model of capitalist economies that takes theoretical account of the necessary internal existence of non-capitalist elements. She does not aim to elucidate the differences between societies and contexts where different non-wage forms are found. In fact the question of differences between these forms is not a central concern to her since she is sketching the general logic of extended capitalist reproduction, not explaining historically-specific cases. It follows from this, then, that she pays no attention to the cultural dimension, apart from the brief discussion of ideological mechanisms which function to conceal the basic processes of capitalist exploitation. Nor does she examine the specific adaptive strategies adopted by particular households or housewives aimed at maximizing income flows or at minimizing the drudgery of domestic work.

She approaches the problem of understanding non-wage labour from Marx's labour theory of value. According to Marx, a key characteristic of capitalist economies is that all goods and services acquire the character of 'commodities' such that their social origins (i.e. the social relations of production involved in producing them) are ignored, and only their 'thing-like' qualities are described. Hence the economy is supposed to run on the basis of the exchange of commodities, with profit being created through the manipulation of prices and through capital increasing in value, rather like a tree bearing fruit (Taussig 1980: 32). Marx demonstrates that this line of reasoning is a mystification of the fundamental process by which goods and services are produced through a specific set of social relations of production, which in a capitalist society involve a basic distinction between owners and non-owners of the means of production. As I suggested earlier, Marx's analysis concentrates upon the *typical* form in which capitalist surplus extraction occurs (i.e. on the way in which the capitalist-owner class appropriates the surplus value of workers). Marx did not, however, extend his analysis to explicate the mechanisms by which non-capitalist relationships and social processes in the family contribute to the creation of the essential labour power of workers deployed in capitalist production and servicing activities; nor did he provide a thorough analysis of non-capitalist forms of commodity production. Bennholdt-Thomsen's discussion of domestic and peasant labour tries, then, to indicate how one might extend Marx's labour theory of value, which aims to explain and measure exploitation under capitalism, to include 'subsistence' work.

Her discussion can be criticized from a number of points of view. While Marx certainly acknowledged the importance for the capitalist mode of production of the privatized reproduction of the labouring class by means of the family-household, he did not demonstrate a direct and necessary link between wage and non-wage labour processes. Indeed there appears to be no theoretically satisfactory way of using the labour theory of value to account for domestic labour and its characteristics, or to establish the socially necessary labour time that enters into the value of the product it produces. As West (1980: 176) has argued, 'There is no way of competition between domestic units minimizing the labour time embodied, and no tendency towards the equalization of working conditions among housewives compensated or matched by differences in their "pay" (their part of the wage)', as found with capitalist enterprise. It also is difficult to show how fluctuations in the price of labour power (wage) might affect the performance of domestic labour (Smith 1978: 204–05). It is therefore analytically impossible, it seems, to demonstrate precisely how unpaid domestic labour is subordinated to capitalist valorization processes, as Bennholdt-Thomsen claims. It becomes difficult then to explain non-capitalist relations of production simply by reference to capitalist principles. These arguments apply not only to domestic household labour but also to peasant forms of production. Another related point is that if one concentrates on subsumption one is likely to miss the important ways in which non-wage, non-capitalist forms (and their supporting institutional structures) resist the penetration of commodity relations or transform them in some way in accordance with existing non-capitalist principles.[8] Bennholdt-Thomsen assumes that, in the end, exchange value is produced and that all these non-wage forms have simply contributed to the process.

A further problem is that, unlike Marx, her analysis gives little consideration to the actual social forms associated with different types of production and reproduction. Had she done so she would have made more of the difference between unpaid housework among working-class families, who possess no means of subsistence independent of the wage, and peasant households that incorporate many different kinds of unpaid labour and can often survive without direct recourse to the market. As Mackintosh (1979) emphasizes, household labour must also be seen in relation to existing cultural norms and values concerning the sexual division of labour, the obligations of marriage, and the expectations of family and kin. It may be correct to regard people's conceptions of the social relations they are involved in (in the family or factory) as in some senses cultural mystifications of patterns of exploitation but, from another standpoint, one can argue, as most anthropologists would, that the social perceptions and symbolic meanings which actors attach to their social relationships are just as valid a guide to the understanding of social process as are imposed analytical concepts, whether these be based on Marxist theory or on neo-classical economics.[9] Certainly, if one wishes to achieve a deeper understanding of the social relations of production within specific economic units, then one should attempt to gauge the social estimation of the value of the labour in question as expressed by the individuals, groups, or classes involved. The relations between men and women in the home or on the farm (or those between worker and capitalist in the factory) cannot adequately be comprehended if one concentrates solely upon the problem of subsumption within the logic of capitalism.

This latter point is well illustrated by Skar in Chapter 2 of this book and by Bradby (1982) who write about Peruvian highland communities. They recognize that remote peasants in the Peruvian Andes are part of a framework based upon capitalist principles. From time to time the peasants engage in wage labour at the mines or large agricultural estates, and use money as a medium of exchange for certain basic necessities.[10] However, in certain important respects, the subsistence side of their economy and the social relations within the family-household context remain governed by principles other than those of the capitalist market.

Skar shows, for example, how non-wage labour exchanges in the community she studied express social relationships relating to village organization and are not, directly or indirectly, affected by monetary values or rewards. Strong attitudes exist against offering wages or claiming wage benefits for working in the maize fields with some neighbour or kinsman, or for contributing to communal work projects such as the building of the village school. Even when labour is hired for a daily wage (*jornal*), which occasionally happens, it seems that the money paid over functions to oblige the worker to reciprocate at a later date: 'In reality the same money, bills and coins, are often paid back and forth, and it seems that the money is rather kept as a security than as a currency for buying and selling' (H.O. Skar 1982: 215).

Differing values are placed on labour depending on whether it relates to the subsistence or wage side of the economy. The latter is closely identified with the haciendas in the nearby valley region where men work regularly for a daily wage. But wage labour still functions as a factor in the subsistence economy, since it is through working on the hacienda that access to necessary additional agricultural land for subsistence is obtained. Skar goes on to argue that money, in fact, has a kind of utilitarian value: it enables peasants to satisfy certain consumption requirements which must be purchased at shops or from traders. Yet subsistence crops, like maize, potatoes and grains, are generally not sold for cash and there is a strong normative rule against doing so. Only livestock are sold, but then not in the central market places of the region but to travelling itinerant traders. In the village context, money also carries with it a special supernatural quality: coins are part of the offerings made to highland spirits and, in many situations, they act to communicate with these spirits.[11] Inter-household exchange of agricultural produce is linked to notions of reciprocity and community and should not therefore be tainted with monetary associations. Nevertheless, both the subsistence and monetary spheres of the economy are essential for the survival of these peasant households and are intricately intertwined.

Bradby's account is similar. She shows the vitality of non-monetary forms of exchange in Central Peru and stresses that these are not hostile to the workings of capitalism but work in tandem with the market and capitalist forces. Also, like Skar, she observes that the presence of money is not necessarily indicative of capitalist production relations (Bradby 1982: 121).

A similar point is made by Long and Roberts (1978b) when referring to another Andean case: *minka* exchange between households who receive payment in kind or money for the labour they contribute to specific tasks, such as helping with the harvesting, or roofing a house, 'is not, strictly speaking, wage labour partly because some subsistence is always provided, but also because *minka*. . . is part of a community-wide set of reciprocal obligations' (Long and Roberts 1978b: 312). In other words, it does not take place within the context of a market for labour which is 'free' and receives a fixed wage. Another way of saying this is to argue that non-capitalist institutions act to restructure the monetary elements introduced into the system, and so as long as peasants retain a relatively independent basis for the operation of their economic affairs, then capitalist relations and principles will not prevail in all situations. Non-capitalist forms are not, of course, outside the capitalist framework but represent the way in which local or subordinate social structures mediate the effects of capitalist penetration.

Taking this point of view, it becomes critical to develop a more adequate analysis of the different ways in which non-capitalist structures interrelate with, and impinge upon, capitalist forms. To do this requires that we look closely at the character and potentialities of existing non-capitalist forms and institutions, both in developing countries and in those parts of European societies where such relationships persist.

An anthropological approach to this problem, giving emphasis to both actor perceptions and strategies, as well as to defining socio-cultural frameworks, is clearly important. This point has been force-fully made by various authors writing of the need to take cognizance of the cultural and ideological dimensions of domestic labour, whether this be in reference to peasant or industrial situations. For example, after reviewing alternative frameworks for analysing problems of sexual subordination, Bourque and Warren (1981) argue for the integration of a social ideology and class analysis. They write (1981: 82, 212):

'In order to specify the mechanisms that perpetuate sexual hierarchy . . . we need to examine links between the sexual division of labour, rural institutions which regulate the allocation of resources and define values for the community, and social ideologies which give cultural meanings to sex differences . . . The social ideology approach, with its focus on the interconnections of sex role stereotyping, sexual divisions of labour, and institutionally structured access to crucial resources, is particularly well suited for documenting the ways sexual hierarchy is perpetuated.'

Unlike some symbolic or structuralist anthropological models, Bourque and Warren attempt to ground their analysis of social ideologies in the material conditions and power structures of society. The final chapter of the present book, by Bowes, attests to the analytical usefulness of such a combined approach.

The importance of considering power dimensions and cultural

expectations when analysing the sexual division of labour in the household is also brought out by Whitehead's (1981) discussion of the politics of domestic budgeting in West Africa and Britain. She focuses upon what she calls the 'conjugal contract' which structures the ways in which products and income produced by the labour of the husband and wife are divided to meet their various personal and collective needs. Such a 'contract' is, of course, often implicit, and based upon unstated cultural rules.

Whitehead shows that in both West Africa and Britain inequalities of power between husband and wife are manifest in the various arrangements by which goods, services, and income are allocated and distributed. The central point in her argument is that relative power exercised within the family is not simply dependent upon the relative wage commanded in the labour market or upon the relative labour input into agricultural production or household tasks. In both cases, she finds that women's duties are closely associated with the collective family aspects of consumption – in the one case, management of the common subsistence fund, and in the other, the housekeeping allowance – while men are much more individuated in relation to their control over resources and in relation to their own consumption. Furthermore, income from wage work is categorized into different types of expenditure (e.g. collective consumption, holiday fund, weekly household food budget, fund for consumer durables, etc.) and there exists a division of responsibility as to these items between husband and wife, with the latter taking the major responsibility for matters concerning the household as a unity.

In Britain, when the middle-class wife enters the labour market, it is generally the man who remains the 'breadwinner'; the wife's earnings are viewed as generating extra money for certain luxury items such as holidays or 'pin-money' (her own recreational fund). She is not expected to contribute to the major running expenses of the household. This is the man's responsibility, although he too will retain a certain proportion of his earnings for his own personal expenditure. This points, once again, to the fact that income from wage labour performed by different household members may be evaluated and distributed quite differently.[12]

According to Whitehead, differences between men's and women's income and expenditure patterns can only be adequately explained by reference to specific socio-cultural and historical factors associated with particular forms of household organization and sexual division of labour. At the same time, it is important to stress that

such differences as may be observed are not only culturally determined but are also rooted in the everyday objective material
conditions experienced by men and women. Whitehead's examples
show how men and women in the two societies have differential
opportunities for obtaining certain types of income and goods and
how these differences tend to reinforce prevailing cultural definitions
of the conjugal contract. A further implication of her analysis is that
the social meanings of 'receiving a wage' and of 'being employed'
shift according to the sex and social status of the individual in
question.

These various studies emphasize the need to move beyond the
rather limited view of household labour processes that concentrates
upon elucidating the benefits of domestic or peasant labour for
capital and for the functioning of the capitalist economy. We must
also deal with the impact that specific sexual divisions of labour,
types of marriage contract, and power relations have on non-
capitalist social relations of production and reproduction. Furthermore, the concept of 'labour' or 'work' (whether domestic or extra-
domestic) cannot be treated as homogeneous since its meaning will
vary situationally and cross-culturally. As Wallman (1979[b]) points
out, we not only have to consider the kinds of activities included in
these concepts and who carries them out but also how they are
evaluated. Work relates to social transactions as well as to material
production and it generates specific identities for those involved in
particular forms of it, and the control of these often implies control
over the values ascribed to them. Cohen (1979: 249–50) shows, for
example, how in the Shetlands the concept of work extends beyond
the idea of 'the economy', 'occupation', or 'subsistence' to include
symbolic and evaluative elements. Crofting in the Shetlands has, he
argues, shifted in meaning as a result of changes in the economy,
from the notion of work with a primary economic rationale to that
with a symbolic one, namely the maintenance of a valued collective
identity associated with the islanders' 'way of life'.

The analysis of non-wage labour, then, inevitably raises questions
of the social value and expectations of such work or co-operation.
Clearly, many of the tasks and relationships involved cannot be
assigned a monetary value. They can only be understood in terms of
the benefits perceived and derived by the participants themselves.
Many non-wage relationships are in fact based on sentiments of kinship, on neighbourhood or community ties, or imply commitment to
some local system of social status. It therefore becomes important to

make explicit the social and cultural frameworks within which these relationships operate and to identify the broader structural conditions under which they arise. The various contributions to this volume highlight these differing social, cultural, and structural dimensions, and show how non-wage relationships reflect both patterns of co-operation and status difference.

THEMATIC OVERVIEW OF THE VOLUME

The chapters that follow aim to explore the above theoretical issues through the discussion of specific empirical cases. They are grouped around three principal themes: (1) the factors that promote or inhibit the persistence of peasant forms of organization and the family farm; (2) the question of inter-household exchanges and community-level patterns of co-operation; and (3) the changing roles of women within the division of labour within the household and the wider community. These three themes are, as I have attempted to show in the foregoing theoretical discussion, closely interrelated and of central importance in the analysis of the social consequences of capitalist expansion among agrarian populations, both in Europe and the less developed countries.

The first three chapters (2 to 4) discuss the characteristics and functioning of peasant household economies in three Third World situations. Each describes internal and external factors affecting the continuity of peasant production based on non-wage labour. The examples, however, relate to different agrarian situations: an Egyptian village, made up of independent smallholders producing a variety of food crops for home and local market consumption, and growing cotton every third year under government compulsion; a group of Argentinian households that live as sharecroppers within a large-scale estate, cultivating tobacco as part of their tenancy agreement; and a community of Peruvian highland peasants who practise primarily subsistence agriculture on the basis of a mixed system of individual-family and communal land tenure, but who also earn wages at the nearby hacienda to obtain some cash income.

As the cases demonstrate, the extent to which decisions on the farm are affected by market and other external forces is partly determined by the type of agricultural crops that are cultivated. In the Egyptian and Argentinian examples we find a high degree of external control exercised over cotton and tobacco production since both cash crops are compulsorily grown. In the Egyptian village, there are government-sponsored co-operatives which organize the rotation of plots to be devoted to cotton and which market the final product. Yet, as Glavanis shows, peasants still manage to devise various strategies to avoid the full brunt of the system. For example, they engage in temporary land exchanges with households outside the designated cotton area so as not to commit themselves so heavily to it; or they plant only a small area, claiming that it is impossible to cultivate more if they are to feed themselves and their animals. The Argentinian sharecroppers are more dependent on tobacco production since their tenancies require its cultivation. In fact, it seems that when they have to choose between giving attention to tobacco or to their food crops, a situation which frequently arises because harvesting periods tend to coincide, they will normally allocate their labour to tobacco. Melhuus gives the example of a complete maize and bean harvest going to rot because of heavy rains at the time of harvesting; it was decided to bring in the tobacco first. Although the sharecroppers recognize the need to take care of their subsistence crops and livestock, they have to give priority to tobacco because the landlord demands a reasonable return on his land at the end of the season, when the harvest is shared on a 50 per cent basis. The demand and price paid for tobacco is determined by the negotiations that take place between the international tobacco companies and the various landowning and commercial interests in Argentina. These negotiations naturally lie outside the influence of the sharecroppers themselves.

The third case represents greater possibilities for developing independent economic strategies. The Peruvian peasants in question maintain an agricultural economy based on community-controlled, irrigated maize and non-irrigated grains and bean production, with access to higher-altitude potato plots and herding pastures controlled by the sugar hacienda in the valley. Like other Andean examples, a striking feature of this economy is the simultaneous exploitation of different ecological zones, enabling households to have direct access to a wide range of tropical and temperate products (Murra 1975). Skar shows that, although the village has independent control of certain production resources essential to the household, the people are dependent on the hacienda for access to the higher-altitude resources and for their cash needs. Hence the village/subsistence sector and the hacienda/cash sector are closely interlocked. At the same time, however, there are moral restrictions against the sale of basic staples, such as maize, and against the making of commercial contracts for labour or goods with fellow villagers. Thus the commoditization of village relationships and transactions is blocked by carefully circumscribed norms of exchange, backed by social and religious sanctions. These Peruvian peasant households, then, retain a relative degree of insulation from the capitalist economy, but they do not lie outside it.

Each of the Third World cases describes the division of labour within the household, highlighting how tasks are allocated to various household members. In none of the situations can the household be regarded as an autonomous unit since extra-household labour is required at certain times in the agricultural and family-life cycle. The Egyptian example documents the level of labour input for different agricultural tasks and describes how exchange labour is recruited. This pattern of labour reciprocities forms part of a wider system of borrowing tools, household utensils, animals for ploughing, cash and produce when households face critical shortages, and plots of land. These data are especially interesting, since frequently exchanges of labour are analysed separately, when they constitute only one among several types of interdependencies that are essential for the functioning of the household economy. The Peruvian example exhibits a similar pattern and illustrates how certain types of labour exchange are reinforced by other social ties. One particularly important strategy involves multiple marriages between two sibling groups. Given the bilateral system of inheritance, landholdings tend to fragment over time. Sibling marriage alliances counteract this tendency by making it possible for people owning contiguous plots of land to continue to work the land together as kin and affines.

Information on inter-household co-operation for the Argentinian case is less full, but Melhuus tells us that households are often large, with as many as ten to fourteen children, who from an early age assist in the picking and curing of tobacco. Some households adopt children of poorer relatives or their own grandchildren, or take in 'employed' hands who receive their keep and a share in the harvest. Hence a series of relationships develop between labour-deficient and labour-surplus households; and sometimes two or more households based on sibling relationships, or father–son ties, form regular work units. Nevertheless, one is left with the impression that, due to the very heavy labour demands of tobacco cultivation and processing and to the lack of mechanization possibilities, most households during peak periods of the year will be hard-pressed to meet their own immediate labour requirements and will not therefore be in a

position to offer their services to other households. Peasant households, then, must often face the dilemma of weighing up the various
costs and benefits of establishing regular exchange relationships with
other households.

Chapters 5, 6 and 7 address themselves to the question of the
viability of the family farm in Europe. The chapters by Abrahams
and Ingold analyse the situation in two contrasting rural areas of
Finland, one where middle-sized properties continue to make a
living, and the other where family farms are finding it increasingly
difficult to survive. The chapter by Kocik describes how, in Poland,
the custom of 'paying off' non-inheriting siblings affects the continuity of the farm and the relations between rural and urban kin.

The Finnish cases examine the problem from both a synchronic
and a diachronic point of view. They provide accounts of the ongoing management problems of the small farmer, focusing upon the
mobilization of labour and on the ways in which farm and off-farm
work are combined to build a livelihood. They also discuss the
continuity of the family farm, dealing with inheritance questions and
the transmission of the property.

Both bring out the specificities of local social structures and family
patterns but also show the importance of historical shifts in the significance of different sectors of the national economy: for example
the expansion of the forestry industry and the question of out-
migration once jobs become available in the urban areas. They draw
attention as well to certain political changes that occurred earlier in
this century as a result of the Russian and German wars. Another
predominant theme relates to the impact of government policies on
land settlement and the kinds of support given to family farmers.
One especially interesting aspect of this is the policy of providing
incentives for farmers to take land out of production in areas where
there is over-cropping in regard to specific crops. Both Abrahams
and Ingold agree that one striking outcome of these various changes
is the marked shift from a strong work ethic tied to the idea of toil
and independence towards the attitude that work equals having a
job, since paid employment is seen as giving 'status'.

Certain differences emerge, however, in their assessments of the
viability of the family farm in the two rural areas. Ingold paints a
picture of depopulation, fragmentation of farms, and the general
decline of smallholder agriculture. Abrahams is less pessimistic: he
argues that farming is still feasible for middle-sized farms and that
many of these are operated through the joint ownership and sharing

of machinery, and use exchange labour of various kinds. He also points out that there is less individualization of the farm unit with non-inheriting relatives leaving the farm for good. On the contrary, close ties are maintained with kin in the towns and cities who return during their holidays to spend time working on the farm.

Both writers, though, describe important inter-generational differences in attitude and commitment to the farm as expressed by the old and the young. There are also changes in the sexual division of labour on certain farms necessitated by the out-migration of family members or by changing production requirements. Ingold makes the additional comment that some farmers now experience difficulty in finding a wife willing to lead a rural life. Inter-household co-operation also presents problems in the area studied by Ingold. This arises principally because many rurally-resident households and families are incomplete socio-demographically and this creates difficulties for establishing regular exchange relationships with other farmers in the neighbourhood. In contrast, Abrahams describes how, for certain farmers, particularly those having roughly equivalent resources, co-operation remains an important element in their farming strategy. In neither case, however, is there any strong 'village community' or sense of 'local place'.

The biggest difference between the two farming situations is the role played by forestry in the local economy. In Ingold's area, forestry is big business associated with the arrival of companies using highly-mechanized methods of timber extraction and taking over the whole process of cutting and transporting. This has replaced the system based on family forest areas exploited by the farmers themselves. Undoubtedly this has affected the economic independence of the small farmer. Abrahams's area has not been transformed in this way and so forest areas attached to individual farms and worked by the farmers themselves continue to function within a diversified family farm strategy. The arrival of large-scale forestry companies, then, signals the end of viable small-scale farming and generates few new local employment opportunities. This leads to increasing marginalization of the family farm and to an exodus of labour seeking work outside.

Both Abrahams and Ingold discuss the problems that arise over the transmission of the farm property when all surviving children are legally entitled to a share and when sub-division of the farm would threaten its economic viability. One solution they describe is the system of 'paying off' siblings or relatives who have moved out of farming. Kocik's chapter explores this practice among family farmers in Poland. The major argument advanced is that paying off should not be interpreted simply in terms of a material or monetary settlement since the various negotiations and attitudes that surround it express deep emotional and moral attachment to the family and to the farm. Even though the forms and levels of settlement now vary considerably, the overwhelming majority of persons of peasant origin (even if they now work in the city) still believe that one should make some provision for non-inheriting children or siblings, and this attitude persists in spite of the practice being legally prohibited. The notion of having a share in a patrimony reinforces feelings of belonging to some sort of supportive and united family and of having identifiable social roots, even if in the end one receives little or no real material benefit. For city people this type of commitment not only perhaps offers some emotional reward and satisfaction but can lead to very definite material advantages. Thus urban families can make claims upon their rural kin for products from the farm and they can stay at the farm during vacations. In return, these city connections may be used by those working the farm to obtain seasonal labour at peak periods, or for getting access to the various urban services they need from time to time.

However, as Kocik stresses, the present-day situation generates considerable pressure on the farmer who requires capital to modernize his operations, and the paying-off system may drain crucial resources from the farm at a time when these are most needed (i.e. at the time of taking over the property). There are, then, conflicting interests at stake that occasionally flare up to create acrimonious situations, possibly leading to the breaking off of family ties. Mostly, though, a balance is struck and rural and urban kin continue to interact and depend upon each other for assistance. This interlinking of rural and and urban families was no doubt crucially important during the food shortages in Polish cities in 1981, when basic items were either unavailable or could only be purchased through the black market at exorbitant prices. The continuing pattern of intra-family relationships centring upon the original family farm represents a remoulding of the earlier peasant smallholder family. The relationships are now stretched out over geographical space to encompass both rural and urban milieux and bring together a diversified occupational pattern. This adaptation is highly reminiscent of similar situations of relatively recent migration of peasants to the city: similar accounts exist for the restructuring of the Indian joint family to form what Epstein (1973: 207–11) calls 'a share family', and for Peruvian highland peasants who make up multi-occupational 'confederations of households', cross-cutting rural and urban locations (Smith 1984). Kocik's brief account suggests, too, the need to investigate further how far paying-off arrangements and similar kin-based networks bind together rural and urban families in Finland.

The final three chapters (8, 9 and 10) give closer attention to women's work and status than do earlier ones. A focus in all three is the sexual division of labour and the social evaluation of women's as against men's work. Bouquet's study of a dairy farming area of south-west England shows how the work roles and social worlds of men and women have diverged, farm work now being defined as 'man's work' and women becoming actively engaged in a search for new commitments and new sources of social estimation that do not depend upon farm work *per se*. Women's roles have also been significantly redefined in the Icelandic case described by Johnson, where the shift from a mixed farming-fishing to a modern specialized fishing economy has resulted in women becoming more confined to the domestic sphere than they were in the nineteenth century. The last chapter, by Bowes, analyses how various ideological, economic, organizational and interactional factors combine to structure the division of labour in an Israeli kibbutz. Bowes exposes the contradiction between official kibbutz ideology, which stresses the equality of sexes and de-emphasizes the household unit in production, and actual practice, which relegates women to lower-prestige, 'unproductive' service tasks, just as one finds in the European bourgeois family.

Chapter 8, on the wives of dairy farmers, illustrates a process that is probably much more general for highly-mechanized farming systems. The introduction of more sophisticated, labour-saving technology often forces women out of agricultural work, leaving them mainly resonsible for domestic matters.[13] Sometimes this has been accompanied by the wife playing an active role in the general administration of the farm (such as in many of the Polder farms of Holland), including such responsibilities as negotiating with the bank for investment loans or dealing with suppliers of animal feed or fertilizers, thus releasing the man to carry out the everyday farm work, which he can usually accomplish without extra full-time labour.[14] Bouquet's case brings out the additional point that farmers' wives may seek new ways of creating independent status for themselves.

Her analysis traces the development of new non-farming activities undertaken by such wives. These relate primarily to two fields. The first involves the taking in of paid visitors during holiday seasons, but occupies the wife also for part of the off-season period, during which she will redecorate or make structural improvements to the accommodation. Bouquet shows that seemingly commonplace or trivial activities, such as carpeting or wall-papering the farmhouse, acquire symbolic and organizational importance for the allocation of status amongst women. Also, a woman's expertise develops around the business of recruiting good visitors, retaining them on a regular basis, advising them about holiday pursuits, and putting them in touch with local shopkeepers who need their custom.

The second major field is community and charity work. They launch appeals for local institutions or raise money or goods for 'good causes'. Bouquet argues that, although these activities are no doubt motivated by the desire to do good things, fund-raising and similar activities become arenas in which women compete for social prestige. Whereas individual farmers are respected for their level of farming knowledge and skills, their wives are frequently judged in terms of activities outside the farm itself.

The different fields of activity of men and women produce different cultural models. Whereas the men tend to maintain egalitarian ideals, stressing status equality and co-operation among farmers, the women articulate an hierarchical view of status which is based upon how 'successful' individual women are seen to be in their social activities. Also, although Bouquet does not fully discuss it, the wives of farmers come to play a crucial role in interlinking the different domestic groups within the locality and it is through this that they develop a stronger sense of commitment to the community than do the farmers themselves.

Johnson's chapter concentrates on the changing domestic and work situation of Icelandic women over the past century. The analysis documents, through a series of censuses, the changing occupational structure of the community. In the nineteenth century, the community was composed of scattered farming homesteads whose residents consisted mainly of a nuclear family composed of male householder, his wife and children, together with foster children, other relatives, servants and parish paupers. The farmer's wife was responsible not only for domestic work but also participated in the farm and in the production and exchange of knitted woollen items. She was usually assisted in housework by female servants. Gradually, this basic pattern, associated with small-scale agricultural production and fishing gave way to a new sexual division of labour based on the marked separation of male and female spheres. Men now work in the modern whaling and herring industry and their wives as full-time housewives, without the help of resident servants or dependants other than their own children. A few women with older children have obtained part-time employment in the fish factory and this has led to some co-operation between women of different households for child-minding and other services. However, for the majority, the incorporation of their menfolk into modern fishing has signalled a narrowing of work tasks for them and has increased their encapsulation within the domestic sphere, reducing their economic independence. On the other hand, one might speculate that some women will have responded to these changed circumstances by pursuing more active, outward-looking strategies such as those adopted by the dairy farmers' wives. Indeed it would seem surprising if they had not, since Icelandic women have vigorously supported the women's movement and have staged highly successful housework 'strikes' and pushed through a number of important legislative reforms improving women's rights.

Bowes's final chapter analyses labour processes in an Israeli kibbutz. Although kibbutzim are not organized in terms of household units of production and, in comparison with the earlier cases, are much larger-scale economic enterprises, several similar issues are raised: for example, the distinction between 'paid' and 'unpaid' work, the social meaning and prestige of different forms of work, the contrast between 'male' and 'female' jobs, the question of inter-household exchange and co-operation, and the articulation of the kibbutz with the wider economic structure.

Bowes emphasizes the need to situate these problems historically. The kibbutzim originally saw themselves as prototypes for the kind of society that would constitute the new state of Israel. The pioneers claimed, according to their Zionist/socialist philosophy, that women would achieve equality with men by engaging in the same manual tasks; but, gradually, sexual differentiation developed, concentrating the men in various so-called 'productive' tasks, while the women were allocated largely to service jobs, such as child care and working in the communal kitchens, which were regarded as 'unproductive' and of lower prestige value. In a similar vein, the kibbutzim deviated from the ideal of relying upon their own co-operative labour by recruiting outside hired hands and by taking in voluntary workers who came to the kibbutzim to spend short working holidays in order to learn about the kibbutz way of life. The volunteers were given their keep but received no official wage.

This lack of fit between precept and practice arose fundamentally, it seems, in response to pressures to achieve high levels of economic growth. Thus notions of efficiency tended to override principles of equity and self-reliance. In the end, then, the particular pattern of labour organization and types of ideological contradiction that emerged must be analysed in terms of the structural problems faced by the kibbutz at different stages of its development. The matter is complicated, as Bowes points out, since ideology does not remain static or internally consistent. Nevertheless, her case illustrates in detail how several dimensions intersect: the economic, organizational, and ideological. The concept of 'productive' labour and the prestige attached to acquiring a 'permanent job' are two central elements in the everyday life of kibbutz members, and negotiations take place in order to obtain such socially-valued work positions.

The kibbutz example, then, rounds off the book by bringing to the fore once again the necessity of exploring the interplay between structural imperatives (e.g. the wider economy and the requirements of particular production systems) and existing cultural means and social resources. Thus, although the kibbutz functions essentially as a modern, commercially-oriented, agricultural enterprise it does so principally on the basis of non-capitalist relations of production. Indeed, one can argue that the efficient organization of labour depends upon the judicious use made of the various types of non-wage workers available on the kibbutz. But, as Bowes demonstrates, the use of such labour generates its own dynamic, as the various categories compete with one another to secure the more prestigious jobs.

In the kibbutz, work takes place in the public domain and each individual's work contribution is public knowledge. Work and its social estimation, then, is a central pivot around which social life revolves.

Notes

1.   The distinction between peasant and simple commodity forms of production rests on the degree of commitment to the market. Peasants characteristically reserve some of their production for home consumption or for inter-household, non-monetary exchange, while simple commodity producers are more heavily committed to the market. The end point of commoditization, as Friedmann puts in, is 'an enterprise, whose relations to outsiders progressively take the forms of buying, selling, and competition' (Friedmann 1980: 163).

Simple commodity producers, then, depend to a considerable extent on commodity relations for reproduction. This is not so much the case with peasant producers who, under certain conditions, may resist full market incorporation. Organizationally, peasant and simple commodity production may, however, be similar, depending on family labour and a similar division of labour within the household. Empirically, it is often difficult, especially in Third World contexts, to differentiate between these two forms.

2. Some parts of this section derive from an earlier manuscript on 'Diversified household enterprise and labour process in the Andes' (Long and Dandler 1980).

3. An interesting historical example of how smallholder peasant production (in this case, tenant farmers) threatened the economic viability of large-scale, agricultural enterprise is found in Brading (1977: 23–58). For further analysis of the family farm in modern agriculture see Hedley (1976), Bennett (1982) and Koning (1983).

4. It is frequently difficult when dealing with economically diversified households with plots of land to determine how far agricultural production constitutes a central element in household livelihood strategies. It is not as easy to identify supplementary sources of food or income as Friedmann suggests (see Friedmann 1978b: 552–53).

5. There are major difficulties in defining the household. It has been used variously to refer to co-residential domestic groups, income-pooling units, or property units (see Wall (1983) for a recent sophisticated discussion of this problem). The most appropriate definition for the present discussion and the papers to follow is that suggested by Wood (1981: 339). He defines the household as 'a group that ensures its maintenance and reproduction by generating and disposing of a collective income fund. As such, the household is differentiated from but not exclusive of the family, co-resident dwelling groups, and kinship structures . . . The dynamic character of household behaviour can be conceptualized as a series of "sustenance strategies" by which the household actively strives to achieve a fit between its consumption necessities, the labour power at its disposal . . . and the alternatives for generating monetary and non-monetary income.'

A provocative critique of the concept of 'household' is provided by Aijmer (n.d.) who argues that one should analytically disaggregate the various task-oriented activities associated with the household and identify instead constellations of people who take part in certain basic activities and express sentiments of belongingness. Hence one would, for example, talk about 'shelter', 'stove', 'eating', 'production' or 'resource-management' groups rather than use the ambiguous notion of household. These groups would not, in most cases, coincide with whatever one defined as a household and would vary situationally within the same social context. This raises issues which lie outside the scope of the present volume, although I believe they are centrally important for developing a sounder comparative analysis of agrarian change and livelihood strategies. See also Deere and de Janvry (1979) and P. Roberts (1984).

6.   For a fuller analytical discussion of these issues, see Long and Roberts (1978b: 297–328). Compare the recent treatment of labour relationships, reciprocity and socio-economic differentiation by Sanchez (1982: 167–83).

7.   Briskin (1980) argues against the view that domestic labour produces use-value. She suggests that domestic work *actualizes* or *transforms* use-values, but does not create them. She has in mind the use of purchased foods, vacuum cleaners and other household equipment. Her argument misses the point that the production and reproduction of labour power is the crucial element.

8.   A similar issue arises in the analysis of the continued existence of the working-class family. Marxist analysis generally explains the survival and role of this in terms of its functional interests for capital. This interpretation, as Humphries (1980: 140) powerfully demonstrates, is unbalanced 'for it assumes the power of capital to be unlimited and fails to recognize that capital's ability to transform existing social institutions, like the family, is circumscribed by the opposition of those concerned'. Humphries argues that the struggle for a 'family wage' (i.e. a level of remuneration adequate for the support of unemployed wife and children) by nineteenth-century British workers both furthered their class interests and, at the same time, protected and reinforced the nuclear family as a basic institution. 'The preservation of non-market relations within the family emerges as neither an obsolete remnant of a less developed mode of production, nor a sociological anomaly, but a result of labour's struggles' (Humphries 1980: 163).

9.   Firth (1979: 200–01) emphasizes a similar point when reviewing Marx's labour theory of value. He argues that goods are 'objects of normative estimation, normative claims and symbolic status' and therefore 'value is the resultant of a complex set of variables of which labour power in the forms of abstract or average labour-time can only be one.'

10.   Data for similar Peruvian highland communities emphasize the dependence on wage earnings: Figueroa (1982: 156) estimates that about half total household income is monetary income, of which four-fifths is derived from the sale of labour. See also Long and Roberts (1984: 171–72).

11.   Coins also figure prominently in Andean marriage ritual and are often believed to give off a powerful vapour which derives from mysterious buried treasures called *waris*. The newly-married couple is advised to keep these coins safely as a guarantee of prosperity. (See Isbell 1978: 121–22.)

12.   The question of how a man's (and woman's) earnings are distributed within the family is an important topic for further research (see Pahl 1980). As Finch (1983) indicates, this relates to the larger issue of how, particularly in industrialized societies, men's work imposes structures and constraints upon women's lives, thus contributing significantly to the social construction of reality by wives.

13.   The extent to which mechanization affects women's work on the farm will vary, of course, according to the type of agriculture and the size of enterprise. Gasson (1980: 169–73) suggests that women normally make major contributions to dairying but that the wife's involvement will sharply decrease with an increase in the scale of the farm. Bouquet's sample of farmers operates relatively large enterprises of between 50, to over 300, acres. The dairy farms produce between 200 and 2,000 litres per day at peak production times. Gasson also describes a category of 'women-farmers' who are essentially 'farm-centred', and other cases where working farm wives show little interest in household or off-farm activities. These variations need fuller comparative investigation.

14.   Recent interviews with 28 farmers' wives in Oostelijk-Flevoland conducted by sociology students from the Agricultural University, Wageningen, point to changes of this type.

2 Aspects of Non-Capitalist Social Relations in Rural Egypt: the Small Peasant Household in an Egyptian Delta Village

Kathy R.G. Glavanis

The continuing failure of capitalist relations of production to become generalized completely within Third World countries as well as within the centres of industrial capitalism has in recent years instigated a re-examination of the nature of capitalism and its inability to dissolve and supplant non-capitalist forms of production.[1] According to Wolpe, this debate about whether capitalism necessarily dissolves and replaces pre-capitalist modes of production or not is by no means new. Marx discussed the impact of capitalist production on pre-capitalist modes of production, but provided no clear and consistent answer as to the likely outcome. Two alternative paths of analysis are to be found. 'The first approach (which has been commonly accepted to be *the* approach adopted by Marx) is based on the assumption that the appearance of capitalism . . . signalled the more or less immediate and inevitable disintegration of PCMPs [Pre-capitalist modes of production] and the subsumption of the agents of these modes under capitalist relations of production.' (Wolpe 1980: 1–2) The second approach recognizes ' . . . differentiated relationships which may be set up between capitalist and other modes of production' (Wolpe 1980: 3).

Some Marxist scholars have attempted to go beyond the theoretical confines of this debate (Roseberry 1978; Bernstein 1979; Taylor 1979). For example, Roseberry, in his historical analysis of small coffee producers in Venezuela, focuses upon the increasing domination of merchant and usurer's capital during the nineteenth century, and later industrial capital in the twentieth century over the production process, but without expropriation of the means of production. As a result of the small farmers' dependency on credit from the usurer/merchant in order to grow coffee, 'coffee farmers were caught in a productive relation with capital which allowed for the *production of surplus value*' (my emphasis). However, the producers still maintained some control over the means of production so that 'the exploitation was not as efficient as it might have been' (Roseberry 1978: 12). Today the state acts as the principal creditor and coffee buyer. Thus, coffee producers continue to be '. . . neither fully peasant nor fuly proletarian . . .' only partly subordinated to the control of capital.

Similarly, Bernstein argues that as household production is increasingly 'subsumed' in the circuit of capital, peasant producers become ' "wage-labour equivalents", that is producers of surplus-value, but in less determinate conditions than the proletariat . . . Thus peasants are "wage-labour equivalents" in a relative sense that limits the subjugation and real subsumption of household labour by capital to the extent that the producers are not fully expropriated nor dependent wholly for their reproduction on the sale of labour-power through the wage-form' (Bernstein 1979: 423–24, 436).

Bernstein's category of 'wage-labour equivalents' is not particularly helpful in understanding the class position of African peasants, who are said to be like wage labourers but yet different. Underlying his notion of 'wage-labour equivalents' is a commonly-held assumption, namely that all non-capitalist forms of production are eventually disintegrated by capitalism. Based on this, the only possible conceptual categories are those arising from an analysis of the capitalist mode of production, given the clear domination of capitalism within the world economy.

Related theoretical issues arise in respect to the agricultural sector of advanced capitalist societies where non-capitalist forms also persist. The tendency here has been to treat these non-capitalist forms as either basically capitalist or as merely transitional, and ultimately doomed. Recently, a few Marxist scholars have begun to re-evaluate these traditional positions, regarding first, the question of the specificity of agricultural as opposed to industrial production (Mann and Dickinson 1978; Mooney 1982) and second, the nature of the internal dynamic of non-capitalist forms of production themselves and their role within contemporary capitalist economies (Hedley 1976; Vergopoulos 1978; Friedmann 1981). Both areas of concern have necessitated a re-examination of some commonly accepted notions about the nature of capitalism itself.

The isolation of the specificity of agriculture as an issue of importance in understanding the limitations of capitalist development in agricultural production is not, of course, new. Marx, Kautsky, and Lenin all, from various points of view, perceived agriculture as being different from industry. Both Marx and Lenin noted the gradual and uneven penetration of capital within agriculture (Marx 1867 (1962): 781; Lenin 1908 (1977): 316). Lenin specifically isolated various factors which he considered to retard differentiation and hence capitalist penetration, namely bondage, usury, and labour-service, all remnants of pre-capitalist rural Russia. However, as none of these factors were structural to agricultural production, Lenin presumed the eventual domination of capitalist relations within agriculture.

Kautsky wrote that 'agriculture does not develop according to the same process as industry; it follows laws of its own'. This is first because of the fixed nature of land, the major means of production in agriculture, which prohibits its multiplication, as occurs with the industrial means of production; second, that 'diseconomies of distance grow at a faster rate than the economies of size' after a certain limit, whereas 'in industry large units of production are always superior to small ones' (Banaji 1976: 2, 31).

Kautsky adds a third factor which he claimed was the most basic cause for retarded capitalist development in agriculture, namely the shortage of manpower. The concentration of agriculture was seen to create its opposite, i.e. the dissolution of smallholdings. This resulted in the simultaneous destruction of the main supply of agricultural labour on the capitalist farm, given the seasonal nature of most agriculture. Finally, Kautsky points to another non-structural factor that perpetuates non-capitalist forms of production, namely 'the conscious political support of the State' (Banaji 1976: 30, 34).

In their seminal article, Mann and Dickinson (1978) characterize agriculture as being unattractive to capital penetration for a variety of reasons, the main one being the normal and natural gap between production and labour time. Other related structural aspects of agricultural production which result from the above gap and which generally act against capital's receiving an average rate of profit, hence making it unattractive to capital, are: (1) inefficiencies in the use of constant capital arising from the very high organic composition of capital in farming (i.e. ratio of the value of land, buildings, and machinery to labour); (2) problems of circulation stemming from the perishability of some crops and the necessity for the long-term storage of others; and (3) problems of labour recruitment and management (Mann and Dickinson 1978: 471–78).

Mann and Dickinson's main contention (1978: 473) 'that the capitalisation of agriculture progresses most rapidly in those spheres where production time can be successfully reduced' and 'conversely

. . . that those spheres of production characterised by a more or less rigid non-identity of production time and labour time are likely to prove unattractive to capital on a large scale and thus are left more or less in the hands of the petty producer' has elicited the most serious criticism (Perelman 1979; Mooney 1982), although other parts of their analysis have likewise been questioned.[2] Perelman points to the nature of the labour supply as having been the crucial factor in the determination of whether capitalist agriculture flourished or not in various parts of England, not the gap between production and labour time (Perelman 1979: 12). Mooney, on the other hand, attempts to disprove the Mann–Dickinson thesis by correlating the actual degree of variance between production and labour time with the percentage of wage labour as an indication of capitalist development. Examining data for eight commodities and/or commodity groups for the period 1944–74, Mooney found that there was no correlation between the degree of variance between production and labour time and the degree of wage labour employed. However, he then states that the percentage of wage labour used in an agricultural enterprise is not an appropriate indicator of the extent of capitalist penetration (although he has relied upon the same indicator to disprove Mann and Dickinson's argument). Mooney's position that American agricultural producers only 'appear' as petty commodity producers, or family units, but are actually undergoing a process of 'on-farm proletarianization' strongly resembles Bernstein's conceptualization of African peasants as wage-labour equivalents.

An alternative view is that of Friedmann (1981), who distinguishes between a mode of production, including the totality of enterprises, and the forms of production characteristic of enterprises. Consequently, Friedmann is not forced to analyse American family farmers at the level of enterprise using capitalist categories. She analyses these family farming enterprises in their own terms. Focusing on their internal logic, she characterizes the form of production as non-capitalist. The labour process is governed generally by the principles of 'the gender division of labor, kinship obligations, and patriarchy' (1981: 12). Thus, this kind of enterprise 'dispenses entirely with the category of profit as a condition of reproduction, and replaces the inflexibility of the wage with a flexible cost of personal consumption' (1981: 17). The simple commodity production enterprise is consequently seen to have important advantages over capitalist enterprises within the same branch (1981: 13).

In many ways, Friedmann's characterization of the internal dynamics of the unit of production within family farming is similar to that of Chayanov. However, for Friedmann, this form of production, simple commodity production, is dependent on a wider capitalist economy for its reproduction, namely the existence of markets in land, labour, and credit. Thus, Friedmann's conceptual categories allow for the analysis of family farming at the level of enterprise and at that of the wider economy without collapsing one into the other. This is a theoretical step forward. She states (1981: 5), that 'as a logical category, simple commodity production implies minimally that all external relations of the enterprise are commodity relations, that is, the enterprise sells all it produces, saving nothing for direct consumption, and buys all it consumes, both for means of production and for sustaining the life of the laborers . . . . The continuous existence of any simple commodity production enterprise, therefore, implies generalized commodity production.'

Some research, by contrast, has shown that the preference of family farmers is 'to maintain a pattern of diversified farming despite the potential higher effeciency of more specialized production' (Hedley 1976: 417; Bennett 1969). Farmers prefer such a pattern of farming as it ensures virtual self-sufficiency in domestic consumption and protects them 'against unpredictable price fluctuations and the vulnerability of a single commodity to the effects of natural hazards' (Hedley 1976: 417). In other words, the *ideal pattern* of family farming is the production of both *use* and *exchange values* or *commodities*, although this pattern has become more difficult to maintain since the Second World War (Hedley 1976: 417–18).

Secondly, according to Friedmann, another result of generalized commodity relations and thus the operation of the law of value within the wider economy is competition between enterprises. However, again, research has shown the centrality of co-operation between relatives and/or neighbours in family farming (Hedley 1976: 416–17; Bennett 1968). One study even shows that despite the reports of farmers who claimed the occurrence of a decrease in co-operative relations amongst themselves as compared with the past, the incidence rate of co-operation (in terms of labour, machinery, etc.) had actually increased (Bennett 1968: 284). In Friedmann's analysis, there is no recognition of the importance of these particular non-commodity relations to family farmers within the capitalist centre.

The debate about whether capitalism necessarily dissolves and replaces non-capitalist forms of production or not is far from resolved. What emerges from an examination of the recent debates is the real paucity of theoretically informed but empirically grounded studies which focus on the relevant issues, thereby helping us to understand better the complex relations between capitalism and other forms of production.

In the following case study, I examine these issues in relation to small peasant households in rural Egypt. This examination is based upon my fieldwork in the Nile Delta. The chapter is divided into two major sections. The first attempts to demonstrate what I call the consolidation of the Egyptian peasant household, a non-capitalist form of production, after the 1952 Revolution, and the major forces that have been responsible for this. The second focuses on some of the various forms of non-capitalist social relations which have helped ensure the reproduction of the small peasant household, despite the increasing commoditization of the Egyptian countryside through the active intervention of the Egyptian state.

AGRARIAN EGYPT AFTER THE 1952 REVOLUTION: THE CONSOLIDATION OF THE EGYPTIAN PEASANT HOUSEHOLD

The predominant *form of production* within the agricultural sector in Egypt today is the small peasant household. While not denying the existence and significance of differentiation within the Egyptian countryside, the position of this household has nevertheless been consolidated since 1952. Two sets of state policies can be isolated which have most clearly contributed to this: the Agrarian Reform Laws of 1952, 1961, and 1969 regarding land ownership and tenancy, and the differential pricing and subsidy policy with regard to field crops and livestock.

Through the Agrarian Reform Laws, a legal maximum limit of land ownership was established in order to undermine the power of the large landowners. In 1952, the first land reform law 'set the maximum limit of landownership at 200 feddans [1 feddan = 1.038 acres] for a single person, with 100 feddans extra allowed for his dependent children, provided that the total did not exceed 300 feddans' (Abdel-Fadil 1975: 8). In 1961, the upper limit was lowered to 100 feddans for a single owner, and in 1969 it was lowered for a third time to 50 feddans per person, or 100 feddans per family (Ikram 1980: 217). By 1970, 12.5 per cent of the cultivated land had been distributed among approximately 9 per cent of the rural population, in plots of at least 2, but not more than 5, feddans per family (Abdel-Fadil 1975:10).

More important, though, was the effect of the agrarian reform on tenancies. Rents had become exorbitant before the 1952 Revolution, but with the Agrarian Reform Law of 1952, they could not exceed seven times the basic land tax of 1949, and sharecropping rents were not to exceed half the income, after expenses were deducted and divided equally between tenant and owner. These changes meant a considerable reduction in rent for the tenants. Although short-term rental agreements exceed the above rates and are quite common in the countryside today,[3] those with rental arrangements from 1952 have managed for the most part to keep their rents low, as it was made almost impossible by law to remove a tenant unless he had failed to pay his rent for several years in a row.[4] Today, about 40 per cent of the total area continues to be rented in one of the legally specified ways (Ikram 1980: 212). Thus, through these changes in land ownership and tenancy, the Egyptian state has ensured the sanctity of private property and reinforced small peasant production as the predominant form of production within Egyptian agriculture.

By 1975, according to Ministry of Agriculture statistics,[5] (Mitwali 1981: 33), the number of small peasant holdings of less than 5 feddans (2,589,000) equalled 92.5 per cent of the total, cultivating 67 per cent of the land, with an average holding for this category of 1.5 feddans. In 1950, holdings of less than 5 feddans (786,700) had equalled only 78 per cent of the total, cultivating 23 per cent of the land, with an average holding for this category of 1.8 feddans (Abdel-Fadil 1975: 14).

Amongst these small peasant holdings, the category which increased most substantially during this period was that of holdings with less than one feddan, which in 1950 represented 21 per cent of all holdings (Abdel-Fadil 1975: 14) and by 1975 represented 39 per cent (Mitwali 1981: 33). Not only did this category increase most substantially numerically, but individual peasant households seem to have been able to consolidate themselves over time, a process indicated by the increase in the average size of holding in this category, from 0.52 feddans in 1950 (Abdel-Fadil 1975: 14) to 0.66 feddans in 1975 (Mitwali 1981: 33).

Let us now turn to the second set of state policies which, it is suggested, have contributed fundamentally to the consolidation of small peasant households in the Egyptian countryside. Since 1952, the Egyptian state has followed a pricing and subsidy policy which has, overall, resulted in the indirect taxation of field crops such as maize, wheat, cotton, rice, and sugar cane. These crops are grown primarily by small peasant producers. On the other hand, meat production has been protected by the government, particularly from 1974 onwards. Between 1965 and 72, meat prices were well over twice the import equivalent, and between 1973 and 76, when world prices for agricultural products rose dramatically, all these except meat were indirectly taxed by the Egyptian state (Cuddihy 1980: 117, 102, iii). The combination of the above policies has led to an increased involvement in and dependence upon livestock rearing amongst most small peasant households. As a recent World Bank report confirmed, 'cattle holding is often the best investment for the small farmer' (Ikram 1980: 193–94; Harik and Randolph 1979: 82). This process has often necessitated, amongst other strategies, such as the temporary rental of additional land, a change in the crop mix of many small peasant producers. In order to help meet the increased demand for winter fodder brought about by the increased number of household livestock, small peasant households have increased the area devoted to the cultivation of permanent Egyptian clover (*barsim*) and decreased the area devoted to wheat and cotton which compete seasonally for the same land and are also amongst those crops indirectly taxed.

Livestock is significant to the small peasant household not only because of its relative profitability vis-à-vis the traditional crops. Adult animals provide the peasant household with draft power, as well as with its most important source of animal protein, cheese. Furthermore, most small peasant households rely primarily upon the selling of approximately two-thirds of their cheese production and nearly all their butter production to meet their daily cash needs, such as the purchasing of cigarettes, tea, and sugar. These depend, of course, on whether the cow or water buffalo is lactating or not. Milk production stops during the latter part of pregnancy, so that for approximately five months out of every one and a half years the peasant household is without milk if it possesses only one adult female animal. Finally, cattle holding is a form of insurance in times of hardship or when a large sum of money is needed by the household, for instance on the occasion of a son's marriage. An animal can be sold, and a younger one bought to replace it, with the difference being spent on the required occasion. Alternatively, a share in the animal can be sold. On the other hand, young calves are almost always specifically raised for the purpose of selling at the end of a fattening-up period which usually lasts for about six months. This gives the peasant household access to a considerable sum of money at fairly regular intervals.[6]

The relative importance of cattle rearing in the small peasant household is also reflected in the high percentage of family labour devoted to it. In a recent field survey in the Delta province of al-Sharqiyya, male peasants who had landholdings of less than 1 feddan were shown to have devoted 70 per cent of their labour to livestock, while women devoted 82 per cent of their time to this activity. A similar tendency was recorded for peasant households between 1 and 3 feddans. However, the labour balance shifted slightly in favour of crops for men with holdings between 3 and 5 feddans, with 50 per cent of their labour time being devoted to crops and 50 per cent to livestock (Richards 1981: 37).

Two additional state policies, perhaps of less significance, have helped to maintain the viability of the small peasant household despite the disadvantageous terms of trade for crops grown by most Egyptian small peasants, as well as the mandatory triennial crop rotation of cotton. These are the building of the High Dam and the formation of agricultural co-operatives.

One of the major contributions of the High Dam, whose construction was finally completed on 15 January 1971, was the more even distribution of water throughout the agricultural year. Among other things, this enabled small peasants to shift from autumn to summer maize, which increased yields by approximately 20 per cent (Richards 1980: 8). The main functions of the agricultural co-operatives, first initiated on agrarian reform lands in 1952 but extended to all rural Egypt by the early 1960s, have been to provide short-term credit in kind, e.g. fertilizers and seeds; to organize and oversee the eradication of cotton pests, and to implement government directives concerning the cultivation of cotton and the other designated compulsory crops.

Together these policies have contributed to substantial increases in yields per feddan, in particular for maize and wheat, through the provision of constant water and fertilizers. Thus, in 1952, the average yield per feddan of maize was 900 kg and of wheat was 742 kg. In 1978, the average yield per feddan of maize was 1,641 kg and of wheat 1,400 kg (Ikram 1980: 422). As a result, Egyptian peasants have been able to devote less land to maize and wheat and more to Egyptian clover (*barsim*) without unbalancing the subsistence needs of the household, as would have occurred if yields had remained constant. Also, these increased yields have meant that the size of the viable holding has effectively been lowered. It needs to be emphasized, though, that the positive gains from the High Dam have already been achieved. Its concomitant negative side-effects, such as increasing salinity, rising water tables, lack of silt, and the increasing occurrence of schistosomiasis,[7] have become increasingly deleterious to agricultural production and the health of the peasant. Peasants have been provided with stable supplies of fertilizers at declining real prices, although many complain about the poor quality or tardiness of supply and that 'these prices have in general been above world parity over the last two decades' (Cuddihy 1980: 64); they have led in the long run to a net transfer of funds out of the agricultural sector.

Other state policies have been indirectly responsible for the consolidation of the small peasant household through their effect on the rural labour situation. Under Nasser, a vigorous policy of industrialization was pursued, with the majority of enterprises being located in Egypt's two main urban centres, Cairo and Alexandria. From 1957–63, 49 per cent of Egypt's new factories were founded in Cairo, while 18 per cent were located in Alexandria. This imbalance was evident from the beginning of Egypt's industrial development in the nineteenth century. From 1865–1956, 48 per cent of all new factories were founded in Cairo, while 20 per cent were founded in Alexandria (Barbour 1972: 129).

Likewise, government employment was dramatically expanded following the Egyptian Revolution. From 1947–61, approximately 40 per cent of all new employment was located in the government sector, more than doubling it (Mead 1967: 138). It is estimated that government employees increased from less than 310,000 in 1947 to nearly 770,000 in 1960, and to 1,035,000 in 1966–67 (Mabro 1974: 209–10). A related policy, and one that contributed significantly to this mushrooming of the Egyptian bureaucracy, was the guarantee given to all graduates of institutions of higher education of a job either in the administration or the public sector. Although this policy was made official in 1962, it had been followed in practice for many years (Mabro 1974: 157). A similar guarantee was given to all participants in the 1973 October War. As was true for the geographical distribution of industrial enterprises, the location of government employment was skewed, the majority of it being centralized in Cairo, Alexandria, and to a less extent, the provincial capitals (Barbour 1972: 200).

Another important source of 'employment' for young Egyptian males, eighteen years and older, and one which grew in importance until the mid-1970s was the military. Within the context of the ongoing state of war between Egypt and Israel up to 1977, most young

Egyptian males were drafted into the army for a period of several years, sometimes more, following the defeat of the 1967 June War. For many rural draftees, this resulted in their eventual migration to Egypt's urban centres following their term of duty. Here, their newly-acquired skills allowed them to compete advantageously in urban labour markets (Abdel-Fadil 1975: 112).

The education system expanded tremendously after 1952 in all sectors, most dramatically in secondary technical and university education. (Mabro 1974: 156). There was a remarkable expansion within the predominantly rural governorates during the first decade following the Revolution, when the number of students in these rose at a faster rate than the urban ones (Mead 1967: 30). Nevertheless, there are still marked rural–urban differences in the field of education. It was estimated that in 1963–64 90 per cent of all urban children were attending primary school but only 65 to 75 per cent of rural children were enrolled (Szyliowicz 1973: 264). This trend has continued into the present.

These developments, taken together, have helped to create conditions for the withdrawal of part of the rural labour force from the agricultural sector, sometimes temporarily, although more usually permanently, and, more often than not, to the urban centres of Egypt.[8] It is reflected in the declining occurrence of landlessness within the Egyptian countryside in recent years.[9]

The overall labour situation within Egypt has been noticeably affected by an additional factor, namely the oil boom that resulted from rises in the price of petrol following the 1973 October War. Egyptians increasingly began to migrate abroad to the Gulf States in search of work for a higher income than was possible within the Egyptian national economy (Ikram 1980: 138).

However, these trends have also had negative side-effects on the small peasant household. The labour balance within small peasant household enterprises is sometimes upset due to the withdrawal of necessary family labour, and in particular of young male labourers at a point in the demographic cycle of the family when they would have normally begun to contribute significantly to work in the fields. Thus, peasant households sometimes find themselves chronically deficient in the necessary household labour.

THE VILLAGE SETTING: MIT QAMAR

The village of Mit Qamar (a pseudonym) is located approximately 70 kilometres north-west of Cairo, in the province of al-Minufiyya. In 1976, Mit Qamar's population was 2,367, an increase of only 70 persons or 3 per cent since the 1966 census. This indicates a high degree of out-migration. Nearly every household with which I was acquainted had close relatives resident in Cairo. This was especially true for the younger generation. This pattern coincides with the generally high rate of out-migration documented for the province of al-Minufiyya (Ikram 1980: 394; Central Agency for Public Mobilization and Statistics 1971: 14–16).

Mit Qamar is almost exclusively an agricultural community. The majority of its inhabitants are engaged in the cultivation of Egyptian clover (*barsim*)[10] and wheat in the winter and maize in the summer – all basic subsistence crops of the peasant household. These same households grow some cotton every third year, as well, when their land falls within an area designated for cotton cultivation by the village co-operative, although sometimes they grow only part of the required amount or none at all. Some cash crops are grown on a small scale, including sweet potatoes, cucumber (for seed), a variety of taro or elephant's ear (*qulqas*)[11], potatoes, tomatoes, and aubergines, as well as an assortment of the latter vegetables for home consumption including two varieties of mallow (*khubbaiza* and *mulukhiyya*).[12] In addition to the above, the majority of households are engaged in the rearing of livestock, primarily mature female water buffaloes (*gamusa,* singular) and small male calves, as well as in the selling of cheese and butter (*samna baladi*).

Land is an essential and scarce resource in Mit Qamar. The total area (*zimam*) is 567 feddans, with approximately 520 feddans being cultivated, or an average of 0.2 feddans per person. Land is relatively evenly distributed amongst the inhabitants. Thus, there was no land reform in the village, and in 1976–77 the largest holding (*hiyaza*) was approximately 15 feddans, with a handful of others having between 5 and 8 feddans. Most holdings, however, are small, being less than 2 feddans. Landlessness is essentially a phenomenon of the past, and those households with no access to land are predominantly those headed by older, widowed women and invalids.

Socially and economically, the residential area of Mit Qamar is divided geographically into two halves, the north (*al-nahiyya al-bahriyya*) and the south (*al-nahiyya al-'ibliyya*). The village headman (*ʿumda*) and all of larger landowners reside in the northern half, in which is also located the village agricultural co-operative (*al-gamʿiyya al-taʿawuniyya al-ziraʿiyya*), the primary school, and the health clinic. The agricultural land is likewise divided between the two halves, with most holdings of those from the northern side located in the irrigation basins (*ahwad*) surrounding their residential area. As a result, there is generally little social and economic inter-action between the residents of the two sides on a day-to-day basis. Marriage between the two is likewise limited, although it does occur. Amongst both sides of the village there is a strong sense of identity, with the northerners stressing their wealth and educational achieve-ments and the southerners their community spirit. As I lived in the southern half of the village with a small peasant household cultivat-ing 17 *qirats* (1 feddan = 24 qirats) of land, most of the data upon which the following analysis will be based is drawn from my experi-ences and research amongst small peasant households within the southern half of Mit Qamar.

NON-CAPITALIST SOCIAL RELATIONS IN MIT QAMAR: CO-OPERATION AND ASSISTANCE

Today in Mit Qamar, various forms of co-operation play an impor-tant role in maintaining the viability of small peasant households and lessening their dependence upon money and market relations, and hence upon wage labour. However, the historical dimension of co-operative relations within the village or in the Egyptian countryside in general is difficult to establish. This is because so little has been written about these kinds of relations, or about the nature of ag-rarian social relations in general.

Despite the total absence of any discussion of co-operative re-lations amongst peasant households in Ayrout's classic study, *The Egyptian Peasant,* first published in 1938, field experience and the few other available sources suggest that it nevertheless existed and was important. Ayrout's suggestion that a peasant household consist-ing of a married couple, their children, water buffalo, and donkey formed a 'sufficient' unit to cultivate five feddans of land without outside help (Ayrout 1968: 60) is difficult to accept. It may have reflected the peasants' ideal, but could not have corresponded to the reality of their conditions. Due to the family demographic cycle, labour self-sufficiency would have been a near impossibility, at least during the first 12–14 years of the family's life, when male children would still have been unable to help their father in the heavy agricultural work. Thus Ayrout's ideal peasant family would have been labour deficient for a good many years of its life, although the peasant's wife could have replaced some male labour during this period. Also, with only one large draft animal, this peasant family would always remain animal-deficient for all field operations such as ploughing (*hart*) and levelling (*zahhafat al-ard*) for these require two large animals.

In contrast to Ayrout, a number of other writers have mentioned co-operation amongst peasant households, although none has focused particularly on this phenomenon. Perhaps Ammar (1954: 26, 37, 44, 56–7, 61) and Morsy (1978: 85–88) present the most detailed descriptions available on co-operative relations, with both attesting to the pervasiveness and importance of these. Neither, unfortunately, provides any historical depth to their descriptions.

However, from other brief references to co-operative relations amongst small peasant households in the Egyptian countryside, there appears to be a contradiction regarding their historical development. Both Berque (1957: 45–51) and Abdel-Fadil (1975: 45) mention their decline, but Berque is specifically concerned with such institutions as village guest houses (*madyafa,* singular) and communal meeting rooms (*duwwar,* singular),[13] and Abdel-Fadil is concerned with the mutual exchange of labour during the harvesting period. On the other hand, Stauth (1979) posits the reinforcement and strengthening of mutual work and exchange of goods (*muzamla*) amongst small peasant households in the village of al-Shamiyats, al-Minufiyya, with the rise of commercialized agriculture.

It is possible to reconcile these apparently different accounts in that all of the above writers are concerned with different facets of co-operative relations. Evaluating available evidence, it seems probable that some forms of co-operation have actually declined, such as those mentioned by Berque (*madyafa,* etc.) and Abdel-Fadil. With the branching out of the dominant families within the village community through marriage and migration to the cities, the economic and social bases for village institutions such as *madyafas* have broken down. In Mit Qamar, each side of the village possessed only one *duwwar* and no *madyafa,* although the physical remains of other such buildings as well as reports by villagers about others no longer standing indicate that these institutions were much more common in the first part of the twentieth century. Likewise, with the decline in the average size of the family holding since the beginning of the century, mutual exchange of labour at harvest time became less necessary.[14]

In Mit Qamar, as well as in the rest of rural Egypt, a large percentage of peasant holdings are under one feddan and therefore most harvesting of wheat and corn can be undertaken by family labour, although peasants reported previous reliance on exchange labour for this kind of agricultural work. On the other hand, other types of co-operative relations seem to have been strengthened or created due to the changing socio-economic circumstances following the post-1952 agrarian policy. Morsy's recent account of *zamala* (partnership), defined as a mutual, non-contractual form of co-operation, in Fatiha, a village without striking differentiation[15] located in Kafr al-Shaikh, reveals the vitality of co-operative relations today in the Egyptian village. In this village, labour, animals, implements and utensils, food items, etc. are exchanged and borrowed (Morsy, 1978: 85–8). Fieldwork in Mit Qamar confirms Morsy's findings, and it is to a more detailed discussion of the extent and variety of co-operative relations, and the role they play in sustaining small peasant households that I would now like to turn.

In Mit Qamar, the general term used to refer to co-operation amongst peasant households was *mugamla* (act of courtesy), but usually an act of co-operation was described by using one of two verbal expressions, *bin-gamil ba^cd* ('we help one another') or *bin-katif ba^cd* ('we stand by one another'), or, more rarely, using the verb *zamala ma^c* ('to co-operate and exchange with someone'). These expressions, which seem to be used interchangeably, covered a wide range of activities. In terms of *mugamla*, peasants from the southern side of the village stressed with pride their superiority over the north. As the head of the household with whom I stayed said, 'They are all right and everything, but they don't really support each other like we do.' He then gave the example of the death of an animal, saying that those on the northern side would probably just sell the animal to a merchant in order to ensure a slightly better price to the owner, rather than follow the older custom of dividing the meat amongst the villagers. Or if the division of the meat took place, perhaps households would refuse and send it back.

However, the same southern peasants bemoaned the decline in co-operative relations in general, stating that 'all relations had become monetized these days'. Fieldwork in Mit Qamar and comparative research on co-operation amongst family farms in Canada, however, should make us sceptical of such statements. From Bennett's research carried out during the 1960s on Canadian family farms, it was established that while farmers spoke of a decline in co-operation, the frequency of farmers' co-operation had actually increased since the Second World War. This was explained as being due to a decline in the economic conditions supporting family farms, which made co-operation as a result a necessity for their mutual survival. As Bennett states, 'exchange was a practical necessity in several types of farming, because the increase in machines and capital had not kept pace with the increased costs and corresponding needs for stepped-up production' (Bennett 1968: 284).

Thus it is possible in the case of Mit Qamar: that (1) an attested decline in co-operative relations by peasants may not accurately reflect reality; and (2) in times of economic hardship, co-operative relations might be expected to increase or be transformed. Economic circumstances have generally got worse for the small Egyptian peasant household over the last twelve years (with the major exception of livestock rearing), with cultivators of traditional crops being heavily taxed, albeit indirectly, through the manipulation of prices, and, in a period of rising expectations and increasing consumerism, through their falling victim to increased inflation, while having little access to subsidized government co-operative stores.

Co-operation and generosity amongst relatives and neighbours for those from the southern side of the village was seen as being a virtue and a duty for all those who could manage to help, while being avaricious (*bakhil*) was a matter for criticism. Two village proverbs embody this notion: *il-balash ghali* ('what is done for nothing is treasured') and *il-gamil luh agmal minnu* ('There is nothing better than an act of kindness'). However, generosity beyond one's means was seen as foolish, and was criticized. As the head of the household with whom I was staying told me, it was customary to give both wheat and maize at harvest time to the poor of the village, but it would be foolish for him to give so much that his own household would have to buy wheat or maize later on in the year. This had actually happened in April 1976, when the family had to buy back from one of their poor neighbours some of the straw which his household had given them the year before. To live within one's own means was a virtue, a morality amongst small peasant households based upon long experience of living on very little. Two common village proberbs. *ᶜAlaᶜadd hasirtak, midd riglaik* ('stretch your legs the length of your mat') and *il-ᶜIyas illi yaᶜuz mahalak, yihram ᶜalaᶜl-gamᶜ* ('your size prevents others from finding room on the straw mat') succinctly express this deep-seated fear of over extending oneself and inadvertently putting one's household in a more vulnerable position.

The various exchanges of goods, animals, and labour within the southern side of the village take place according to a general notion of village social structure. It was a matter of open discussion amongst small households as to whom on their side, (*nahiyyitna*), were well-off and who were poor and needed assistance. At the bottom of the socio-economic ladder were those who were without land and animals, usually aged widows. Next on the scale were those with a little land (4–12 *qirats*), a milk-producing animal held in partnership (*shirk*), and having to work regularly for wages. Above them were households which possessed approximately 1 feddan, with a milk-producing animal held in partnership, but who rarely had to resort to wage labour. Those households that held between ½ and 2½ feddans were seen as being self-sufficient in terms of wheat, maize, *barsim,* and straw. On top of the social scale were those with 3 or more feddans, who were expected to be able to lend animals, money, etc. without suffering hardship.

However, the above scale does not indicate 100 per cent agreement amongst peasants in Mit Qamar as to who is poor and who is not. For instance, the head of the household with whom I stayed stated that Afkar's household was amongst the poor of his area. She and her family possessed 4 *qirats*, rented 4 more on a short-term basis (*sagil*) and possessed 2 animals held in partnership, 1 female water buffalo and 1 small calf. Both her sons worked for wages. On the other hand, Afkar told me that she thought her family were in the middle (*mutawassitin*), which she described as those who sometimes had to buy wheat and maize and sometimes had to work for wages. The villagers' conceptualization of the social scale is important in determining from whom a given household can expect help, and to whom the same household should give help.

Given the above, help and co-operation amongst households are not necessarily nor directly reciprocal. Households deemed poor, without land and animals, receive help and assistance without the donor having expectations of it being returned at any time in the future. For all other small peasant households, most help is given without the expectation of immediate reciprocity. However, underlying the giving of help is the notion that it might be returned one day, though not necessarily in the same form, to the original donor, when he or she is in need of help. A common village expression,

'Whoever helps me one day, I'll help them at another time' incorpor-ates this notion of building up a reserve of good deeds amongst friends and relatives which can be drawn upon at a later date.

Having presented a general view of co-operation in Mit Qamar, I would like to turn to the specific forms it takes within the village.

Labour co-operation

To be self-sufficient in labour, land, animals, and the subsistence crops of wheat, maize, and *barsim,* is the ideal of every small peasant household in Mit Qamar. However, many small peasant households are often temporarily or chronically labour-deficient, even though they are engaged in the cultivation of a limited area of land and the rearing of only a few animals. This is primarily due to the kind of traditional technology still employed which is basically labour-intensive. Before turning to a discussion of how small peasant house-holds attempt to rectify labour imbalances within their enterprises, it is necessary to outline briefly the nature of agricultural requirements in Mit Qamar.

It is first necessary to distinguish between the necessary labour requirement of a given operation and the average or optimum labour input. This distinction is important because it highlights the extent to which a small peasant household, given its family composition, is absolutely dependent upon additional labour external to it. The majority of agricultural operations required for cultivation of the four basic crops grown by all small peasant households in Mit Qamar can be done by one or two adult males. Ploughing usually requires two adults, one, male or female, to lead the team of animals and one (male) to guide the plough. When sowing wheat and maize, a third adult (for wheat, male or female; for maize, usually female) is needed to sow the seed in the freshly ploughed earth. The sowing of Egyptian clover, wheat, and cotton is done after ploughing and can be done by one adult male for Egyptian clover and cotton or by one teenager for cotton. Flattening (*zahhafat al-ard*) with a plank (*loh*) attached in place of the plough requires one adult male, as does making the long irrigation ridges (*bitun*), with another traditional instrument, the *batana,* also attached in place of the plough. Divid-ing the cultivated area into smaller irrigation areas (*tahwid*) with the *loh,* for the cultivation of wheat, Egyptian clover and maize, re-quires two adult males. For the cultivation of cotton, the land is divided into furrows (*mash al-khutut*) which can be done by one adult male with the hoe (*fas*).

Irrigating (*raiy*) usually requires one adult male, but may require another person, possibly a child of either sex, when the source of water is far away from the land. The child is responsible for keeping the animal turning the water wheel. The thinning (*takhfif*) of cotton and maize plants requires one adult male, as does hoeing (*ta'zi'*) cotton. The digging and spreading (*sabkh al-ard*) of natural fertilizer (*sibakh baladi*) requires one adult, male or female, but the transportation between the house and field can be done by a child of either sex.

The cutting of Egyptian clover requires one adult or teenager (usually male), while the harvesting of wheat with the sickle (*sharshara*) and maize with the small hoe (*man'ara*) requires one adult male. The bundling of wheat and the harvesting of cotton requires the labour of one child, teenager, or adult of either sex. The threshing of wheat by the traditional threshing machine (*norag*) requires one adult, usually male, and one child of either sex to ride it in order to keep the animal moving. Mechanized threshing requires a team of four or five, usually male adults, to move the wheat bundles to the machine, to feed them into it, and to rake the threshed wheat away from the machine. Winnowing (*diri al-'amh*) is done by a team of three men hired by the owners of the machine.

The pulling of cotton bushes from the ground (*ta'li'*) requires one adult male, while beating off the dried mud from the roots of the bushes requires one adult female or teenager, male or female. Finally, the transportation (*na'l*) and storage (*takhzin*) of wheat and maize require one adult, usually a male for the former and a female for the latter.

From the above it can be seen that the majority of agricultural jobs can be done by one adult man, with a few requiring two adults, including ploughing for Egyptian wheat, or two adult men for jobs such as irrigation ridgemaking (*tahwid*). Likewise, only two operations require three adults, namely ploughing and sowing wheat and maize, and only one operation requires more than three, namely mechanized threshing. However, a number of operations, such as making furrows for cotton, thinning, hoeing, digging, transporting, and spreading fertilizer, harvesting, and pulling out cotton bushes, which can be done by one adult, usually male, can be accomplished through teamwork, shortening the duration of the operation.

Most households possess at least the eventual potential of becoming labour sufficient, with the average family size being 5.5 in the province of al-Minufiyya (Central Agency for Public Mobilization and Statistics 1977: 56). However, many factors intervene to make this quite often an impossibility: the family developmental cycle, infertility, ill-health, imbalance between the sexes, education, employment, migration, etc. Many of the small peasant households with whom I had contact faced one or more of the above problems, and therefore had a permanent or temporary labour deficiency for those operations requiring two adult men or more, i.e. they had an *absolute deficiency*. In addition, many households possessed only the minimum in terms of labour input, and therefore female and children's labour became disproportionately important. In this kind of household, flexibility in the division of labour between the sexes and age groups was an important factor in the internal fulfilment of household labour requirements. For instance, women would lead the team of animals while ploughing, cut Egyptian clover and help in the digging, transportation, and spreading of natural fertilizer.

Likewise, flexibility in the timing of jobs is an important way in which such households can fulfil more adequately the necessary labour on their holding. For example, despite the fact that Mit Qamar's co-operative and the peasant radio broadcast (*Iza^cat al-Sha^cb*) told peasant producers in the fall of 1976 to plant their wheat by 25 November, many small peasant households planted it later, even into the second week of December. This means that the planting time for wheat was effectively approximately one month long. Thus, the peasant household with less labour than another can extend their time in digging, transporting, and spreading natural fertilizer if they need to, without any serious consequences.

Finally, certain short cuts in agricultural operations can be undertaken to decrease the required labour input. The primary method of achieving this decrease amongst small peasant households in Mit Qamar was to use less natural fertilizer (*sibakh baladi*) per *qirat*, as the traditional process of digging, transporting, and spreading the fertilizer is extremely time-consuming. Thus, instead of using 30 loads (*na'l*, singular) per *qirat* for the planting of maize, which I was told were required, the household with whom I stayed used only 15 loads per *qirat* as the husband and his wife had to do the majority of the agricultural work on their own 17 *qirats*, plus the 8 *qirats* of his invalid brother, with only occasional help from their son who was in his final year of high school; neither husband nor wife had very good health.

However, as has been indicated, certain households have an *absolute labour deficiency* and thus the above methods cannot overcome this, given the type of technology utilized. In this situation, small peasant households must rely upon extra-household labour, or adopt new technology, e.g. ploughing by tractor. However, the substitution of tractor ploughing for the traditional method involves an outlay of cash, £E0.15 per *qirat* in 1976–77, to rent the tractor. This cash outlay, although seemingly small, goes against the small peasant tradition of minimizing cash transactions in agriculture and within the household when possible. Hence, in Mit Qamar, most small peasant households still plough by the traditional method. The rapid adoption of threshing machines by small peasant producers in Mit Qamar from 1977–80 may appear to contradict the above. However, such a process can be explained by the increasing number and importance of livestock in these households, and thus their need to thresh more quickly than they used to be able to with the traditional thresher.

Extra-household labour is provided through informal and non-reciprocal co-operation or through more formalized labour exchanges. The occurrence of one or the other depends upon the overall socio-economic status of the household and the nature of its labour force, i.e. whether the adults are young and healthy or old and in poor health. Contrary to Richards's and Martin's findings (1981: 8), hiring extra labour is not an additional method adopted by small peasant households in Mit Qamar. Such households always seek to avoid such cash outlays, and only those with 3 feddans or more hired labour in Mit Qamar. However, those households with 1 feddan or less often talked about the hiring of labour for a certain job which they did not want to undertake, but the hiring of such labour never occurred to my knowledge and the jobs were performed by family or co-operative labour.

Informal and non-reciprocal co-operation tended to occur in cases where the given households were judged to be in need of such assistance, i.e. an older couple with no children and in poor health or a widow with no adult male children. In these cases, relatives and neighbours would generously and often spontaneously help in agricultural tasks. Bennett noted the same phenomenon amongst Canadian family farmers. He noted that most of the work on a small ranch, operated by an aged and enfeebled man, was carried out by neighbours who 'regarded him as a neighbourhood charge' (Bennett 1968: 288).

However, for small peasant households with at least one healthy adult male, co-operation in labour is usually more formalized and reciprocal. Usually these kinds of exchange are based on close kin-ship ties. Similarity in holding size is also a factor in the formation of such co-operative relations. Thus, two peasant households, each possessing one fit adult male, will co-operate in making the irrigation ridges by hand, with the plank first on one and then on the other's land. Reciprocal co-operative labour does not take place merely for jobs which require more labour than the households possess. Some agricultural operations, especially those involved in the cultivation of cotton, such as making furrows, hoeing, harvesting, and pulling out the cotton bushes, are often done by co-operative labour teams which may vary in size from two to five adult men. The exception is for harvesting, where women and children are capable of performing the job. Such teams provide small peasant producers with a more conducive social environment, which psychologically lightens the burden of this labour-intensive and difficult work, as well as short-ening the time required to perform the task. However, such co-operation is not an absolute gain, as each member of the team will have to contribute approximately the same amount of labour on the holdings of the rest of the team.

Borrowing

Borrowing is a pervasive and accepted social custom in Mit Qamar. Through it, many small peasant households are able to gain access to some of the necessary means of production, both for agricultural and household production, without much expenditure. Likewise, tem-porary loans in kind and money give the household breathing space for meeting its needs without having to resort to the market or being forced to work for wages.

Tools

Many small peasant households do not own the basic agricultural tools and equipment besides a hoe which is used for digging and spreading *sibakh,* the sickle (*sharshara*) which is used for cutting Egyptian clover and harvesting wheat, the small hoe (*man'ara*) which is used for planting cotton and harvesting maize, and a canvas donkey sack (*ghabit*) which is used to transport manure, additional earth (*ratch*), and clover. Thus, the main tools for ploughing and land preparation must be borrowed. These include a plough drawn by two animals (*mihrat*), a *loh*, the plank used for levelling which is attached in place of the plough, an *'asabiyya*, a wooden box-like

instrument used in levelling by hand, and a *batana*, a wooden instrument attached in place of the plough to make long ridges (*bitn,*
singular) within a field for irrigation purposes. Another *loh* with
handle and rope is used by two people to make short ridges within a
field for irrigation purposes.

These tools are borrowed from better-off relatives or neighbours
in the field, without any sort of payment or exchange. This lack of
ownership did not seem to cause any major problem in carrying out
cultivation on time, as ploughing operations were staggered amongst
peasants with holdings in the same irrigation basin (*hod*) in any case,
and no field went unploughed due to a lack of tools.

Other tools and items necessary for agriculture are borrowed by
many small peasants. For instance, the traditional tool for threshing
wheat, the *norag*, which is a wooden sledge with metal discs on the
cross bars drawn by a large animal, is often borrowed.[16] Also, only a
few households own the rope sack (*shilfi*) used to transport straw and
maize and thus they must borrow one at least twice a year. Although
none of the above tools and equipment is expensive, with a plough
costing approximately £E5.00,[17] the fact that small peasant households do not need to purchase and maintain these tools and equipment means that the cost of productive consumption of the peasant
household enterprise is decreased.

Household Utensils

A similar situation exists within the domain of the home of the
peasant household. Many basic household utensils and equipment are
borrowed constantly back and forth amongst neighbours, again without any direct reciprocation. However, in order to borrow freely,
one must be willing to lend one's own possessions when others are in
need of them. For instance, peasant women borrow the basic bread-
baking tools and often make use of a neighbour's hot oven to bake
their flat, unleavened pastry/bread (*fitir*), or cook horse beans (*ful*) or
a traditional dish of rice, butter, and milk (*ma'ammar*), contributing
perhaps some dung briquets (*gilla*) and dried maize stalks, the fuel
used in traditional ovens. Other common items borrowed are copper
pots (*halla*, singular), basins (*tisht*, singular), sieves (*mankhul,*
singular), knives (*kaslak*, singular), mortar and pestle (*hon*), a kind
of wooden beater used in the preparation of *khubbaiza* (*mafrat*), a
large wooden spoon (*maqhraf*), a chopping instrument (*makhrata*),
and primus stove (*wabur qhaz*). When guests from outside the village visit, extra mats ('*iyas*, singular) and pillows may be borrowed.

Again, although these household items are not expensive, the most expensive being copper utensils, with a large copper pot and lid costing about £E10.00 to £E15.00,[18] being able to borrow means that small peasant households can forgo buying certain necessary utensils and equipment and still complete all of their household tasks.

Animals

As most small peasant households 'possess' only one large animal,[19] another *must* be borrowed to undertake the ploughing and preparation of their land, since the traditional plough requires two large animals. However, this is not the only situation when a peasant household needs to borrow a large animal. If its water buffalo is pregnant or sick, which happened regularly during the period I was resident in the village, the people are forced to borrow two animals instead of one for ploughing and levelling.

A brief look at the pattern of animal borrowing of the household with whom I lived will help us to understand more clearly the nature and pervasiveness of this form of co-operation within Mit Qamar. During the agricultural year 1976–77, Mustafa's household borrowed 10 animals from seven owners to accomplish six field operations: to plant wheat (twice); to carry cotton bushes from the field to his house; to irrigate clover; and to plant maize (twice). Of the seven owners, all from the southern side, five were considered close relatives, the other two being neighbours in both field and *darb,* the narrow lane in which he lived. In terms of socio-economic status, five of the owners were considerably better off than Mustafa, with four of them possessing around three feddans of land as compared with Mustafa's 17 *qirats.* Of the remaining two, one possessed slightly more land than he did, 21 *qirats,* and the other less, 12 *qirats,* but the latter was also a government employee and therefore had a monthly salary of about £E12.00.

What emerges from the above data, and was corroborated by other cases within Mit Qamar, is that animal borrowing takes place primarily between closely-related peasant households from the same side of the village, with the lender having a considerably higher socio-economic status than the peasant household borrowing the animal. As far as I could determine, the borrowing of these animals was gratis, and no labour was returned in exchange, although I was told by Mustafa that the one who borrowed animals could repay with his labour by helping the lender plough, harvest maize, etc. In this particular case, the health of the peasant was so poor that it would have been difficult for him to engage in more agricultural work. As it was, he was also the recipient of labour from a large number of neighbours and relatives. However, at the same time, Mustafa lent out his own water buffalo a number of times to his widowed sister, who had loaned him hers once, and to two other relatives, neither of whom had lent him an animal, when their own animals were sick.

Another case of animal borrowing illustrates the necessity for more direct and immediate repayment. A young peasant, Subhi, who owned seven *qirats* of land and rented another five seasonally by short-term rent (*sagil*), and who worked for agricultural wages within and outside the village, borrowed a donkey from a relative for two days. However, when he borrowed it for a third day, he agreed with the lender to hoe his nine *qirats* of cotton in exchange. His father-in-law, on the other hand, did not demand any exchange labour when he borrowed a donkey from him. The fact that the peasant who was borrowing the animal was healthy and worked normally for wages, and that the relative who lent him the donkey had no sons to help him in agriculture, combined to result in the borrowing peasant having to partially repay his debt. These two cases illustrate the number of factors that can come into play in determining the actual arrangement between lender and borrower.

The importance of such co-operation over animals in preventing the small peasant household from having to resort to market relations in order to undertake necessary agricultural tasks is clear, and most small peasant households make use of such co-operative arrangements. However, some do not. For example, Musi, the same small peasant/employee who lent Mustafa his water buffalo for irrigating, chose to plant his maize by the ʿafir as opposed to the *harati* method, because the former could be done by tractor. This kept him from having to borrow another animal, which he considered a bother. The fee to plough his field of 12 *qirats* (12 × £E.15/*qirat*), i.e. £E1.80, was not much, given his monthly salary. However, for most peasants, no regular salary is available and hence such 'unnecessary' costs are avoided if possible.

Money and Produce

Certain difficult moments in the life of a small peasant household are temporarily overcome through the borrowing, without interest, of small sums of money and produce from other households. Repayment is required eventually, but not immediately. One of the most common items borrowed amongst peasant households was straw. This occurred especially during the month of May before many peasants had been able to finish their threshing and winnowing, which of course coincided with a period when there was very little other fodder available. The extended length of possible repayment time is illustrated by the case of the household with whom I stayed. They had borrowed a basket of straw before they had finished threshing their wheat in 1976, and at harvest time of the following year, had still not returned it in kind. This shows that immediate repayment is not necessary. The debt is not, however, forgotten.

Land

Another form of co-operation takes the form of land exchanges (*tabaddul or badl al-ard*) which occur when two peasant households agree to exchange an equivalent piece of land in order to avoid the full brunt of the government's directive to grow cotton every third year. The system works as follows. For example, peasant A, who possesses 8 *qirats* of land in a given irrigation basin (*hod*) which falls within an area of the village designated for cotton cultivation (*tauhid al-'utn*), exchanges four *qirats* of this with peasant B for four *qirats* of his land, which falls outside the cotton area. The exchange will be reversed the following year. Consequently, neither peasant has to give up the cultivation of wheat and maize, which overlap with the growing season of cotton. Such exchanges help to increase the self-sufficiency of peasant households, despite government directives. Likewise, they allow both peasants to avoid going against the co-operative's directives and hence becoming violators (*mukhalifin*), liable for a fine of £E20.00.

The frequency of such exchanges is hard to determine as, like other illegal, informal forms of tenancy, they are not recorded in the records of the co-operative. Peasants involved in such exchanges legally maintain control over their own land, but must deal with the co-operative in terms of credit, etc. for the exchanged piece of land.[20] I personally heard of three pairs of exchanging households, while many peasants when questioned about exchanges, stated that they did not do it because it was difficult to find an equivalent piece of land.

However, two points stnd out: first, that *tabaddul* was more likely to occur amongst small peasant households with very small usufructuary rights to land; and secondly, that *tabaddul* was likely to be supported by close kinship ties, as it involved long-term commit-ment. Thus, the household with whom I stayed, possessing 17 *qirats* of land, had a long-standing exchange relationship with the widowed sister of the head of household, possessing 36 *qirats,* based on the mutual exchange of 4 *qirats* of land. Two neighbouring households also had a long-standing exchange arrangement whereby one ex-changed their entire permanent usufruct of 4 *qirats* of land with a close relative who possessed 3 feddans. The latter obviously carried out the exchange more for the sake of his poorer relatives than for his own household. However, he was unable to fulfil his informal obligation one year when nearly all his land fell within areas desig-nated for cotton cultivation, and hence the household with the 4 *qirats* ended up growing cotton that year.

The apparent infrequency of such land exchanges can be partially explained by the incomplete control of the co-operative in enforcing the cultivation of cotton. The flouting of the government's directives to plant cotton is widespread throughout the countryside and not just a phenomenon of Mit Qamar. In September 1976, the agricultural inspector for one of Mit Qamar's neighbouring villages told me that of the village's 300 holdings (*hiyazas*), 150 had disobeyed the government directive. Another agricultural inspector from the dis-trict of Abu Kabir, al-Sharqiyya, told me that in the villages in which he worked, there was a positive correlation between the number of those who broke the government order and the number of small-holdings, i.e. those villages with a large percentage of smallholdings had a large number who disobeyed. His observation confirmed my own research in Mit Qamar. This suggests that they could not afford to sacrifice scarce land to a low-return crop just to meet government directives. Most peasants in Mit Qamar continually failed to plant the stipulated amount of cotton because of its low profitability and because of lax government enforcement. Sometimes peasants failed to plant any of their land with cotton. This occurred, for example, in 1977, when peasants cultivating one of the cotton areas in Mit Qamar collectively decided to ignore the co-operative's directives.

Peasants also often planted cotton in only that part of the land which fell within the cotton area, that part in the centre of the field, farthest away from the top. In 1981, some peasants with land in this area in 1977 followed the second tactic, planting approximately half their holdings with cotton. When they were called before the local police regarding this violation, they were able to say that they had planted part of their land with cotton, but they would insist that they could not plant more as they had to feed themselves and their animals. These tactics seem to have worked for peasants in Mit Qamar, as only one peasant had ever been fined £E20.00, the penalty for not cultivating cotton, and that was because he had failed to attend his court hearing despite three notices from the authorities.

The continuation and frequency of the practice of land exchange in Mit Qamar is, as indicated, dependent on a number of factors. Being forced to grow cotton every third year has been the basic cause for the formation of *tabaddul* relations, along with the low price of cotton and high input costs. On the other hand, incomplete control over the production process and failure to fine violators has decreased the necessity for it amongst small peasant households. However, indications are that even if the government makes cotton a more lucrative crop to grow, as it has tried to, with the price of a *qantar* (1 *qantar* = 44.93 kg) of cotton rising from £E20.00 in 1976 to £E50.00 in 1980, the fodder demands of the small peasant households prevent them from devoting most of their land to cotton cultivation. Hence, they will continue to violate or evade the cooperative's directives *vis-à-vis* cotton. If fines are actually increased and imposed, small peasant households will probably find land (*tabaddul*) arrangements for their survival.

My analysis of one village in the Egyptian Delta has attempted to show the importance of various forms of non-capitalist social relations in the reproduction of the small peasant household which remains the predominant form of production within the Egyptian countryside. In spite of increased commoditization within agrarian Egypt, help and co-operation amongst small peasant households continues to take numerous forms, be it in terms of labour, tools, utensils, etc., which together help make it possible for Egyptian peasants to continue to reproduce themselves as peasants and not as full-scale proletarians, wholly dependent upon wage labour. Through these mechanisms small peasants can decrease their dependence upon market relations and hence contribute to the inability of capitalist relations of production to become predominant within agrarian Egypt.

Notes

1. I would like to take this opportunity to thank Norman Long for giving me this opportunity to explore further the field of rural sociology as a part-time staff member in the Department of

Anthropology, University of Durham, 1979–82 and for encouraging me to participate in the Working Group on Non-Wage Remuneration and Informal Co-operation in Rural Society, XI Congress of European Society for Rural Sociology, Espoo, Finland. Secondly, I would like to thank the participants in the above working group for their comments and suggestions on an earlier version of this chapter. Thirdly, I would like to express my appreciation to the Department of Sociology and Social Anthropology, University of Hull, and the Centre for Middle Eastern and Islamic Studies, University of Durham, for the financial support which made my research possible. My initial fieldwork and research was carried out in Egypt from January 1976–September 1977 for the writing of my PhD for the Department of Sociology and Social Anthropology, University of Hull, England. It was funded by the University in the form of a three-year scholarship. In March–April 1981 I returned to Egypt to do some follow-up research, financed by a travel grant from the Centre for Middle Eastern and Islamic Studies, University of Durham, England. The transliteration of Arabic words in this chapter has been done in accordance with the local dialect of the village of Mit Qamar. Finally, it is impossible to express adequately my deep appreciation of my husband, Pandelis M. Glavanis, from whom I have received support and encouragement since the inception of my project on rural Egypt.

2.   For instance, both Perelman and Mooney point out that 'capitalism is not alone in seeking a greater unity of production time and labor time' (Mooney 1982: 5). Likewise, Mooney criticizes the authors' contention that perishability forms a major obstacle to development, stating that the authors themselves in a footnote acknowledge 'that capital has penetrated areas of highly perishable agricultural commodities such as fruits and vegetables' (Mooney 1982: 9).

3.   Short-term rents are nearly five times what the legal rental rate is in the village in which I carried out my study. Thus, instead of paying £E3.00 per feddan per annum, the peasants of Mit Qamar are obliged to pay between £E144.00 and £E168.00 per feddan (or £E6.00 to £E7.00 per *qirat*).

4.   The government has, in the last few years, been re-evaluating land for taxation purposes, which will lead to higher official rental rates.

5.   These statistics, based on co-operative records, do not completely reflect the actual pattern. For instance, short-term rental agreements are not recorded, which means that the given piece of land remains registered in the name of the owner. Likewise, a certain landholding might remain in the name of the father, although in actual fact it might be divided and cultivated by the sons.

6.   The preceding information on the role of livestock in the small peasant household was gathered during my fieldwork, carried out in the Egyptian countryside, on the transformation in the peasant household post-1952.

7.   Schistosomiasis or bilharziasis is a debilitating parasitic disease which is widespread amongst Egyptian peasants. It is contracted primarily through contact with contamined water from irrigation canals.

8.   From 1960–1976, the urban population increased 68.3 per cent, while the rural population increased by only 27.5 per cent (Central Agency for Public Mobilization and Statistics 1978: 159).

9.   Recent studies (Richards and Martin 1981; Morsy 1978) and my own fieldwork indicate that landlessness (i.e. no usufruct rights to land) amongst households with potential male agricultural workers is relatively small, and certainly much less than the 40 per cent cited by Abdel-Fadil (1975: 44).

10.   The scientific name for Egyptian clover is *Trifolium alexandrinum L.*

11.   The scientific name for elephant's ear is *Colocasia antiquorum.*

12.   The scientific name for *mulukhiyya* is *Corchorus olitorius.*

13.   In Sir al-Layana, District of Minuf, al-Minufiyya, where Berque carried out his research, there were 15 communal meeting rooms and guest houses around the time of the First World War, but by 1953 there were only 6 (Berque 1957: 49).

14.   Abdel-Fadil (1975) claims that this type of labour exchange broke down as its precondition, namely an equitable distribution of

land, did. This may have been true for the period of 1900–52, but with agrarian reform, land became more equitably distributed, and by the 1970s, indications are that landlessness was no longer a dominant feature of Egyptian villages. However, small peasant holdings under 5 feddans, especially those under 1 feddan, have increased dramatically in number. Hence I would argue that exchange labour for harvesting wheat and maize is no longer needed as much as before, but that is not to say that these small households do not give or receive help in the form of labour.

15.   The largest holding in Fatiha in 1974/75 was 8 feddans, and 42 per cent of the holdings were under 1½ feddans (Morsy 1978: 8).

16.   During the wheat harvest of May 1977, the majority of small peasant households in the southern side of the village of Mit Qamar used the traditional wheat thresher (*noraq*) to thresh their wheat. However, three years later, in May 1980, the villagers reported that only one household had used the traditional thresher within the entire village. The rest of the village relied upon tractor-powered threshers, two from the village and others from the area. It seems that the main factor for the change to mechanized threshers was the increasing pressure for animal fodder, i.e. straw, at this time of the year, given the general increase in animal population within the village.

17.   By April 1981, the cost of a plough had risen to between £E15.00 and £E20.00.

18.   Most peasants buy aluminium pots these days because of the rapid increase in the price of copper and the disadvantage that copper utensils must be recoated with nickel every few years. An equivalent aluminium pot with lid cost around £E2.50 in 1976/77.

19.   The animal deficiency amongst most small peasant households was partially alleviated when I returned to Mit Qamar in April 1981. A number of small peasant households had acquired a second large draft animal, but that is not to say that all small households now possess two large animals.

20.   Stauth mentions exchange of land (*badl al-ard*) for the village of Shamiyats, but does not indicate how prevalent it is (Stauth 1979: 26).

3 Cash Crop Production and Family Labour: Tobacco Growers in Corrientes, Argentina

Marit Melhuus

Contrary to earlier notions, it seems that the peasant is here to stay. The peasant problem is not merely a discussion for theoretically-oriented scholars, but a reality – and in parts of the world, a rather brutal reality at that. Despite unfavourable social conditions generated by national and international policies, the peasant has shown an extraordinary ability to adapt to changing conditions (Esteva 1978). The 'ignorant', 'conservative', and even doomed, peasant of the 1950s has, to a certain extent, become a flexible and viable agricultural producer. It seems that, instead of being the Achilles' heel of an economy, impeding capitalist development, under certain conditions, the peasant is susceptible to integration into the capitalist economy.[1]

The tobacco growers of Corrientes provide a case in point. They are sharecroppers dependent upon a landowner for access to land and produce an industrial crop for marketing by international tobacco companies. The three main actors in this social setting, then, are peasants, landlords, and industrialists, and it is, in fact, the logic of peasant production that contributes to the maintenance of this particular agrarian form,[2] although it is also important to keep in mind that these producers are involved in a highly developed commodity market. They are first and foremost producers of exchange-value, engaging in simple reproduction, where the money obtained is used to buy necessary consumer goods, and they live and work in a society where wage labour dominates most economic activities.[3]

In this chapter, I aim to illustrate fundamental aspects of the integration of this peasant economy into the wider society. My intention is to isolate the conditions for the reproduction of the specific agrarian system found in the tobacco area today. Emphasis is placed on the internal organization of the household, focusing upon labour organization and questions of household viability under precarious

economic circumstances. The point to be stressed is that the concrete observable processes and strategies at the individual household level must be comprehended within a broader context; but that
this context must not be perceived as solely external since many of its
features are internalized and reflected in particular household
strategies.

The argument revolves around three basic assumptions: the logic
of the peasant economy, the conceptualization of peasants as 'parts
of the whole' (Kroeber 1948; Redfield 1956; Shanin 1973; Alavi
1973; Ennew, Hirst and Tribe 1977) and the idea that this reflects an
asymmetrical relation between producers and controllers of surplus
(Wolf 1966). The fact that a peasant runs a household not a business
concern implies that the categories of wage, rent, and profit are
absent in his economic calculations. What he sees and what he cal-
culates is the result of his labour, irrespective (more or less) of the
number of hours of work he and his family have invested. At the
centre of this statement lies the postulate that for the peasant, his
labour power has no direct exchange value. In other words, it is the
concrete organization of tobacco production which is crucial. This is
reflected at various levels and in relation to various factors, land
distribution, labour power and marketing channels being the most
important. The logic of a peasant economy implies a particular organization of production embedded in a model of family labour and
self-exploitation. The household is both a unit of production and one
of consumption. An examination of the production process must
take as a starting point the crop or crops produced, and relate this to
the demands for labour power and the pattern of the division of
labour that emerges. The running of a family farm is a complicated
administrative task. Specific demands on co-operation and flexibility
must be met, not only in relation to the agricultural cycle, but also to
the developmental cycle of the domestic group. Households may
vary in size, in this case from four to sixteen members, and pose
quite different demands for the internal organization of the household which it must be able to meet as it expands and declines over
time.

On the assumption that peasants do have a specific economic
rationality separating them from other agrarian types, and accepting
the basic premiss that they produce a surplus, I attempt to reveal, in
this particular case, the structural relationship which ensures that this
surplus is siphoned off. In other words, I will show that the social
incorporation of this peasant society, in the tobacco area, into the

economy at large, is one based on economic exploitation. Furthermore, I will show that this form of exploitation as it exists today, is contingent upon the maintenance of a peasant rationality, based on a specific sharecropping system, in combination with capitalist market mechanisms.

Central to my argument is the concept of surplus. A few remarks are necessary to the determination of this concept. In order to identify a surplus product we must first take into account surplus and necessary labour, as a surplus product is the result of surplus labour. Surplus labour is not an absolute concept but is relative to what is culturally and socially defined as necessary labour. Necessary labour (according to Hindess and Hirst, 1975) is that labour time necessary to secure the conditions of the reproduction of the labourer. Surplus-labour, then, is that labour which exists over and above necessary labour.[4]

Being sharecroppers within a landlord system, the tobacco growers of Corrientes are obliged to produce a surplus. This surplus they are not able to realize themselves. It is transferred, overtly, to the landowner, through a rent relation of direct appropriation and, it may be inferred, covertly, through an unequal exchange in the market transaction, where the market price does not cover the individual costs of production.[5] We are thus operating on two levels, that of production and appropriation, and that of circulation and realization.

In order to elaborate the argument, it is essential that certain contextual features be presented. This will clarify the problems related to defining the relations of production and, moreover, will specify the conditions under which these particular agrarian relations have evolved. One point to be stressed is the specific historical process which resulted in the introduction of black or Turkish tobacco to this area. Another aspect which demands attention is the cultivation of Turkish tobacco itself, taking into consideration the specific demands on production and organization that this cultivation implies. Having thus presented the external factors relevant to the household production unit, we may then proceed to examine the internal processes: the structuring of the production unit, the internal division of labour, and the possible strategies that may be pursued under these constraints.

PROPERTY STRUCTURE AND THE LAND TENURE SYSTEM: ECONOMIC CRISIS AND THE INTRODUCTION OF TOBACCO

The province of Corrientes is located in north-east Argentina. Brazil and Paraguay border it to the east and north, and the Parana River to the west. Corrientes has always suffered from her marginal economic and geographical position with respect to the powerful economic and political centres concentrated in the Pampa region. The economic development of the tobacco area in Corrientes has primarily evolved around cattle ranching.[6] However, because of unfavourable ecological and climatic conditions, combined with a specific property structure, cattle ranching has, until recently, been dominated by extensive management, with few capital investments, no systematic breeding and a lack of scientific method and expertise as compared with the more mechanized and capitalized ranches of the Pampa region.[7] Low productivity and marginal market position are the characteristic features of cattle raising in the region.

The principal production unit has been the *estancia* (estate). In its traditional organization, a policy of minimal risk has prevailed. Production has not been organized as a capitalist enterprise, but rather as a rent maximization unit, without the capitalist connotation of rent. The landowner, being the proprietor of a vast extension of land, runs his *estancia* with a minimum of monetary outlay and practically no capital investment. Labour does not enter as variable capital, but is contracted through various individual agreements. A form of labour-rent dominates in the cattle sector: the local cowboy is contracted to care for the herds of the landowner, and, in return, given a piece of land to cultivate. Wage labour may be employed, but to a much lesser degree.

Before going on to discuss the introduction of tobacco to the province, it seems pertinent to present some of the basic aspects of the property structure and land tenure system of the area. As I have already mentioned, land is a commodity in limited circulation. The large estates have developed over hundreds of years, and there has been little modification in land distribution since the turn of the century.[8] In the department of Goya, where most of the tobacco cultivation is concentrated, 70 per cent of the total area pertains to estates of 1,000 hectares or more, these representing only 5 per cent of property units.[9] On the other hand, property units of 50 hectares or less, which total 56 per cent of all units, control only 5 per cent of the total area. This extreme concentration of land has resulted in a specific socio-economic structure, converging around a complex land tenure system. We find that the majority of production units, as opposed to property units, are under 50 hectares, and most of them are under 10. Only 22 per cent of all production units under 50 hectares own the land they are cultivating. In Goya, for example, of 3,404 registered production units of less than 10 hectares only 280 of them own the land they are cultivating. Within the tobacco region of Corrientes this is the general trend: of a registered 7,816 units of tobacco production, 5,638 did not own land i.e. around 70 per cent. Of these, 73.3 per cent held under 9 hectares (Ministerio de Agricultura y Ganaderia de la Nación, Investigación Sociologíca Rural 1970).

Land is a scarce commodity, and the extensive cattle ranching has had a very low capacity for incorporation of the rural labour force. In addition, industrial development at local level is insignificant. The result then is a critical employment situation for the local Correntino, and unemployment is met by out-migration. Corrientes has always exported people from the province. As early as 1914, 15 per cent of the Correntinos were to be found in other provinces. Today, there are 280,000 of them living in the Buenos Aires area alone. Of a provincial population of about 600,000, this is a substantial figure.

The collapse of the world stock market in 1929 drastically affected the Argentinian economy. Traditional export markets were closed and prices of products dropped by 50 per cent. A period of stagnation within livestock breeding and agriculture was unavoidable, and Corrientes, being on the periphery, felt the full effects badly. But the crisis did not force the Correntinian landlords into bankruptcy. Having accumulated few debts, they were not forced to sell land. Their land monopoly was maintained and alternative sources of rent income were sought. Industrial crops seemed to be a solution.

The economic policy of Argentina in this period (due to immense problems with the balance of payments) was based on import substitution: the country itself was to produce some of the products it until then had been forced to import. Tobacco was among these. However, in the first phase, it was the textile industry that led the import substitution process, resulting in a great demand for cotton, which was planted in Chaco, Santa Fé, and Corrientes. In Corrientes, the cultivation occurred mainly on the larger estates, on a sharecropping basis. However, the uncertain climate, plus the rent to be paid to the landlord, made the relative production costs of cotton higher in Corrientes than in the neighbouring provinces. Regional specialization emerged, northern Santa Fé becoming the dominant cotton producer.[10] But as cotton left the fields of Corrientes towards the end of the 1930s, tobacco entered them.

At this point, the traditional landlords of Corrientes were still seeking new forms of rent. In a situation where land was abundant, but under the control of an exclusive landed élite, specific labour relations developed. A relationship of exploitation based on the appropriation of rent-in-labour or rent-in-product came to be the form under which tobacco cultivation evolved.[11]

Taking advantage of a situation with high rural unemployment, it is easy for a landlord to 'contract' families to cultivate tobacco on a 'sharecropping' or *aparcería,* basis, as it is called locally. The *aparcero* pays the landlord a stipulated percentage of his harvest, sometimes as much as 50 per cent. The landowner specifies the crop and supplies the land, and has no further involvement in the production process. The tobacco grower provides labour, means of production and builds his own house. This arrangement is an expression of the 'minimal risk' mentality which is prevalent among the traditional landed élite. The cultivation of tobacco, being extremely labour-intensive and land-intensive, favours a peasant adaptation, with the logic of the family farm and self-exploitation permeating the production units.[12]

The demand for tobacco, or a similar crop, that did not compete with cattle raising, exploited little land and gave a good price, gave the Correntinian landlord a 'niche' to exploit. He could continue to maximize land rent while keeping his own expenses at a minimum. If this, or a similar product, had not appeared at the critical moment, when the Correntinian landlord was being displaced in the race for cattle, we could question the continued viability of the then existing production units, and wonder what the situation would be today.

Today in the tobacco industry, it is in fact the industrial corporations that hold the future of the tobacco growers in their hands. Until 1934, the production of tobacco was relatively stable, but from then on, production increased. However, since 1964, there has been a reduction in the production of Turkish cigarettes, resulting in a reduced demand for Turkish or dark tobacco; this, in turn, has affected the tobacco growers of Corrientes, for they are producers of the dark tobacco used in them. Simultaneously, there has been an increase in the production of light tobacco ('Virginia' and 'Burley') in the Northern provinces of Salta and Jujuy. Nowadays the cigarette industry shows a clear preference for light tobacco.[13]

In contrast to many other agro-industrial enterprises in Argentina, the cigarette industry has managed to keep pace with other branches of industrial development, such as the petro-chemical and electro-metallurgical industries, for example (Dorfman 1970; Ramos, 1972). Following a general trend, the cigarette industry has also undergone a marked process of centralization and concentration of production,[14] and today is almost totally controlled and/or owned by foreign firms.[15] These international cigarette monopolies, striving to maintain their place among the leading industries in Argentina, are forever pressing for higher profits. Reducing costs is one method of increasing gains. Decreased expenditure on outlay for raw materials is one way of achieving this, hence the pressure to lower the price of tobacco.[16] However, since there are various parties that are interested in good tobacco prices — the grower, but also the landowners, and local commercial enterprises and tradesmen — there are many interests seeking better tobacco prices. Although the fundamental relation of exploitation for the tobacco grower is his relation to the landlord, through the land-rent paid as a percentage of his harvest, the *price* he receives for his tobacco is critical.

We will briefly consider some price-related aspects of tobacco growing, hoping in this manner to disclose why it seems that a peasant logic at the level of production is a rational adaptation. It is essential to keep in mind that we are considering commodity producers of an industrial crop, and that the conditions for its marketing are set by the tobacco/cigarette industries. Our contention is that it is the family-based farm which, in this case, will produce the cheapest raw material. Our argument is based on the assumption that, at the market level there is a transaction of unequal exchange, where the market price obtained generally does not cover the individual costs of production, were this to follow a capitalist evaluation; this is, nevertheless, a hypothetical supposition.[17]

This situation is made possible because a peasant producer does not calculate the exchange *value* of his own labour power, let alone strive for profit and rent. Were he to give himself and the rest of the household members a reasonable wage for the labour expended, and allow for a profit, his production would definitely not be profitable, at the going rate for tobacco; he would, in fact, be producing at a deficit. Whether this underpayment of labour power already consumed actually expresses an 'individual surplus' which is transferred to the industry, perhaps contributing to the formation of a super-profit, should be discussed. Friedmann has stated that to benefit from low prices is not the same as to exploit (Friedmann 1980).[18] However, the issue at hand is not so much whether the tobacco industry exploits, as I am inclined to think it does, but that it is able to obtain a cheap raw material because the producers of tobacco, operating with a peasant logic based on self-exploitation, can produce at lower cost prices than a capitalist enterprise could. Herein lies one of the conditions for the social incorporation of a family farming economy into a capitalist economy.

TOBACCO CULTIVATION AND FAMILY LABOUR

It has already been stressed that tobacco cultivation is extremely labour-intensive. Let us briefly look at some of the labour operations involved in the cultivation of Turkish tobacco.

The tobacco seeds are first sown in beds, at different time intervals in late winter or early spring, from July through the end of August. After 10–12 weeks, the small plants, having reached approximately 12 cm high, are transplanted to the fields, which in the meantime have been prepared and fenced in. The transplantation, starting in August and continuing until December, takes place after rains have thoroughly wet the earth. This process is done manually, with each plant being rooted up, transported to the field and then replanted. Only a month after transplantation, the plant may have reached the height of 1 m and developed 10–12 leaves. At this point the bottom leaves may show tendencies to yellow, which is a sign that they are ready for harvesting. Harvesting begins, leaf by leaf, plant by plant, in December. Harvesting is manual, starting with the bottom 4–5 leaves of each plant. As the plant continues to grow, and new leaves develop, harvesting continues, and in the course of 3–4 pickings, the whole plant is finally stripped, leaving the stalk and a few top leaves. In the period of early harvesting many activities run parallel to one another. The total growth cycle consists of 3 months in seed beds and 3–5 months in the field. As sowing and transplantation occur in stages, there may be tobacco plants with differences of 1–2 months in development, growing side by side. So the cultivation process for a household stretches over a period of 7–10 months, whereas the total production cycle will be longer. Before sowing, the seed beds and fields must be prepared, and after harvest, the tobacco must be dried, cured, classified and marketed.

It has been calculated that between 150 and 160 work days are necessary to cultivate 1 hectare of tobacco. An average household will cultivate 3–5 hectares, each holding 18,000–25,000 plants. If they are evenly distributed, at different stages of the growth cycle, the top season may stretch from November to the end of April, totalling nearly 80 per cent or 125 work days of the total labour input of the whole production process. If the plants are more concentrated, i.e. not so evenly spread over time, around 60 per cent of the labour input is spent within 3½–4 months from the middle of December to the end of March.

Few of the most labour-consuming operations have been mechanized. This is partly due to the expense involved in mechanization, which is not deemed lucrative in relation to price, but there are also certain operations which do not permit mechanization. In contrast to light tobacco, which is harvested mechanically by cutting down the whole plant and stripping the leaves, and then dried under shelter, on gas stoves, dark tobacco, as mentioned, is harvested leaf by leaf, as they mature, and dried in the sun. It is this sun-curing that gives the tobacco its special flavour. These operations are done by hand. In fact, it is the harvest period which is the bottleneck of the whole production cycle, and it is the harvesting potential of a production unit which will determine how much tobacco is to be planted. As the operations involved in the harvest are never subject to mutual aid or exchange labour situations (as is, for example, the transplanting of seedlings from beds to fields) a household head cannot take into account more hands than he actually controls.

Tobacco cultivation, however, is not and cannot be the sole preoccupation of the household. Its running also entails a series of household chores which must be done in order to meet the social and physical requirements of the individual members. These include cooking, washing clothes, taking care of children and old people, shopping, and also observing religious festivals and maintaining beneficial relations with the saints. In addition, subsistence production from the kitchen garden of more basic food crops, as well as the upkeep of cattle, sheep and poultry, are necessary. So there are a multitude of tasks that have to be organized and co-ordinated, all requiring both careful planning and extreme flexibility.

The organization of a household is based on a combination of a clear-cut division of labour for some tasks and a pooling of labour resources for others. Basically, the main division of labour is structured by gender and age. However, this is not absolute. It tends to have a female bias, there being certain tasks which are exclusively female, and not interchangeable, whereas there are many other tasks which are predominantly male but, depending on circumstances, can well be carried out by women. This can be illustrated if we look at the socialization of children.

Children are, at an early age, incorporated into the general running of the household. Young boys may already at the age of 7 be given small tasks to fulfil, of which running errands over large distances are the most important. A girl is considered really useful by the age of 10, when she is capable of doing most of the household chores: washing clothes in the nearest lake, cooking food, keeping house and taking care of children. If the children are sent to school, they are usually withdrawn at the ages of 11–12, or, for girls, when they have their first menstruation. A boy will then move out of his parents' room and go to live with his older brothers, in a room of their own, normally a partition of the store-house. He then belongs to the male world, and his older brothers are mainly responsible for teaching him the necessary agricultural skills.

Girls are in a different situation. They not only learn all the skills of running a large household, but are also trained to participate in the work of the fields, and are expected to do their share when this is deemed necessary, the period of transplanting and harvest being the most obvious. Where sons are scarce, girls are in some cases taught to plough. In any case, their obligations to the household cannot be separated out and reduced to household chores. In fact, it is hard to draw the line between productive and reproductive labour, since cultivating maize is as much reproductive labour as cooking it would be. Girls are responsible for the general upkeep of the domestic domain, and, under prevailing conditions, this is an arduous and time-consuming as well as administratively demanding task (fetching water, gathering wood for the fire, slaying chickens, washing clothes etc.). However, girls are by no means exempt from agricultural tasks, and in large households they may be working in the fields alongside their brothers.

What we are describing is a situation where both the field work and housework are characterized by being extremely labour-intensive, the former, however, being susceptible to seasonal variations. This makes it impossible for one and the same person to both cultivate tobacco and take care of the household chores.[19] This in turn imposes specific demands on household composition and co-operation. In a sense, the prevailing division of labour expresses a form of necessary economic complementarity. The form and content of housework affects the limits of viability of the household as a whole. When considering the personnel available for tobacco production, a household head must take into account those necessary for these other reproductive tasks. This situation is most clearly expressed when a tobacco producer becomes a widower. If the household composition is such that there are no grown-up daughters to take over the tasks of the wife, the household will dissolve, the children being placed with relatives, and the widower possibly joining the household of a brother or sister.

The point to be stressed is that there is an intimate and necessary economic connection between housework, reproduction, and production. A woman is necessary for the carrying out of domestic tasks while at the same time she may be expected to participate in the fields. It is the household as a unit of production which will define the total field of work in which a woman is to participate. At the same time, the character of the housework, i.e. the actual labour process involved, sets clear and definite practical limitations on how time may be utilized. There is no question of negotiation between men and women as to who is to do the housework, though there may be discussions as to the field activities. This is one aspect of the structuring of the household which obviously will permeate organizational processes.

Taking into account the constraints inherent in tobacco cultivation, and keeping in mind the overall structural features related to land, labour and market, we will illustrate the internal dynamics of these units of production which we have characterized as peasant. We hope to indicate certain patterns in household organization which crystallize as adaptive processes working towards the reproduction of household units in a situation of social and economic uncertainty.

Tobacco production is organized in and around the household where *labour* (available or potential) is the central factor of production. We have already stressed that the harvesting capacity of a production unit is the crucial factor in the planning of the productive cycle. In the period of the harvest, all available hands, men, women, and children, are to be found in the fields, picking, or at home stringing the leaves. This pooling of labour resources expresses the maximum production unit, which during slack periods, is dispersed and engaged in other tasks, such as household chores or subsistence farming. In addition, both land tenure relations and the availability of specific means of production, such as possession of draught animals, size of storehouse, fencing etc., will together form a set of constraints to which the household must respond. Efforts must be directed towards maintaining an optimal balance between labour, land, and technology.

To secure the necessary labour, different strategies are pursued. Most obvious is the effort to prolong the natural family expansion phase. Women give birth to the bitter end. Households with 10, 12, or 14 children are not uncommon. Furthermore, we also noted a system of 'adoption', whereby many households prolong their natural expansion phase by taking in children of poorer relatives, illegitimate grandchildren, or by asking for the first male child of their eldest son. This continual mobility of personnel can be explained as an effort to make up for an unfavourable household composition, where the balance between productive and non-productive members is critical. However, another logical explanation for this behaviour springs out of the very special situation of the sharecropping peasant. He has the right to cultivate and reside on the land as long as he, his family or household, is productive. The moment he no longer produces, or cannot produce, the amount necessary to keep himself and pay the landlord, his time is up; his tenancy is not 'inheritable'. Therefore, it is important to put off as long as possible the dissolution of the household.

In many cases where the labour situation is unfavourable, other labour arrangements are made. A young boy may be 'employed', living with the family and working alongside the rest, and receiving part of the harvest as pay. Or close kinsmen, often widowers or single men, are recruited with various remuneration agreements. In some cases, 'joint ventures' between separate households may be established, where brothers, or father and son, join to work the fields. Of course, the reverse process, where households expel superfluous labour, is also apparent. In most cases, women leave to seek work in the urban centres, while boys are urged to stay. Once there, young women are usually employed as domestic servants, and once they have left a rural area, they rarely return to live again. They will marry and settle in the town. For young men, obligatory military service may represent an important turning point. It may in fact be a first contact with the outside world and a last farewell to the rural area. This may be a critical moment for the household as it loses able-bodied men, either temporarily or, worse, permanently.

However, for a sharecropper within a large estate, where restrictions on land are rarely imposed, the crucial factor is to maximize the available labour potential so that stable units can be maintained. We can observe large variations in the labour potential of a unit and the actual realization of this. Explanation for this variation can primarily be sought in the composition and size of the household, related to a more or less efficient internal division of labour. However, relation to the landlord, technology employed, agricultural expertise, and organizational talents, along with the quality of land, will of course affect productivity.

One possibility, which increases productivity and reduces labour-intensity, is to use a tractor. Traditional methods of ploughing are time-consuming. Where oxen take 5 days, and horses and mules 4, a tractor can plough the same amount of land in little more than an hour. But for some, time is really not a problem, and the improved condition of the soil after a tractor ploughing of minor consequence. A household head will not opt to pay for a job which he feels he can perfectly well do himself. There is no point in 'freeing' the labour force to a point where it is unemployed. It is the larger households, planting more than 4 hectares of tobacco, that tend to use a tractor. In these instances, the preparation of the soil will be quite time-consuming and require many sets of draught animals and ploughs to complete the task. Few households are in the position of possessing such a quantity of animals and implements, and, in addition, the necessary labour force to set them all in motion. Another aspect which should be taken into account when considering the use of a tractor is whether or not there are alternative tasks to which labour can be dedicated, such as subsistence production.

Some subsistence production is an integral part of all households, but it is always incidental to tobacco production. Similarly, it is clearly related to the prime factors of production: labour, land and technology. Obviously, if these barely cover the essentials necessary for tobacco production, allocations to subsistence production are rendered near-impossible. The peasant producers are primarily commodity producers, and are so integrated into the market economy that a minimum of cash income is essential to cover their daily needs. Because of this market integration, subsistence production cannot function as a buffer in times of crisis. Pulling out of market-oriented production to concentrate on subsistence is just not an alternative. Nor will a producer, having once satisfied his immediate consumer needs, related to the market, cease to produce tobacco, and concentrate his energies on subsistence production, maize being a partial exception. Cash crop and subsistence production are not interchangeable categories. This is not (as our budget studies show) because the peasants are, like Western workers, forever more consumer-goods minded, with the buying of commodities as a goal in itself. There are other mechanisms, such as generally high inflation, increased productivity in other units of production dedicated to tobacco, lower prices for tobacco, at work, forcing the poorest units to produce more and more tobacco. Generally speaking, it would be correct to assert that at the outset their material resources or 'wealth' are so reduced that any possible means of increasing cash income will readily be sought. This is true whether the tobacco grower owns his land or is tied to a landlord, although the latter group is more limited in its allocations, as it is the landlord who will specify what is to be produced. He may also limit the access to land available for other products which do not directly increase his land rent.

Subsistence production, however, does have many advantages. Where possible, much time and energy is directed toward these activities, especially where it can replace a commodity which otherwise must be bought on the market, the most obvious example being maize. Money is a scarce good, and much of the year is passed soliciting credit in the local store. There are also many essentials that must be bought, implements, clothing and food, for instance, which cannot be produced. So any reduction in monetary expenses is helpful. However, this strategy can only be pursued if the minimal requirements in connection with tobacco have been fulfilled, and there is labour available.

The labour involved in subsistence production is mainly concentrated at the beginning of the tobacco's growth cycle, when land preparation, sowing, and/or planting takes place. The tobacco is then still at an early stage and does not require all available hands. So this excess labour which would otherwise be wasted or 'dead' can instead be converted into food production. (We came across one example of a household choosing to send one of its older daughters to town to work during this slack period, as it was a 'waste of energy' to have her around the house.) However, the harvesting of the food products tends to coincide with the most labour-intensive period for the tobacco. The results of subsistence production are destined for the pot, with often only an amount sufficient to fill the casserole for a few days being harvested at a time.[20] So harvesting is gradual, and does not demand that tobacco be neglected in order to gather other crops. On the other hand, subsistence production is neglected in periods where tobacco production suddenly (due, for example, to rain) demands total concentration of effort. In these circumstances fields of maize and beans have been left to rot. Here only a fraction of the work involved in subsistence production, if any, can be perceived as competing with, or being convertible into, labour dedicated to tobacco.

Another observation is that those households that hardly engage in subsistence production, except perhaps some maize, would not normally buy the products they do not cultivate (including beans, pumpkins, peanuts, and melons). Thus, those who have considerable subsistence production have a net energy intake source, denied others, which has important nutritional consequences. Of the ten households where we made a detailed registration of data (and it must be admitted that exact data on subsistence production were extremely hard to obtain and calculate), it was striking to note that, although there was a large variation in the amount of tobacco produced, and hence cash income, the amount of consumer goods purchased per household member was more or less the same. This holds true even when taking into consideration that the larger households had more mouths to feed and bodies to dress, and in spite of productivity differences favouring some households with an absolute surplus in relation to others. The largest differences in consumption patterns were in relation to such products as sugar, potatoes, and bread.

There is, it appears, a direct correlation: larger households, producing more tobacco, having more spare labour in slack periods, also have a larger and more varied subsistence production, given that land and technology are available for this purpose. Of course, there are quite marked differences as to how well this latent productive capacity is exploited within the larger households, some maximizing efforts and others being not quite so efficient. But in any case, their subsistence production is larger than that of smaller households.[21]

The advantages of being tied to a large estate are quite apparent when we consider subsistence production. This activity costs no more than the labour expended, the landlord having in this particular case relinquished his demands on the products. The main constraints lie in the labour force that can be spared for these activities. Yet, as subsistence production does not compete with tobacco, and as labour is not a calculated cost for these units, subsistence production will mainly employ labour which is idle and thus incidental to tobacco production.

We see, then, that there are complex forms of management and decision-making related to the various tasks which confront the household. Securing an optimal balance between production and consumption, in other words, securing household viability, requires a fairly mobile and flexible labour force, both within and partially between households. It is essentially the allocation of the labour force, made up of women, children and men, to the various farm and household tasks, which is central to this process. It is the logic of peasant rationality which allows for the allocation and abuse of this labour, which thus contributes towards the continued maintenance of this particular agrarian structure.

CONCLUSION

In this chapter we have tried to expose some of the mechanisms that maintain a form of peasant adaptation in respect of the cultivation of Turkish or dark tobacco in Corrientes, highlighting those aspects which seem pertinent to our interpretation, which is far from exhaustive. Central to the exposition has been a presentation of significant external factors: the regional specialization of agriculture in Argentina; the specific rationality of landlords in the tobacco area, where incentives for major investments were lacking, and which allowed for the development of a sharecropping system tied to tobacco production; certain qualities inherent in tobacco cultivation (such as labour- rather than capital-intensive); and the demand on the part of the industry for a cheap raw material. These factors together form the basic conditions and impose certain constraints on the form that tobacco cultivation takes. The household-based production unit is, in fact, a product of circumstances. The external features converge and are in a sense internalized as the individual household units engaged in tobacco cultivation, respond and adapt their strategies to prevailing conditions.

Emphasis has also been placed on the internal organization of the units. Household composition, according to age and sex, combined with other factors, such as the relationship to the landlord, control of sufficient means of production, and agricultural expertise, set basic constraints on the actual production process. We have also stressed the importance of recruiting labour, and the effective utilization of the available labour within the household. The production unit is flexible, expanding, according to need, by employing women and children in critical periods. As has been made clear, however, it is the harvesting capacity of the household unit, taking all hands into consideration, which determines the amount to be planted; the harvesting capacity is, in turn, contingent upon the stage the household has reached in the development cycle. The fact that production time in the agricultural cycle and available labour time do not coincide, permits, in certain situations, an alternative use for labour in slack periods. Subsistence production thus becomes an important asset. As we have shown, it is the larger households which can exploit this possibility to full advantage.

To grasp the logic of this particular adaptation, the concept of surplus was introduced. This shows how the tobacco producer is integrated into the wider economic structure. In addition to covering his own consumer expenses and replenishing his productive equipment, he must produce over and above this, namely the rent which the landlord demands (in this case 30 per cent). Furthermore, because of the self-exploitation inherent in peasant production, tobacco cultivation, as it exists today, is conducive to the needs of the cigarette industry, providing a relatively inexpensive raw material. Hence it is the rationality of self exploitation which makes it profitable to exploit the peasants. The existence of production units that are both 'willing and able' to cover their own labour expenses, provides an extremely cheap labour force. We can speak of incomplete remuneration of labour power expended which, according to Cook, is 'the hallmark of smallhold peasant production operating within a commodity economy' (Cook 1977). The peasant is the sole controller of his own reproduction and it is therefore he who decides, more or less voluntarily, his lower limits for reproduction, i.e. he can manipulate, to a certain extent, the costs he deems necessary for his own reproduction and will in certain periods press himself and his household to the limit. Evidently, under such conditions, any process of systematic accumulation for the peasant producer is effectively hindered.

The rent the landlord receives is determined by two factors: the price of tobacco and the productivity of each unit dependent upon him. The industrial sector, along with public policy, fixes the price for tobacco and they thereby not only determine material conditions for the tobacco growers, but also the size of the rent a landlord will obtain. At the level of production, there is a relationship of direct exploitation between the peasant producer and the landowner, expressed in terms of rent. However, it is at the level of circulation that this rent, along with the tobacco growers' individual portion is realized. It is here also then, that the two economic rationalities intertwine, and the capitalist sector will dominate and set the upper limits of the continued advantages of this adaptation.[22]

Notes

1. This chapter is based on my thesis, 'Peasants, Surpluses and Appropriation: An analysis of the structural integration of the tobacco growers of Corrientes', presented for the *magister artium* at the Institute of Social Anthropology, University of Oslo, Norway in 1978. The fieldwork was carried out from June 1974–July 1975 and was financed by NAVF, the Norwegian Research Council for Science and Humanities. In this further elaboration of the argument I am again indebted to Jorun Solheim. Her patient involvement and careful, acute suggestions have facilitated the revision of earlier drafts. The critical comments of Eduardo Archetti, Gunnar Sørbø and Svein Duus were also appreciated.

2. A very interesting discussion as to the rationality of family farms is presented by Mann and Dickinson (1978).

3. The issue to be explored is the integration and mutual dependency between different economic rationalities. In Argentina capitalism is the dominant mode of production, and other forms of production are subsumed under this capitalist rationality. The 'survival' of the family-based production unit in a social formation where the capitalist mode of production is dominant, is contingent upon conditions external to it. That capitalism is the dominant mode of production entails that it is this mode of production that poses the limits as to how far and how long other relations of production can be tolerated. In social reality there may exist a combination of relations of production, but the basis for the reproduction of these lies in the condition set by the dominant mode (see Bettelheim 1972: 297; Hindess and Hirst 1975: 161).

4. Or, as Marx claims: 'It is every bit as important, for a correct understanding of surplus-value, to conceive it as a mere congelation of surplus labour-time, as nothing but materialised surplus labour, as it is for a proper comprehension of value, to conceive it as a mere congelation of so many hours of labour, as nothing but materialised labour. The essential difference between the various economic forms of society, between for instance, a society based on slave-labour, and one based on wage labour lies only in the mode in which this surplus-labour is in each case extracted from the actual producer, the labourer.' (Marx 1867 Vol. I: 209)

5.   This point has been argued at length elsewhere and will only be briefly touched in this chapter (see Melhuus 1978).

6.   The problems discussed in this chapter are relevant for the tobacco area only. This area is located in the south-western area of the province. The ecological conditions are relatively favourable, compared with other areas of it. As a whole, Corrientes has a diversified pattern of agricutural production, tea, citrus, and rice being among its products.

7.   Today, there is a new tendency for investment and capitalization in Corrientes. This has been made possible with the introduction of the Sebu and the subsequent breeding of local stock (*brangus*) suitable for the prevailing conditions. This new adaptation allows for successful competition with other cattle-raising areas of Argentina.

8.   To the extent that there has been a reorganization of land distribution, this has taken the form of colonization projects. However, these are limited compared with other projects in surrounding provinces. By 1916–17, the amount of land parcelled out to colonies amounted to 75,604 hectares, equalling only 1 per cent of the total usable area of the province (Investigación Sociologíca 1970). Furthermore, there seems to have been a process of ecological adaptation, where more fertile areas have been transferred to smaller, more dynamic production units. In areas with poorer or mixed soils, the large estates (over 1,000 hectares) dominate.

9.   The province of Corrientes is divided into 25 *departamentos*, the tobacco area being limited to three, Goya, Lavalle and San Roque, Goya having the most producers.

10.   For a more detailed analysis of the development of cotton in Santa Fé, see Archetti and Stølen (1975) and Stølen (1976).

11.   It is important to underline that this rent is not a profit in the strict sense of the word, nor a capitalistic ground rent (in the Marxist sense), as the formation of the rent is not a direct result of capitalist exploitation, wage labour not being the basic premiss for the appropriation of surplus labour. The economic rationality of the *estancia* is in effect not capitalist, the relations of production being centred around a system of sharecropping on the one hand which is

primarily related to an industrial crop, and on the other, to a system of labour obligation, where the labourer receives the right to cultivate a limited amount of land in return for working for the landlord for a stipulated number of days per year. This labour is employed in the cattle sector. However, it must be made clear that at the level of circulation and realization of this rent capitalist market mechanisms dominate.

12.   And here it is important to keep in mind that tobacco could not have developed on a plantation basis as the wage costs for the labourer would have been too high compared with the market price obtained for tobacco.

13.   The most likely explanation for this preference lies in the type of product and the type of enterprise which light tobacco represents, within the ecological and climatical zone where it is cultivated. Harvests are much more stable and yields are higher. The uncertain climate and the poor ecological conditions of Corrientes have resulted in an average loss of 20 per cent of each harvest (sometimes even reaching as much as 45 per cent). The production of tobacco in Corrientes is typically small-scale and the average producer is in a critical situation as a sharecropper, landless and without access to credit.

14.   In 1935, there were 152 registered enterprises, with the 11 largest accounting for 87 per cent of total production (Ortiz 1971). By 1967, there were only 5 large companies left accounting for 99.5 per cent of national consumption.

15.   *Transfer of national industries to international companies.*

Original firm	Buying firm	Nationality
Manufacturas de Tabacos Imparciales	Reemtsma Cigaretten Fabriken	German
Manufacturas de Tabacos Piccardo y Cía	Ligget and Meyers (L&M)	USA
Massaling and Celasco	Philip Morris	USA
Particulares UF Grego SA Compani	Brinkman A.G.	German

| Companía Nobleza de Tabacos SAIC y F | British/American Tobacco Co. | USA |

(Source: Investigacion Sociologíca 1979: 49)

16.   In 1967 the 'Fondo Especial de Tabaco' was created. This, financed by the consumers of cigarettes, pays the tobacco producer of Corrientes an additional sum or subsidy (*sobre precio*) over and above the price paid by the industry. In Salta and Jujuy (areas for production of light tobacco) the fund is employed more as a credit institution for technical improvements than as a direct payment.

17.   Price is here an expression for the income a producer receives for a certain amount of tobacco delivered, which in turn represents a certain amount of labour expended.

18.   For a further discussion of this issue, see Melhuus (1978) and Vergopoulos (1978).

19.   This is in contrast to our own society where we find that not only are single-person households viable, but also single-parent ones. To be fully employed and at the same time have the responsibility for one's upkeep are not mutually exclusive. The problem of the conceptualization of housework in a cross-cultural perspective has been elaborated elsewhere (Melhuus and Borchgrevink 1982).

20.   Some do cultivate maize as fodder for domestic animals. In such cases the maize must be harvested, de-grained and stored.

21.   We are not here taking into consideration poultry-raising or the keeping of domestic animals such as sheep or cattle. However, we can observe the same phenomenon, though smaller households may keep relatively large numbers of fowls. Cattle are kept as a 'savings account', as they can more readily be converted into cash.

22.   Obviously, the rent makes the tobacco more expensive, and is an effective barrier to any systematic accumulation, impeding a rapid expansion of the productive forces. The land rent not only expresses the contradiction between landlords and sharecroppers, but also between landlords and industrial sectors/interests, just as the price expresses the contradiction between the peasant producer and the

industry as well as that between the industry and the landlords. In short, the land rent and the price are the two key points around which the two economic sectors evolve and converge. The 'landless' peasant has vested interests in both higher prices and in a land reform.

The question of land reform has many implications and is an extremely complex matter. If we follow our surplus argument, it is clear that any surplus earlier forfeited to landowners, would, with land reform, be open to new alternatives (or other vultures!). Under ideal conditions, this surplus could then be realized by the grower for productive or non-productive consumption. However, it is not unreasonable to assume that the price of tobacco would fall, and further that new financial obligations (financing of land, productive equipment etc.) would quickly tap the surplus now present in the market, giving rise to new forms of vertical integration. To lift constraints on access to land does not necessarily therefore entail a bettering of the conditions of the peasant producer, but only alters the frame of reference and may leave the arena open to others. Land reform in itself, then, does not solve the immediate problems of the grower. There remains the threat of over-production, the problem of price-fixing and continued expansion in the production of light tobacco and the manufacture of Virginia and Burley cigarettes, replacing *negros* (Turkish cigarettes) on the internal market. Nor are the miserable social conditions alleviated by mere land reform. Obtaining land does not imply the building of schools, hospitals, or better roads. At this point, I am tempted to begin a discussion of class relations – class struggle – and its possibilities for the future. However, this would be extending the limits of the chapter and is perhaps a theme for further consideration.

4 Interhousehold Co-operation in Peru's Southern Andes: a Case of Multiple Sibling-Group Marriage

Sarah Lund Skar

The following chapter is a discussion of work processes and family organization in a traditional Quechua community in Peru's southern Andes.[1] An overriding characteristic of the community's economy is the persistence of social forms which may be seen as barriers to the encroachment of capitalist expansion. This is not to say that villagers do not participate in market transactions but rather that cultural norms largely expressed through the quality of work relationships effectively protect the subsistence sector of the economy from market intrusion. Other barriers also exist, particularly those of geographical isolation and a poorly developed infrastructure. Thus this case can be viewed in contrast to the situation described by Long and Roberts (1978a) for Peru's fertile Mantaro valley, where accessibility to larger urban centres is an important factor in capitalist expansion. From the Mantaro study we find that social differentiation is pronounced among this mestizo population and that the area's economy is fully integrated into the national one (Long and Roberts 1978b: 305). Not surprisingly, traditional forms of non-wage labour relations in the Mantaro are advantageously manipulated by richer peasants in their own market transactions.

The case material presented below will be treated from the perspective of two economic sectors,[2] capitalist and subsistence. These are interconnected in such a way that the traditional forms of labour are vitalized and their normative value enhanced. In other words, this particular peasant economy has not been weakened through its contact with capitalist markets and wage labour. This will be shown to result from both external and internal factors restricting the nature of the economic interface between the two sectors. The significance of different types of non-wage labour processes for both of these economic sectors will be explored.

At this juncture it should be emphasized that such a situation is never static and that the degree of market integration will undoubtedly change as capital and commodities become more accessible. Rather it should be underlined that it is the flexibility of the relationship between the capitalist and subsistence sectors of the economy that is crucial to village autonomy, as well as household (and inter-household) viability. The relative complementarity of these two economic sectors is a basic element in cultural as well as social well-being, in that the impact of fluctuations in one of the sectors is buffered by the successful outcome of economic activities in the other.

THE ANDEAN SETTING

Peru's southern Andean region (southern *sierra*) is an extremely complex landscape of semi-tropical valleys, temperate uplands, and high mountain moorlands (over 4,000 m) called *puna*. The dramatic geographic variation is perhaps nowhere as articulated as in the northern valleys of the department of Apurímac. There the rivers of the region deeply dissect the mountainous terrain and flow as much as 2 km below the peneplain (Gade 1973: 38) before joining the Apurímac River. The steep canyon walls rise from 800 m up to the high *puna* at 4,500 m. The tremendous span in altitude results in extreme ecological variations compressed within small areas (Troll 1968). Exchange of altitude-specific produce between one zone and another within a single valley complex, as well as at greater distances, has a long history in the entire Andean region (Murra 1975). Andean anthropologists (Webster 1972; Brush 1977; H.O. Skar 1982) have elaborated on Murra's notion of verticality and have shown in a number of studies how the gaining of control over a maximum number of ecological environments is an important adaptive technique for most Andean populations.

In the Andean context, indigenous ecological and geographical specialization has not automatically involved the population in a market system for the exchange of specialized produce (Harriss 1982: 71). Rather, other processes of circulation have developed and persist alongside, and in conjunction with, the market.

In most Andean areas a system of large landed estates or haciendas has been superimposed upon indigenous forms of ecological adaptation. Much of the logic of the former relies heavily on the constraints of the latter. The subsistence economies of Andean households depend on controlling resources in a variety of altitudinal zones. For example, a viable household in a maize-producing region must have access to irrigated plots at an altitude of about 3,000–3,500 m for their maize production, as well as higher-lying potato plots (3,500–4,000 m); to *puna* pasturelands if the household combines herding with agriculture; and perhaps to a number of lower-lying non-irrigated plots for growing grains and beans. A hacienda which might have specialized market-oriented production in one or several of these areas can seriously disrupt the balance of control over a maximum number of ecological environments of the peasant household, by monopolizing resources in one of the crucial zones.

In the case which concerns us here, that of the haciendas of the northern Apurímac valleys, market production was concentrated in the tropical valley bottoms where sugar cane was grown and locally manufactured into rum which was then marketed throughout the local region. Originally the tropical valley bottoms were not an integral part of the environmental adaptation of the agricultural communities further up the slopes, but maize and pasture lands higher up the slopes were gradually brought under the control of the haciendas in order to force the upland communities into relationships of dependency (*yanakunaque*). Their labour on the haciendas was exchanged for access to land in the crucial ecological zones of the mid and upper slopes. The essential element in this dependency relationship between hacienda and community rested on the divergence of economic emphasis in the two disparate social settings, the one focused on a basic subsistence orientation, and the other on market production. This is not to imply, however, that relations of dominance were not present, nor that the dependency is symbiotic in nature. On the contrary, the relationship has been designated by H.O. Skar (1982: 119–22) as parasitic, in that the competition for resources is completely dominated by one set of group interests, at the expense of the other.

The area of the most crucial resource competition between hacienda and Indian community in the northern Apurímac valleys was located in the altitudinal zone where maize was grown (i.e. 2,500–3,500 m). In some cases these lands were completely taken over by the haciendas, and the Indian populations became totally dependent on sharecropping. In others, as for example the village of Matapuquio with which we shall become more familiar as the discussion proceeds, the core of the irrigated maize lands remained under the jurisdiction of the communities. In such instances the hacienda became the source of desirable, though not essential, commodities. More importantly, through working relations with the hacienda, one was granted use rights to potato plots and pasture lands in the *puna*. The intensity of dependency on the hacienda for supplementary resources would vary from household to household but the communities' control over their own maize plots meant not only a degree of independence from the hacienda, but also comprised the corporate estate necessary to gain legal status as a Comunidad Campesina (literally, Peasant Community).

A Comunidad Campesina is an autonomous village whose rights in land are legally recognized and protected by the state. As is brought out in David Lehmann's discussion (1982: 22), a Comunidad is not only a creation of the state, but is also an institution of land tenure regulating individual access to land. Much of this regulation is communal in nature, plots being divided out among members on a yearly basis according to need (*laymi*). Control of other lands may be in the hands of families, with rules of inheritance being the regulating factor. Ideally, Comunidad lands are inalienable, and cannot be bought or sold. In the more traditional communities there is a certain moral sense that those who live and work in the community should enjoy rights to land, and if it is scarce, outsiders are not welcome.

VILLAGE AGRICULTURE IN A VERTICAL ENVIRONMENT

The village of Matapuquio is a legal Comunidad. Because village marriages are 97 per cent endogamous, residence and Comunidad membership are nearly synonymous. Comunidad land tenure, which includes the transmission of the highly-valued maize lands through inheritance, and the yearly distribution of *laymi* plots for growing tubers, overlaps with hacienda land tenure. This is so inasmuch as the potato and pasture lands of the heights are owned by the hacienda but are administered by the Comunidad through the traditional *laymi* system. This interface between privately held lands on the one hand and communally-distributed *laymi* plots for growing subsistence crops on the other, is one of many in which wage and non-wage labour will be found to converge.

The village settlement pattern is one of dispersed households ranging up the slope from 3,000–3,400 m. This is the crucial area of maize cultivation, and houses are spread throughout the landscape at the edge of the all-important maize fields. Plots for potatoes and grain are located at a greater distance, outside village-held lands, at an altitude of approximately 3,800 m. Herding cattle and sheep, which is of secondary importance and largely the responsibility of women and girls, is also carried out on the hacienda lands of these upper slopes.

Men and boys from the village work on the Hacienda Pincos[3] to maintain their use rights of these resources. In recent years they have received monetary payment for this labour. Up to a half of an adult man's working time could be claimed for the hacienda, depending largely on the extent to which the household depended upon the hacienda for land. On those occasions when monetary needs were high, as, for example, before a fiesta (H.O. Skar 1982: 287), there was an obvious tendency to put in more working days at the hacienda. When subsistence agriculture on the slopes required intensive work during certain times in the agricultural cycle, work on the hacienda fell off. In other words, there is a clear strategy carried out by the village men in co-ordinating the subsistence and market-oriented sectors of the economy as the need arises. This flexibility has largely been possible because of the nature of the cane production on the rich irrigated bottom lands (2,500 m) and the impact of relative altitude for maize production on the slopes.

In Pincos, cane production is not influenced by the fluctuating of the seasons between dry periods and the rains. All the fields under cultivation have cane at different degrees of maturity throughout the year. The source of irrigation, water from the Pincos River, has made this constant production possible. In such a situation labour needs are also fairly constant.

On the other hand, subsistence agriculture on the slopes is greatly influenced by two factors: timing in terms of the beginning of the yearly rains and the altitudinal location of one's maize plots, the latter affecting the amount of time needed for the maturation of the crop. For example, a period of particular labour intensity in the production of maize is during planting. The rains crucial to irrigation usually begin in October and mark the beginning of the planting season for the maize plots furthest up the slope. Gradually households further down the slope take up the work, the lowest-lying fields being planted up to three months later than those located in the highest region. Because plant growth and development at higher altitudes requires more time, the labour requirements of subsistence agriculture in the village are staggered, freeing different groups of men from up and down the slope to work on the hacienda during the course of the agricultural year.

VILLAGE HOUSEHOLD ORGANIZATION AND TRADITIONAL FORMS OF NON-WAGE LABOUR

Household organization is based first and foremost on the bilateral kindred (Lambert 1977: 1–27). In groupings based on the kindred, blood relations traced through both one's parents are of equal importance. As kindreds are not corporate groups residing over a joint estate but are, rather, shifting constellations of individuals brought together in relation to a single ego, joint activities beyond the context of the nuclear family are characterized by recruitment strategies and factionalism. As only full siblings share the same kindred, solidarity of the sibling group is a crucial component in wider group action. Nowhere is this more evident than in the traditional forms of non-wage labour.

At a very elementary level of analysis we can say that the household in Matapuquio ideally consists of the nuclear family. Houses are occupied by a man, a woman, and their offspring. This basic group shares the products from fields held individually by each adult partner. At their death or when the children begin to marry, the land, animals, and belongings will be scrupulously divided up between the children of both sexes. To counteract the resultant fragmentation of landholdings, the recombining of resources at marriage is an important strategy. In the village it is said, 'we marry the land'. When seen in the light of the complex ecological adaptation outlined above, this strategy becomes even more crucial to household viability. Spouses work their fields together. To minimize labour requirements it is obviously advantageous that one's spouse's fields are located as near as possible to one's own. The necessity of guarding the crops from pilfering is another reason why this is advisable. A third consideration is the strenuous demands altitudinal differences of dispersed fields would mean in terms of co-ordinating the work input between the family subsistence plots and labour requirements at the hacienda.

As can be expected, the forming of a new household in the village is characterized by careful planning by the two families. The wider kindreds of the future couple are also heavily involved. Here older married siblings may play an important part. Because of the political importance of the kindred group shared by siblings, it is a frequent pattern to form multiple ties between kindreds through the numer-

ous marriages between members of two sibling groups. As will later
be shown, the most frequent pattern of several sisters marrying
several brothers is a pragmatic arrangement, arising from the sharing
of tasks between sisters and between brothers. The pairing up of
sisters and brothers begins even in childhood, and in adult life continues in modified form. The persistence of co-operation between
sets of siblings after marriage[4] results in strong relations of affiliation
between households similar to those described by G. Smith (1984) in
another Andean context, under the term confederated households.
These relations represent important economic, as well as emotional,
bonds.

Considering a particular example will be the best way of illustrat-
ing the point. In the lower half of the village there are two bordering
barrios or neighbourhoods called Churupuquio and Visitapampa. In
Churupuquio three of the children of Luis Huaman and Teresa
Leguia still reside, two sons and one daughter. Across the path in
Visitapampa is the large family of Juan Yuto and Santosa Quispe.
Three daughters of Juan and Santosa married sons of Luis and
Teresa. When Victor married Marcosa they moved in and lived with
his parents, just across the path from Marcosa's home. Later, when a
son had been born to them, a corner of the cornfield was partitioned
to Victor. This is where the couple built their adobe house. The
move to the other end of the field had partly been precipitated by
Sixto's marriage to Eugenia, Marcosa's sister. As Sixto was the
youngest of his sibling group, he held special rights in his parents'
house and had a responsibility to look after them in their old age.

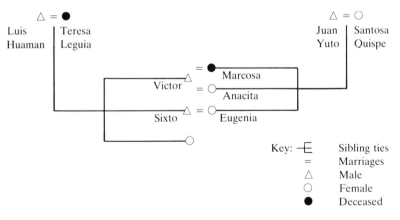

Figure 1   **An Example of Multiple Marriages between Sibling Groups**

With Sixto's marriage, it was necessary for Victor and Marcosa to establish their own household. Marcosa became pregnant again, but both she and the infant died during delivery. Marcosa's lands, turned over to her at marriage, would now have to be worked and held in trust by Victor for their young son. At her death, however, Marcosa had not received all her rightful inheritance. Her parents were still raising younger siblings and withheld sufficient land to maintain their own household. Because of a system of gradual inheritance, much of Marcosa's lands would now be divided between her surviving siblings at their parents' death. This placed the two families of the Huaman Leguias and the Yuto Quispes in a difficult position. In theory at least, Sixto's children could well inherit land through their mother which had originally been set aside for Marcosa. Because Marcosa's parents held much land, the loss to Victor and Marcosa's son would have been considerable. To resolve what otherwise could have been a situation full of conflict and animosity, Victor married Marcosa and Eugenia's younger sister, Anacita.

The example of Victor and Anacita and Sixto and Eugenia is particularly suitable for illustrating the importance of multiple marriage bonds between sibling groups in assuring individual household viability at the early stages of the development cycle. In this case residence near both the parent households gives added support during the gradual process of household devolution, as well. Sixto's marriage to Eugenia marks the transition stage between the old and the new household. As Teresa Leguia died several years before Sixto's marriage, it is his responsibility as youngest son to care for Luis when he can no longer care for himself. Luis has retained 1 *tarija* (1,250 m^2) of his irrigated land and this he works with Sixto's help. Sixto is also beginning to make quite a lot of improvements on the house which on his father's death will become home for himself and Eugenia. In their first years of marriage they had a daughter and a son. Until these children are 6 or 7 years old, the work load on the new household group will be considerable. Sixto and Eugenia must work their own fields (they have between them ½ *tarija* of irrigated land), as well as Luis's fields, and must also help Juan and Santosa across the way with their own fields (Juan and Santosa have 3 *tarijas* of irrigated land, 1 *tarija* of unirrigated, and 2 *tarijas* of pasture, as well as many animals). On top of this, Sixto works at the hacienda to secure rights over sufficient lands. Eugenia is expected to help her mother with herding their numerous cattle and she must also pasture her own animals and Sixto's horses. All of this is a considerable burden on a new household, one made easier however, by the fact that Victor and Anacita are also helping out.

Victor and Anacita have more land to work together (1 *tarija*) than do Sixto and Eugenia, and they also have Marcosa's son Isaac to help with the animals. Nevertheless, they are both expected also to help out in their parents' homes, and Victor is gone for days at a time to work at Pincos. Anacita has two small boys and Isaac is away much of the time attending school in Andahuaylas. The only possible way these households could manage is through mutual assistance, this being facilitated by the fact that one doesn't resent helping one's spouse's sibling when that help also aids one's own sibling.

At Pincos Victor, Sixto and Luis share lodgings. Each brings from the village potatoes, corn, and cheese for the week, and they cook together in their room. On Wednesdays Luis's daughter, who lives next door to her father, comes with a freshly prepared meal for them. In the village Eugenia may herd her own animals, together with her mother's and Anacita's, while her mother looks after the children. Eugenia will no doubt be helped in pasturing the animals by her younger unmarried sister. Anacita would then be free to stay at home to watch over both the houses and fields, with only short excursions to gather grass for the guinea pigs or tether the pigs. Her sister-in-law will certainly visit her on returning from Pincos and they will sit together spinning. It is good to have a day of relative in-activity for on the next it will be Anacita's turn to be up and gone at day-break, with the animals.

During times of intense agricultural activity, these households will again join forces. Not only do Sixto's and Victor's fields lie flush with each other but the fields of their wives do as well. All the maize fields are close together and when that particular part of the village is able to irrigate its fields before planting, this can be done as a single process. As all agricultural work is an occupation for both sexes, all the families and the children who play at the edge of the field join together to irrigate, hoe, and plant maize, a process taking several days. On such days the animals are not taken so far afield and the women are freed to help in the planting by younger sisters and cousins who help watch the animals. Both Eugenia and Anacita will be expected to prepare food and drink for everyone. The group may well include more than simply Sixto, Victor, and Luis. Work in the Huaman Leguia fields will no doubt also include the sister-in-law with her husband. Later, when working the Yuto Quispe fields, Eugenia and Anacita's brothers and wives will also help out. In this way not only are their own fields quickly planted but also the remaining ones of both parents, which are particularly extensive and a considerable burden for a couple in their fifties to plant alone.

In this way younger and older households are able to help each other through these most difficult periods of their life cycle, that of establishment and devolution. The two younger households give of their coveted labour at peak times during the agricultural cycle. This is something older households, having lost many of their young adult members, are in desperate need of, especially as the older members become physically incapable of meeting the hard demands. The young households find security in the presence of the older one. For Sixto and Eugenia these are virtually one and the same. Luis still holds some of his own land and is the rightful owner of the house and the household belongings but working for him is like working for themselves. As the young households grow they can count on aid from the parent ones. More land will be turned over to them to meet the rising needs. As small children grow, they can begin to help with the animals or care for younger siblings, but until this time the women of both older and younger households need each other's help to watch over the toddlers when the men are absent, and to care for the animals.

The case of Sixto and Eugenia, and Victor and Anacita is only one of many such inter-household groupings within the village. Two brothers marrying two sisters seems to be the favoured sibling (and first cousin) grouping. Such agreements, based on the institution of marriage, give outside support to both emerging and dissolving households. The pattern of work arrangements seems to be the same throughout. There is a definite preference for sisters and for brothers to live near one another, whether sets of brothers and sisters from two different families actually inter-marry or not. This preference is based on the nature of the division of labour, in which women almost exclusively care for the animals and men often live for weeks at a time at the hacienda in the valley below.

From this example we can see that the household in Matapuquio is far from an autonomous unit. Despite the fact that residence and most consumption occurs within the content of the nuclear family household, production is dependent on institutionalized forms of inter-household co-operation. Such labour exchanges are embedded in a strong sense of reciprocity, a principle defined by some authors (D. Nuñez del Prado Bejar 1972) as the single most important element in Quechua social organization.

In the case cited above, labour was freely exchanged between family groups without a record being kept of who did what for whom. Such work co-operation, called *ayuda* (Alberti and Mayer 1974, H.O. Skar 1982: 212), is the rightful claim of one's closest family. I would argue that between sibling groups with multiple marriage bonds *ayuda* approaches its most institutionalized form. In Andean society there are, however, other institutionalized forms of non-wage labour employed in inter-household assistance involving wider family and unrelated groups.

Not all members of a sibling group maintain working relations of the kind outlined above. In our example I found that brothers from one group and sisters from another family joined together in the closest of working relations, involving daily inter-household assistance. However, Sixto and Victor have a married sister living a short distance from their own houses and fields. She and her husband have a reciprocal labour exchange known as *ayni* with Victor and Sixto. *Ayni* work exchanges involve a careful tabulation of what kind and length of work is owed. One day's maize cultivation is exchanged with another. In *ayni* one can lay claim to another's time in a very specific way. Relationships based on *ayni* exchange, like those of *ayuda,* can be maintained over a lifetime and are a tangible display of wider group loyalties.

Agricultural techniques in the rugged Andean setting are primitive and labour-intensive. Only in some cases is ploughing done by oxen on those maize fields that are not too steep. All other work is done by digging stick and hoe. Working a large field can thus require many labourers, often more than one can mobilize through *ayuda* and *ayni* ties. The answer to this problem is to hold a *minka* in which often unrelated people will work in exchange for food, coca, and free-flowing alcoholic beverages. At the end of the day some special gift of food, eggs or cheese, may be made, whereupon all obligations have been met.

All these forms of non-wage work exchange have important social implications beyond their purely productive function. They are an expression of social relations in a largely acephalous village organization. Because of their strong emotive quality based upon reciprocity, wage labour is nearly non-existent in the subsistence sector of the village economy.[5] This is despite the fact that virtually all village men have been involved in wage labour relationships in the hacienda for some considerable time. Even though the type of work being carried out in each instance is nearly identical, cultural evaluation of the situational context places differing values on labour for subsistence as opposed to labour for wages. These cultural norms are carried further and are reflected in the results of labour: agricultural produce and money.

CULTURAL VALORIZATION OF VILLAGE SUBSISTENCE AND CASH ECONOMIES

As we have seen, many forms of non-wage labour are culturally specific. The situational context also places differing values on produce and money, as well. In Matapuquio reciprocal non-wage labour arrangements are largely restricted to subsistence activities and to communal work projects (*faena*), such as digging a water reservoir or building the school. Wage labour is a factor in the subsistence economy inasmuch as it is through a wage labour relationship with the hacienda that sufficient land for subsistence agriculture is obtained. This relationship with the hacienda is one marked by ambivalence and deep-seated distrust, springing from generations of exploitation. Even for those families with enough land to satisfy subsistence needs, the hacienda is still a crucial factor in the household economy, and good working relations must be established, because it is the single most important source of cash in the valley.[6]

Obviously, Matapuqenians have monetary needs, and from their wages they are able to satisfy some of these. There is no local market in the valley, however, and people must make a day-long journey to come to a market town in order to spend their wages on essential purchases such as salt, sugar, matches, rubber-tyre sandals, certain items of clothing, cooking utensils and ingredients necessary for making religious offerings.[7] In this context money has a utilitarian purpose, a use-value. However, other village practices reveal a contrary attitude toward money that gives it certain supernatural qualities quite above and beyond what can be bought and sold. Villagers hoard their money for its own sake. Coins are an essential part of any offering made to their mountain gods, the *apus*. Old coins are felt to have special power and are sometimes found laid out on a path over a high mountain pass, often in the form of a cross (Ray O'Sullivan, personal communication).[8] In such a context money becomes a medium of communication between the natural and the supernatural world of the villagers and it is treated with great reverence.

The result of labour in subsistence agriculture is produce: maize, potatoes, grain, and beans. It is a normative rule that such items should never be sold for money. In the case of Matapuquio we do not have a situation in which a typical peasant farmer sells off his surplus subsistence crops. Villagers do not sell in the markets in the region; they only buy there. Even animal products which are occasionally sold by women for money are never brought to the markets, but are sold to travelling middlemen who may come to the village and beg to buy from them.

Ideas about agricultural products are also coloured by beliefs in the supernatural, particularly mother earth, Pachamama. The slightest squandering of grain or corn may cause her displeasure and bring famine upon the entire village. Great respect is given to all products of the land, which are felt to be given in trust to those who live off it. This attitude, however, does not bar agricultural produce from being exchanged (*trueque*) between villagers, requiring only that it should not be sold to outsiders.

In the Andean context *trueque* usually consists of the exchange, often within the context of kinship networks, of altitude-specific products from one level to another, in some cases over great distances, and in others within a very compressed area. *Trueque* in Matapuquio is largely characterized by this latter type, i.e. maize may be exchanged for potatoes, especially when one family's crop happens to fail. The exchange is always carried out in a highly ritualized atmosphere of sharing drink and food, and helps to redistribute more evenly essential products throughout the community.

Agricultural produce is also given as gifts of friendship, when asking favours, or to repay some specialized service (for example, receiving a cure, a midwife's assistance, or help in breaking in a horse). In a region as isolated as Matapuquio, *trueque* often occurs with a purchased object already brought to the village being exchanged for produce. However, in such exchanges the person receiving the produce is really being done a favour, one that he has no doubt had to go to great lengths to persuade his partner to go along with.

RECENT DEVELOPMENTS

Since Peru's land reform of 1969, the Hacienda Pincos has been expropriated and formed into a co-operative, the majority of members coming from Matapuquio. Though all men in the village continued to work in the valley for wages, it was only the men from those families most dependent on Pincos for additional lands who actually became members. However, when in 1976 a percentage of the profits was first redistributed solely amongst members, it became apparent that membership meant great advantages beyond those of simply securing land rights. There was a marked increase in membership, and because redistribution was based upon the number of days worked in a year, there was in addition a great increase in the number of workers coming to the co-operative to work. At one stage workers were so numerous at the co-operative that there was insufficient ready cash to pay the weekly wages. Luxury items such as corrugated roofing and radios began making their mark on the village scene. Of course, during this period, subsistence activities were not abandoned but were rather neglected, and left in the hands of older sons and women.

Perhaps because of the conflict of interests between the two forms of production, we found co-operative marketing practices transformed when we made a return visit in 1981. To avoid the accumulation of profit which would in part be claimed by the government and various co-operative funds before redistribution to the workers, the co-operative product, rum, was no longer marketed. Instead, it was sold in quantity at reduced prices to the workers, in rotation. They would pay the co-operative to transport it to town for them and there they would make sales on an individual basis, pocketing the profit. Thus the co-operative itself no longer had funds to redistribute. All workers could earn a share in the profits without being bound to working as many days in the year as possible. It seemed a very astute way of getting round state regulations.

Alas, the co-operative at Pincos, with its emerald cane fields and small factory for rum production, is no more. In 1982 guerillas blew up all the installations in the valley and laid waste all the fields (El Comercio 23 January 1983: 11–12).

From this great distance one can only speculate as to what this means for the villagers in Matapuquio. Their isolation up in their village seems enhanced, with the valley enterprise in ruins. There is no longer reason for the men to make the 1,500 m descent to work during the week, and there is no more opportunity to work for wages in an area where the sole source of money has always been the hacienda. Some villagers will no doubt migrate away from the unrest of the countryside and into the security of the towns. But the very interesting question arises: in what way will those that remain behind solve the problem of creating new avenues for acquiring money? One suspects that some form of village-wide co-operation in producing a cash crop quite separate from individual subsistence production, will arise. Whatever the solution, it is certain that the village subsistence economy is crucial in seeing them through this crisis.

I have tried to show how both external and internal factors have restricted the interface between capitalist and subsistence sectors in the economy of a traditional highland village in southern Peru. In the complexity of the Andean valley system, ecological adaptation is most successful when households are able to combine their work. This basic principle has been institutionalized through multiple marriages between sibling groups, particularly of the kind where two or more sisters marry two or more brothers. The resulting inter-household co-operation, *ayuda,* is an essential component in house-hold viability. Widening groups of kin and affines are brought in to help with specific tasks through the equally balanced exchange, *ayni,* or through the semi-festive *minka* in which food is exchanged for labour. All of these forms of non-wage labour have an obvious significance for village subsistence. Their significance for the capitalist enterprise in the valley is also obvious, if more indirect. During the time when the men worked for wages and were absent from the village for weeks at a time, such co-operation made it possible for the women to carry on alone. For the men, who had to do their own cooking and bring their own food while working in the valley, mutual help between brothers or fathers and sons was essential. Without working together, one would never have had time to rest. And so forms of non-wage labour were necessary elements in keeping the capitalist system in operation.

Finally, sentiments about co-operative work forms and money and produce are important factors restricting capitalist expansion in the village economy. Attitudes to both produce and money, the former being restricted for sale and the latter being in part removed from its capitalist context and given a different symbolic value, make the distinction between the two economic sectors a complex one. Social relations based on non-wage labour exchange present further problems of definition. One is left with the conviction that in the case of Matapuquio any discussion about the distinction between the two economic sectors is most fruitfully approached from the viewpoint of the non-exclusiveness of the sectors. Rather it is the interaction which occurs at their interface which gives us the deepest perspectives.

Notes

1.   The fieldwork on which this article is based was carried out in 1976–77 over an eighteen-month period. I wish here to acknowledge the generous grant given by the Norwegian Research Council for Research in Science and the Humanities and the Lumholtz Fund, the University of Oslo, for making the research possible.

2.   The crystallization of my ideas in this respect has greatly benefited from conversations with Norman Long who, along with Harald Skar, made astute comments during the final preparations of the manuscript.

3.   For a discussion of division of labour in Matapuquio I refer the reader to my article 'The Use of the Public/Private Framework in the Analysis of Egalitarian Societies' (1979).

4.   In another work (S.L. Skar 1980: 96), I have termed the sibling pair a *masi* relationship, literally 'sharing in the state of' or 'comrades in . . .'.

5.   Harald Skar (1982: 214) discusses the *jornal* system as practised in Matapuquio, where monetary wages of a kind are given for a day's labour. However, it is expected that money paid out in this fashion will be returned when the hireling becomes the hirer. In this system the money becomes a forfeit to be reclaimed when like labour is exchanged for like.

6.   The women's sale of animals and animal products is the other possibility.

7.   These include products from the jungle and the *puna,* as well as cigarettes and rum.

8.   One is tempted to speculate that, especially in the case of the large older Peruvian *sol* (main unit of currency, literally meaning 'sun'), the symbolic content of the coin has been somehow connected with the messianic return of the Inca (Inkarrí, also referred to as the sun). Worship of the mountains is strongly associated with beliefs in the ancestors, the Inca being the first ancestor.

5 Co-operation on and between Eastern Finnish Family Farms

Ray G. Abrahams

Finland is a large country with a relatively small population, and is one of the most northerly countries in which intensive agriculture is practised. The main cities and the most fertile land are in the south-west of the country and a majority of the population (*c.* 2.85 million out of a total of 4.8 million) is located there also, with the rest spread increasingly thinly towards the north and east. The North Karelian area, to which the present chapter refers, is one of the poorer ones in which agricuture is still possible.[1] As one progresses north and east from Helsinki towards the Russian border and the village of Vieki where I worked, one moves from a zone of relatively mild climate, stone-free fertile soil, and comparatively fast timber growth, to a region of more hilly country, where the farmers tell you that stones are the easiest crop to grow, and where the summer, jokingly described to me as being shorter than the winter but less snowy, has an almost butterfly-like short-lived poignancy and beauty.

The main crops in this North Karelian area are barley, oats, and rye. People also grow potatoes, and wheat is cultivated on higher ground. Some people also produce strawberries. Farmers stress, however, that the climate is not suitable for agriculture based on crops alone, and two other main sources of farm income are typically found on a farm itself, in addition to attempts to find some off-farm income. The first is an animal herd of dairy cows and/or beef cattle, or, in some cases, pigs. The second is timber, which can be a farmer's main productive capital and is used to help finance such things as new buildings and the purchase of machinery. The further north one goes, the more timber a farmer needs, owing to the longer growing period involved, and in North Karelia, as much as 60 hectares is desirable as a capital base for a farm whose field area is perhaps 12 hectares.

In trying to understand farming in North Karelia, and to a varying extent in other parts of Finland also, a number of social and economic factors are of great significance. Some of these have exhibited considerable persistence over a relatively long period of time, while in other cases one sees relatively strong and rapid change. Among the more persistent factors has been the private ownership of land by nuclear families. Moreover, although a tenancy and labouring system was an important feature of nineteenth and early twentieth century farming, the number of landowners in a locality has tended to be large, for it is only in Southern Finland that there has historically been any real approximation to large manor-type estates. In addition, although details have varied from one period to another, the system of inheritance is a potentially fragmentary one, in which all children share some rights. A further long-standing feature of the property system has been the right of farmers to sell their farms. This was often, though not always, exercised under the duress of actual or looming bankruptcy during the nineteenth and early twentieth centuries; and it was for many a preliminary to becoming a tenant or labourer on someone else's farm, or even a more or less destitute member of the community, though others used their money to buy farms or emigrate. After the Second World War, land sales became more straightforwardly a function of the rapid rise in migration to Southern Finland and Sweden, though this process has also led to a rise in absentee ownership of farm and forest land, since some people have not wished to convert land to cash in a period of inflation. It is perhaps worth noting here that the land-ownership system I have outlined seems to be accompanied by a strong 'Protestant' ethic of individualism, and a pioneer spirit that stresses the importance of a person's work and their ability to enjoy its fruits as a relatively independent operator. This does not typically mean that people are unwilling to co-operate with one another, as we shall see, but they are nonetheless often rather wary of any such co-operation if it appears likely adversely to affect their status as independent actors and decision-makers.

As in several other rural areas of Finland, population growth and subsequent decline has probably been the single most important changing feature in North Karelia. Taken as a whole, Finland's population grew fairly steadily from about 1800–1950, and the rate of growth then declined to more or less nil by 1975. This process was felt strongly in the rural areas, and among its implications was a tendency for the average size of farms to become smaller through fragmentation by inheritance. This was further exacerbated by national-level political decisions of the 1920s and 1930s to endow tenants and some other landless villagers (themselves in part a product of land and population pressure) with their own small farms; it was additionally reinforced in the late 1940s by the re-establishment of displaced Karelians in some Finnish villages, including Vieki, and the granting of farm land to some ex-servicemen. The period after 1950, when the population of the country as a whole was relatively stable, was, however, one of serious depopulation for the rural areas, and the nature of the fall has led to distortions of age structure and sex ratios. The average age of farmers tends to be high (about 55 in 1980) and young successors to family farms are all too often unavailable. Vieki's population fell from about 2,500 in 1960 to 1,139 in 1980, and the distortions in its structure are clear from *Figure 2* below.

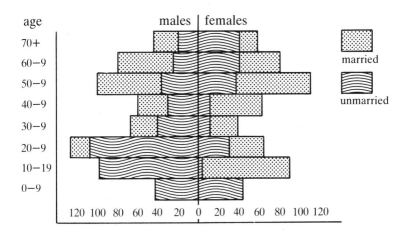

Figure 2   Age/sex composition of Vieki village, 1980

The period of heavy migration has provided some possibility of reversing the trend to smaller farm size. Opportunities to buy, or at least rent, others' holdings have increased, and the owners or potential heirs of many small, non-viable farms and plots have moved away. Not surprisingly, such migration has also meant that the last remaining farm labourers have left many areas, and this, along with the shortage of young people generally, has meant that remaining farming families have had to become more efficient, through increased mechanization and the use of improved raw materials and techniques.

I will turn now to a closer examination of the idea of a family farm and of the forms of internal and external co-operation necessary for its successful functioning.

FAMILY AND FARM

When the two English words 'family' and 'farm' are thrown together to produce the convenient and catchy shorthand label 'family farm', it becomes easy to gloss over ambiguities and shifts of meaning both in time and space, and it is perhaps too easy to forget how difficult the intrinsic combination of social and technical elements involved can be.

Even ignoring the broad spectrum of cross-cultural variation, one knows that the word family has a range of different referents within the confines of English usage. In a fairly recent publication about Elmdon (Richards and Robin 1975), Audrey Richards writes of 'six well-known families which have been represented in the village for a very long time, in fact as long ago as the seventeenth century in two instances'; and I need scarcely add that this is a rather different concept from that of the family as a marriage-centred reproductive and domestic group. Significantly in the present context, this well-known distinction is partly tied to types of property in England. The term 'family car' seems most likely to evoke the idea of the relatively short-term elementary family, whereas the term 'family farm' seems to be a more ambiguous concept which suggests both its connection to a living family group and its inter-generational transmission within the longer-term framework of Richards' usage, noted above. This of course relates to the special qualities which land, at least potentially, possesses as a form of lasting property, and which have long been of interest to economists, lawyers, sociologists and social anthropologists. On the other hand, we know that the heritability of land and farm varies greatly both within and between societies (e.g. as between landlord and tenant, chief and subject, and on a systemic level betwen fixed and shifting patterns of land use) and can be a major influence upon other aspects of the connection between farm and family.

The connection rarely seems to be a simple, trouble-free one. Families of whatever sort have their own developmental processes and inner conflicts, and the relation between these and such factors as the availability and quality of land and the reproduction rates of livestock are often problematic, as a number of studies from East Africa and elsewhere have shown. And the situation becomes more complicated when one adds to such more or less 'internal' factors the effects of wider social, political, and economic forces, including warfare, state structures, trade, money, and technical developments, all of which have influenced the forms and functions of family farms in most parts of the world.

This brief discussion provides a starting point for understanding some of the main features of Finnish family farms as I have studied them in North Karelia. The distinction between family as a descending surname group and family as a more or less contemporary marriage-centred unit is linguistically more clearly marked in Finnish than in English. The former is *suku* and the latter *perhe*, and the compound word *sukutila* denotes a particular ancestral farm which has been in the same 'family' for some generations (*tila* = space or place in general, but contextually an estate or farm). The term *perintötila* (literally an 'inheritance farm') is also used to refer to a farm as a heritable possession. There does not seem to be a term *perhetila* to denote a farm worked by a family (the term *pientila*, literally 'small farm', typically implies this), but the relatively recently-coined term *viljelijäperhe* (literally 'cultivator family') is used in professional literature, and has spread to some extent to more general usage, to denote a family group who work on a farm.

If Finnish is more exact than English in this *suku/perhe* distinction, there are also interesting areas of relative vagueness, or perhaps more accurately 'diffuseness', in its family farm vocabulary. The term *pientila* is one example of this. Others, more used in the past than now, have been simple derivatives of the word *talo* (literally 'house') such as *talollinen* (used for 'owner-farmer') and *talonpoika* (literally 'house-son' or 'boy' but also used for farmer or peasant). Then there are the terms *isäntä* and *emäntä* which relate to *isä*, the usual word for father, and *emä* (an old word for mother which occurs in various compound forms). These words, for which an apt general translation might be 'master' and 'mistress' are in very common usage among villagers and elsewhere to denote a farmer and his wife, although etymologically they contain no reference to farming.

I realize that one can easily make too much of such diffuse vocabulary. Historically it stems in part from the fact that agriculture has only relatively recently ceased to be the main economic activity of the majority of Finns, and the related one that even today, perhaps more than ever, the ties of Finnish urban dwellers to their rural roots are noticeably stronger than those of their English counterparts. In such circumstances, it is not wholly surprising if people talk of farms and farmers without literal reference to farming, or in terms which pay more attention to distinctions of status and ownership than the form of livelihood (the word *talollinen*, for instance, was used especially in the past in contradistinction to a variety of terms for tenant farmers and labourers). Nor are more specific terms wholly lacking. Thus the word *maanviljelijä* (literally land cultivator) seems to have come into increasing use as a word for farmer since the 1920s, when the growing differentiation of the national economy and its occupational structure was accompanied by a levelling out of status in the rural areas, through the dismantling of the tenancy system.

This said, however, it is still possible to argue that the relatively unspecific terminology outlined above reflects real features of the rural situation. For Finnish farmers are by no means simply cultivators and/or livestock breeders but tend to try, if and when they can, to supplement their income from timber work and other sources. Moreover, although farming is these days predominantly a family affair (a relevant factor in itself), the farm-working family does not necessarily exactly coincide with the family (even in the sense of *perhe*) as a farm-owning group, or as a social group defined purely in terms of kinship and marriage criteria. Nor is it generally wholly self-sufficient as a labour force or an equipment-owning unit.

FARM VIABILITY AND CO-OPERATION

A farming family's need for extra labour or equipment has obvious implications for a farm's viability, for co-operation among farmers, and between them and others. In this context, however, it may first be worthwhile to say a little about the concept of viability itself and different areas or aspects of it. Thus one may note that the viability of a family farm involves at least three inter-connected but analytically separable phenomena, namely the persistence of the family as a social unit, the persistence of the farm as a technical one, and the persistence of a connection between the two. Second, it seems useful to distinguish between problems that affect the season-by-season management of a farm by a family, as some form of *perhe*, and those that affect its longer-term transmission between generations, which is, of course, more closely tied to the idea of *suku*. In the former case one is dealing mainly with such factors as labour bottlenecks and temporary illness, and in the latter with the availability of heirs, and problems of potential fragmentation. There are, of course, also close connections between these two areas, deriving from the fact that members of the same nuclear family are centrally involved in both of them.

The transmission of a farm from one generation to another can take place through the retirement or death of members of the senior generation, or a combination of the two, provided that a successor is available. In either case, the rules of inheritance are crucial. Unless a specific contrary arrangement is made, husband and wife typically have joint rights in their farm as do, ultimately, their children. On the death of either one of the spouses, an inheritance group (*perikunta*) is established, which consists of the surviving spouse and children. Half the farm belongs to the spouse while the children have equal shares in the other. On the death of the surviving spouse, equal shares in his or her half similarly devolve to the offspring. In the case of post-mortem succession, the main problem is to adjust arrangements between the heirs without damaging relations between them and without excessive partition of the farm. This problem may be temporarily shelved, for example during the lifetime of a surviving spouse, but it has eventually to be solved. In the case of succession through retirement, which has a long history in the area, as elsewhere in northern Europe, an agreement is commonly drawn up between holder(s) and successor(s), in which the terms of pension, dwelling and other rights of the retiring generation are laid down, and purchase prices of land, buildings, and machinery are specified. Arrangements are also made concerning the inheritance rights of other members of the junior generation who may not wish to take over the actual running of the farm. A son is the usual successor in such circumstances, but succession by a daughter and her son-in-law husband (*vävy*) is a quite common and long-established stratagem, especially if male heirs are not available.

The successful handling of the inter-generational transmission of a farm may demand a great deal of co-operation between those concerned. Often a farm is too small to divide without excessive damage, and this means that some heirs must surrender their rights to it. The costs of buying such heirs out at economic prices may in turn be crippling, especially when a young successor also wants to renovate a farm and perhaps invest in new machinery and buildings.

Such refurbishing in turn may be a source of conflict with retiring members of the senior generation, who will have their own ideas about how to run the farm, and who may find psychological adjustment difficult. Discord between retiring parents and their children, and not least their children's spouses, and also that between inheriting siblings, is well known in the area, though the worst quarrels seem to take place when ageing parents simply refuse to retire at all. In such circumstances, it is all the more notable that many parents and siblings cope successfully with such problems and display impressive patience, sympathy, and generosity in doing so. Parents, for example, may transfer a farm to one of their children on much more favourable terms than those that economic factors alone would dictate. Siblings, especially if already established in a town, may forgo their rights to a share in a farm. This happens more often than appears in official documents, since parents and siblings may not ultimately insist upon the payments which are allocated to them in such papers. An interesting corollary of this is when large areas of a farm remain formally undivided between siblings long after their parents' death, for this seems more likely to be a result of conflict and a failure to agree over division than a simple expression of sibling solidarity.

Retired parents and urban-dwelling siblings may also give some help in the season-by-season functioning of a farm. If farming is predominantly a family affair, a farming family is rarely self-sufficient as a labour force. As one might expect, farm-working families often differ considerably from one another in accordance with varied incidence of birth, marriage, and death, in addition to such other factors as migration and the buying-out of siblings. Thus, in addition to situations that approximate more closely to a simple elementary family, such a farm-working group may consist of a widowed mother and her unmarried daughter, or a group of unmarried adult siblings, or an old married couple with a daughter and her husband. In many cases, moreover, one may find a farm run mainly by a man and wife who have several children living and working away, and one is tempted to remark that the tractors and other machinery which help make such arrangements possible have started to replace children as the junior members of farm-working families. Farmers have, of course, themselves contributed to this problem by their own eagerness to see their children educated and in good jobs, and the situation has been intriguingly compounded by the commonly reported presence of allergies to farm animals or materials among farmers' children. It seems likely that such allergies existed in the past but were treated with less interest and respect than is the case these days.

For the sake of simplicity, variation in the structure of farm-working families has been played down somewhat in the discussion that follows. It should perhaps be explicitly stated, however, that not only is such variation partially intrinsic to the nature of the family as a unit, but it also poses problems for the viable connection of a family with a farm. To some extent, other features of the family help to counteract these difficulties, especially the flexibility of the family as a working group on its own farm, for example with regard to hours worked and tasks performed, though the sexual division of labour can be a hindrance here. Such flexibility, and the commitment of its members to each other, helps to make the family here, as elsewhere, a particularly well-adapted work-force for the varying demands of agricultural production and its successful combination with ancillary activities, though I am aware that it would be folly to attempt to understand the widespread prevalence of family farming purely in these terms. Moreover, flexibility is clearly in itself incapable of overcoming all the problems which are created or exacerbated by fluctuations in family size and structure, and here mutual help between families may become especially important. I may add that a farm's size, and, of course, its machine resources, are, at least in North Karelia, also of significance in this context of co-operation. Predictably, inter-farm co-operation seems to be most prevalent among medium-sized farms. The owners of very small farms are more likely to be able to cope independently, providing they can cope at all, and may well have less to offer other farmers, though this is not always the case (cf. horse-work on potato cultivation below). The owners of very large farms in their turn are sometimes mechanically self-sufficient and may prefer to try to hire help commercially when necessary rather than receive it in reciprocal return for their own. Such larger enterprises are, however, very few in the area.

Broadly speaking one can distinguish the following main forms of co-operation:

(1) *Internal,* such as between a farmer and his wife and children.

(2) *External but intra-familial,* as when absent family members such as a farmer's siblings or children temporarily return at hay-making time.

(3) *Other external*, for instance, the exchange of labour and machinery and the co-ownership of machinery between different farms.

Patterns of internal co-operation on Finnish farms have archetypically involved a sexual division of labour in which a man's main concerns are forest and field work, while a woman looks after a dairy herd in addition to general housewifely duties. On bigger farms in the past, male and female labour was brought in from outside the farm and worked there the year round, but nowadays the employment of paid labour is unusual except on a casual short-term basis. The traditional division of labour still persists to some extent between husband and wife, or sometimes other family members, but it is much less common and tends to be less rigid than it used to be. This partly stems from the fact that fewer farms nowadays have dairy herds as compared with other forms of livestock. Herds themselves, moreover, tend to be bigger than they previously were, and in such cases men have tended to play their part alongside women in milk production, especially when the dairy side is a farm's main source of income. There are, however, still cases where this work is left for a wife to do alone. Such wives often complain about the heaviness of their work load – the shifting of manure can be especially arduous – and they receive a great deal of sympathy from other women and at least some men. On many farms, however, even when a fairly clear division of labour exists, a great deal of mutual help and support is given between husband and wife, and in such cases one gets a strong impression of them as members of a work team confident in, and respectful of, one another.

The availability of husbands to do dairy work and other tasks to some extent depends on what else they have to do. This in turn depends on the extent to which a man attempts to supplement his income through seasonal forestry work or other off-farm employment. Some wives also take work off the farm. If there are able-bodied children, or sometimes the members of a senior generation who are technically retired but still active, a great deal of useful work-sharing can take place, though there are of course limits to how many people a farm will support. Not surprisingly, some old parents and children are less helpful than others, and relatively little can be done about this beyond grumbling. A retired parent is within his or her rights to be just that, and not to work, and within the limits of a farm's capacity to support a family, farmers are not usually anxious to have all their children leave (unless they are all particularly well-educated), and many go to substantial lengths to make life pleasant for them, such as in allowing the frequent use of a car to a teenage son. I should add that there is also considerable variation in parental attitudes and behaviour so that, as I noted earlier, inter-generational conflict and occasionally even homicide occurs, especially when an older farmer or his widow tries to retain excessive control over a farm and its finances against the wishes of an adult child. Again, although there are exceptions, the position of an in-marrying daughter-in-law is notoriously difficult on Finnish farms. There are numerous references to this in folk and other literature, including a brilliant, well-known cartoon in which a large and aggressive mother-in-law asks as she holds up a scrap of food, 'Will daughter-in-law eat it or shall I give it to the cat?'[2]

As I have mentioned, dependence on the labour of others has to a considerable extent been replaced by a dependence on machinery for a farm-working family. Most farms of any size now have tractors instead of horses, and a large amount of supplementary equipment is also often owned. This may include harrows, ploughs, trailers, weed-killer sprayers, mulching machines, mowing machines, balers, and many others, and with these a farmer on his own can do work which formerly took much longer and often involved others' help. Mechanized or partly-mechanized milking systems are now also the general rule. As long as a farmer and his wife and/or other helpmates are in reasonably good health, and have a good stock of machinery, they can nowadays cope quite well with a large part of the everyday running of a substantial and quite profitable farm.

This does not, however, mean that a farming family can survive without outside help. The proviso about health, for example, is not an empty one. In an area where the average age of farmers is so high, heart disease and other problems such as back trouble caused by heavy timber work in younger days are quite common. If a farmer or his wife becomes ill, their situation can be rather hazardous, especially if there is no potential successor living on the farm. Prolonged ill-health has often led to premature retirement coupled with involvement in one or other of a number of state-aided schemes in which the state may buy a farm for later sale to other farmers, or may enter into a so-called 'non-production agreement', in which the farmer receives a special pension provided he stops growing crops and selling milk. Such agreements reflect the position of farming within Finland's economic and political system where it is deemed to be over-producing beyond the nation's needs, despite its dwindling man-power.

Shorter bouts of illness can be dealt with by the help of neighbours and visiting kin. Some professional stand-ins also exist but there are not enough of them and they mainly help with fixed amounts of dairy work. In a recent case I witnessed, when a farmer experienced some heart trouble at the beginning of the planting season, he got help from both neighbours and kin. One neighbour, with whom his relations are especially good, helped with harrowing and planting, and a son-in-law who happened to be visiting also stepped into the breach. A son in Helsinki was able to arrange to take a few days' holiday to come and help, but the farmer recovered in time to avoid this. Once back in action he received help from another neighbour with some heavy loading work. Some years previous to this, the same farmer had experienced a serious bout of heart trouble and was unable to work for some months. Here again many neighbours had stepped in to help as best they could, and hc was able to get through this period successfully, though at some financial cost, since others' labour and machine time is commonly charged for in such cases, and a farmer often gets help in paying for it through insurance schemes. The farmer in question was a particularly well connected and well liked individual and it is possible that this was crucial in enabling him to get enough help to tide him over his difficulties through so long a period.[3]

In addition to sickness, there are periods of the agricultural year when extra help may be essential for a farmer. The most important of these is typically hay-making time in July (appropriately called hay-month, *heinäkuu*, in Finnish) and early August. A problem with this particular bottleneck is that it lasts some time, and everyone usually needs extra help at the same time. So it is not generally easy to call on neighbouring farmers for this, though one can sometimes borrow a baling machine. Commonly, close relatives such as absent siblings, own and siblings' children, and sometimes their spouses, come on holiday to the country at this time, and are a vital source of extra labour. The work, especially if done on more than a very casual basis, is quite arduous and help is much appreciated. One farmer commented that there seem to be some kin who always come at this time and some who always don't. The work is not usually paid for in cash unless the help is very concentrated and, as it were, full-time, in which case a grateful farmer may thrust money on a kinsman or kinswoman who, at least on the surface, is reluctant to accept it.

In addition to such help in times of sickness and in labour bottlenecks, farmers often engage in various other kinds of mutual aid with their neighbours. One form which this takes is the provision of equipment and possibly labour for another farmer when he happens to need it. Few farmers, for example, own combine harvesters and may hire these from others in the village who happen to possess them, just as in the past they hired the use of tractors before tractor ownership became more general. Interestingly, however, it is not only the most modern equipment which is in demand. Many farmers still like to use horses and horse ploughs for potato planting and subsequent tillage, and horses are nowadays as rare as tractors used to be. In Vieki, one farmer I know with a relatively small farm of his own does a great deal of this work for others, sometimes in return for the use of tractors and auxiliary equipment which he himself does not possess. Thus in one case where he did such work, the farmer he had helped asked him, as is customary, how much he owed him. The man replied that he wouldn't say anything about that at the moment. 'I'll let you know if I've got anything to complain about,' he said. This was taken to mean that he wanted help in due course for his mowing and would ask for it when the time came, as indeed he did.

In the cases I have just mentioned, the use of equipment was coupled with the use of manpower, as when the owner of a combine harvester drives it when it is hired. The owner of a horse will typically drive that, too, on potato or other work. In such cases payment, when made, will usually be both for the labour and for the equipment. In other cases equipment alone will be borrowed. This is either paid for separately, or works on a loose reciprocal basis, in which a farmer exchanges the use of some piece of his own equipment for the use of another piece at some time in the past or future. The general attitude in such cases is one of 'Help and be helped' and this is often extended to other situations, for example when a farmer's car slides into a ditch in winter and he asks a neighbour to bring a tractor to pull it out. Such a neighbour may well refuse to accept any offered payment and will say that he never knows when he himself may need a similar helping hand.

A further form of mutual help between villagers is the joint ownership of machinery, though relatively small numbers of farmers are involved. In general such joint ownership makes much sense, since many machines are not in continuous use and machine costs are often high; it may well be that the pattern will become more widespread in the future. In the cases I know of, relations between the farmers concerned are quite long-standing, and participants have stressed that it is crucial for them to be able to trust each other, not simply in terms of honesty and reliability but also in terms of general temperament, since joint ownership can otherwise quite easily lead to dissatisfaction and quarrels. It was also pointed out that the farms involved must have more or less equal needs for the equipment concerned. In some cases, use of the machinery is not confined to the co-owners, and hiring out a machine such as a combine harvester can be quite a profitable venture providing that too much use does not unduly shorten the machine's working life. I should perhaps add that some commercial hiring-out of combine harvesters is also done by individuals who own them. Overall, it seems clear that where co-ownership is successful it provides a further strengthening of already existing ties between farmers, which may initially be based on a wide range of foundations such as friendship and collaboration in village and church activities. It is interesting in this regard that often no written agreements and contracts exist between co-owners, and one detects a feeling in such cases that the arrangement would be doomed to failure if these were necessary. As with more general co-operation, farm size appears also to be a relevant factor here, since it seems especially to be some of the bigger farms, though not usually the biggest, who often own all their own equipment, who engage in such activities. Smaller farmers I have spoken to, whose farms are still big enough to be decently viable (e.g. 10 hectare fields and 40 hectare forest) and who engage in other forms of reciprocity, tend to say that they are too individualistic to engage in such activities. As I have noted, individualism is strongly developed in the area, but there may also be an element here of reaction to a lack of opportunity and sufficient capital to engage in such a venture without stress. It may also be that such farmers have less need actually to own a wide range of machinery, and it may be added in this regard that joint ownership seems typically to involve machinery which is additional to a farm's most basic machine requirements.

To this general framework of family farms and mutual aid between them there has recently been added a new option in the wider municipality to which Vieki belongs. This is the possibility of establishing a grant-aided so-called 'agricultural village' (*maatalouskyla*). Farmers in such a scheme should ideally be relatively young, number about 8–12, and be interested in planned farming, and in improving their technical expertise. The municipality has allocated about £3,000 to help the scheme, and the services of the local area agricultural adviser and access to computer planning are also made available. The scheme is likely to involve some rationalization of machine ownership and use (though not necessarily joint ownership as such) and will last in the first instance for five years. About half a dozen such schemes have already been established in North Karelia and reports on these appear generally to be favourable. Ideally, of course, those who participate should know each other well and get on well together.

Despite considerable initial hesitation and suspicion about the implications of the scheme for the independent action of participants, six applications were in fact received from different parts of the municipality, and one of two from Vieki was ultimately successful. Eleven farms of medium-to-large size from the locallity are involved, while several farms in the same area are not. They are linked together by a variety of ties, including kinship, neighbourhood, village-committee membership, and a past history of co-operation. They are also linked by a common commitment to hard work and to making a viable go of farming. Such commitment is stressed time and again by villagers as a *sine qua non* of farming success, which they feel is ultimately more important than anything else, while not denying the significance of other factors such as favourable inheritance and availability of credit. The 'agricultural village' in question is quite new and has scarcely yet got under way, but the most recent information at my disposal reflects a continued optimism on the part of the participants.

CONCLUSION

It is clear from my discussion that a great deal of co-operation within and between farming families takes place in this area of rural Finland. It remains to add that in the course of fieldwork I was often made aware that the forms of reciprocity involved are highly valued, both for their practical worth and also for what one might call their contribution to the quality of community life on a social and moral plane. Indeed, it seems to be the case that, under present conditions at least, a recognition of one's moral responsibilities to one's neighbours often also makes sound practical sense. As I have noted, the patterns of co-operation in question operate against a background of farm ownership by families, who provide the main farm workforce and who value highly their equality with others and their freedom of choice. It is possible that this last sometimes restricts co-operation, but it may also be that it more positively serves to mould it, since it gives a farmer a keen sense of his own and others' self-respect. Thus on one occasion a farmer on whose farm I was staying was asked by a farming neighbour to come to help him with some hard manual work for which he was paid. It was clear both from my observations and from subsequent discussion that strong efforts were made to ensure that, despite the payment, the situation differed sharply from that of employing a hired hand. The farmer worked very hard, but breaks in the work were longer and more frequent than was strictly necessary, and refreshment was relatively lavishly provided. When it came to payment, the neighbour insisted on paying considerably more than the farmer himself thought was a reasonable amount for the work done. My host would have been upset if he had felt in any way exploited and demeaned by his neighbour, and the neighbour would himself have been unhappy to be thought of as doing the exploiting. Having avoided this, however, both sides were amply satisfied, and the way was kept open for further fruitful collaboration in the future.

If the combination of individual and family autonomy with a need for co-operation is a complex one in eastern Finland, it should also perhaps be noted here that the autonomy in question is further tempered in quite serious ways. Farmers in the area have for generations pitted their wits against the stony soils and inhospitable climate, but the terms and conditions under which this struggle is conducted, and even the structure of the families which conduct it, have in substantial measure been determined by state legislation, political and economc policies, religious culture, and indeed developments beyond the boundaries of the nation. These are forces which farmers can sometimes influence but which are far from being under their control.

This general point is relevant to a final topic which I wish to discuss briefly, and which has been to some extent implicit in my account of co-operation. This concerns the relationship between kinship and neighbourhood in the village community, and particularly the fact that co-operation between kin *qua* kin seems largely, though not wholly, confined to close kin on the same farm, either regularly or as occasional visitors. This would be expected in a community where ties of kinship between its constituent families are relatively rare, as was the case in some of the Tanzanian villages I have worked in (Abrahams 1981). In villages like Vieki, however, there is a great deal of relationship through common *suku* and other kin ties between villagers, and indeed rather more than is in fact realized, since more distant ties tend to be forgotten. The extra-farm kin living in a village do not, however, form a special group or category of people for inter-farm co-operation, though it is true that a kinship link can sometimes provide a basis on which a co-operative tie is first established and later developed. One factor in the situation is the recent patterns of emigration and undivided inheritance which tend to isolate an individual spatially from his brothers (the situation can be rather different with regard to sisters), and to leave him with a set of cousins of varying degree. The potential closeness of these is in turn diminished by the emphasis of the legal and economic system upon the elementary family as a bounded, independent, property-holding unit. It seems likely that collaboration between brothers living on separate farms in the same community would have constituted a more widespread special case in the early days when farms were more often divided and emigration was less common, though there is ample evidence that the 'ambivalence' of siblings can generate as much dissension in North Karelia as elsewhere. However this may be, the present tendency appears to be that many of the more practical, everyday aspects of extra-farm co-operation are left to friendship, neighbourhood, and 'achieved' relations from a universe of kin, while, to some extent mirroring Malinowski's distinction between magic and religion, more 'spiritual' and symbolically important areas of life such as birth, marriage, major birthdays, and funerals, loom large as contexts in which kinship solidarity beyond the elementary family has maintained a special though not exclusive place.

Notes

1.   The work on which this paper is based was carried out in 1981–82 in North Karelia with the support of an SSRC research grant.

2.   The cartoon in question is one of the many published by the distinguished Finnish cartoonist, Erkki Tanttu.

3.   Since I left the field the farmer became ill again and died. His farm is now, for the present at least, closed down under a state non-production agreement.

6.   The Estimation of Work in a Northern Finnish Farming Community

Tim Ingold

A farm is not a static thing, but an evolving testimony to the life's work of those who have left their mark on its buildings, fields, and forests. Hence the past and future of the farm are inseparable from the intertwined biographies of its personnel, and the developmental history of the domestic group which they compose. But every domestic group, as surely as it grows, must eventually disperse. A fundamental problem, in all systems of peasant agriculture in which the household is the unit of production, is how to safeguard the continuity of the farm in the face of this periodic fragmentation. This is not just a matter of settling the inheritance of the estate, viewed as a parcel of durable, landed property. A farm must be worked as well as owned – its livestock tended, its fields cultivated, its forests thinned, and its buildings maintained. The more prolonged any interruption or dereliction of these tasks, the more difficult and costly it is ever to return the farm to an operational condition. The situation that I will describe in this chapter is typical of much of rural Finland. The essential continuity of management has been broken, and the prospects for one farm after another are collapsing for want of a successor generation. In seeking the reasons for this state of affairs, I shall focus on the changing character of work both on the farm and in the forest, as well as on changes in the perception of what it means to 'work' or to 'have a job'.

The material on which my discussion is based derives from 12 months of fieldwork carried out in the district of Salla, in north-eastern Finland, during 1979–80.[1] As the analysis of this material is still incomplete, any conclusions I present must be regarded as tentative, and I am not yet in a position to draw from them any grand comparative or theoretical generalizations. I shall concentrate my attention on four factors that are of particular importance for understanding what has happened in Salla. The first is the close interdependence, in this region, between farming and forestry: as I shall show, the mechanization of forestry has had a profound (and in many ways disastrous) impact on the viability of local agriculture. The second is the redefinition of men's and women's work, especially on the farm, that has accompanied the transition from a broad-based, subsistence-oriented economy to specialized dairy production for the market. A third factor lies in a rather specific set of historical circumstances, which have to do with the policy of resettlement and colonization implemented during the immediate post-war period. Finally, and perhaps most importantly, I shall emphasize the trans- formed aspirations of a younger generation blighted in their native region by chronic unemployment, whose only hope of fulfilment lies in educational qualification for jobs in the urban sector, taking them far from home and often abroad.

I shall begin by sketching in the background of the place and its history. This is followed by an account of the distribution and tenure of forest-bearing land, and the conditions of its exploitation. I continue in the subsequent section with a discussion of work on the farm, with reference to the sexual division of labour, problems of succession, and their implications for inter-farm co-operation. To conclude, I consider briefly the general significance of work as a source of personal standing in the community.

PLACE AND PEOPLE

The district of Salla lies hard up against Finland's border with the Soviet Union, in the south-eastern corner of the province of Lap- land. Its southern boundary falls just 'below' the Arctic Circle, from which it extends over 100 km to the north. In area it covers almost 6,000 km^2, of which little more than 1 per cent consists of fields. The rest is covered by forest, swamp, and towards the north, patches of barren tundra.

The district was originally inhabited by small and scattered bands of forest Lapps, who lived by hunting, trapping, and fishing. The first Finnish settlers arrived towards the end of the seventeenth century, bringing with them cattle, and subsequently horses and sheep. From the Lapps they obtained domestic reindeer. The annual cycle was largely dictated by the needs of the cattle, which for nine months of every year had to be confined within the cowshed. To tide them over the long winter, large quantities of hay were cut during the summer from natural meadows that were to be found here and there in widely scattered locations throughout the forest. In addition, the settlers gradually cleared small fields around their homesteads where they grew turnips and cereals — principally barley, but also rye. Reindeer were gathered up during the autumn and early winter, and were used principally for hauling sledgeloads of hay from racks and barns located on the meadows, which could be anything up to 70 km distant from the homestead. If supplies of hay were sufficient, cattle yielded milk for most of the year. This was churned into butter, and only the sourmilk residue was consumed. Most butter was reserved for trade, in exchange for grain, in which few households were entirely self-sufficient. Meat came from reindeer and wild game, whilst hides and furs were marketed. The surrounding forest was exploited for fuel, fencing, and building materials.

For two centuries, despite a steady increase in population, this mode of livelihood remained basically unchanged. However in the 1890s, the newly-established timber industry began to look towards the huge reserves of forest in the north for its supply of raw materials. All at once, the vast forests of Salla came to acquire a commercial value of almost incalculable magnitude. The timber boom attracted such an influx of labour to the lumber camps that the population almost doubled in the decade 1890–1900. There developed a class of crofters and cottagers, dependent on logging work for a livelihood, in contrast with the established peasantry, whose income was derived from a combination of agriculture and reindeer management. This division was the source of much political bitterness, particularly in the confused years after 1917, when Finland became an independent republic. But old grudges were forgotten in the emergency of the Winter War of 1939–40. At a few hours' notice, the entire population of Salla had to be evacuated, as their villages were burned by advancing Soviet troops. A second, and much longer period of evacuation followed in 1944, during which the retreating German army set about the systematic destruction of every building in Lapland. Throughout the war, Salla was the scene of many particularly bloody battles, the remains of which still scar the landscape, and which have left an indelible mark on the minds, and often the bodies, of the men who experienced them. At the conclusion of hostilities, one half of the area of the original district of Salla was ceded to the Soviet Union. Returning from years of evacuation and life 'in the corners of strange houses', the people of Salla set about the reconstruction of their homes and farms with a vengeance. Those from villages lost behind the new frontier were directed to remote areas of almost untouched forest and swamp, from which they literally hacked out their farms. Within a decade, Salla had become a prosperous agricultural district, held up as an example to the rest of the country. People talked of the 'Salla miracle'. A decade later, at the end of the 1960s, the miracle had gone. Faced with a massive 'mountain' of dairy produce, the state did all it could to encourage farmers to give up. Persuaded that there was no future in agriculture, those of working age, particularly of the younger generation, moved in their thousands to take well-paid industrial jobs in the south of Sweden. One homestead after another was left deserted, as in the space of a few years the population dropped from almost 11,000 to a little over 7,000. Today, only one in three farms is still operative.

THE FOREST

To every farm is attached a large area of forest, commonly covering between 150 and 300 hectares. Though a proportion of the area is economically of no value, consisting of barren, rocky ground or un-cultivable swamp, at least 90 per cent of the remaining area of every estate consists of taxable, forest-bearing land. Pine predominates, though mixed with spruce and a certain amount of birch. At this latitude trees grow extremely slowly – it can take at least a century for a seedling to reach maturity. It is for this reason, and because the forest is relatively less dense than farther south, that the areas belonging to each estate are so large. Until the mid-1930s, the forests of Salla remained undivided, in that final boundaries had yet to be established both between private land and state land, and separating individual estates. Pending the final division (*isojako*), each village was provisionally allotted a block (*lohko*) of surrounding land, which was held in joint possession by every independent, tax-paying estate in that village. The size of the block was estimated in proportion to the aggregate number of tax-units (*manttaalit*) represented by these estates. The tax-value of each, in turn, was based on its yield in agricultural produce, and its wealth in livestock and buildings. A similar principle was adopted to determine the size of each individual estate, when the *isojako* was finally effected. The process of division was extremely long and involved, for both the established peasantry and the state were concerned to claim as much as possible of the fine stands of almost virgin forest which, with the development of the timber industry, had acquired the quality of 'green gold'. It was of course in the local landowners' interests to exaggerate the yield from their meadows and fields, for the additional burden of tax was far outweighed by the value of the forest that would accrue to their estates.

Until the last war, virtually all commercial forest felling was conducted by one or other of the major companies operating in the region. Having obtained the 'concession' to fell a particular block, the company would set up a lumber camp (*savotta*), placing it under the direction of a salaried foreman or 'boss' (*ukkoherra*) who was responsible for the recruitment and organization of labour. Once news of the *savotta* had spread around, men would arrive to seek work, often having travelled many days from home by sledge or ski. They were usually organized into groups of three: for every man with horse and sledge there were two equipped with axes and a double-handled saw. Whilst the latter worked together to fell the trees, the former transported the trunks to the stack by the riverside, from which, in the spring flood, they would be floated downstream. To each horsedriver, the 'boss' would allocate a particular 'patch' from the total block to be felled. Generally, the horsedriver had to recruit his own tree-cutters, who often included a son, brother, or other close relative or neighbour. He was paid in proportion to the volume of timber extracted from his 'patch', and from this he in turn had to pay his tree-cutters, as well as provide for their subsistence.

When commercial felling operations began on a large scale in Salla, around the turn of the century, hundreds of landless labourers from central and eastern Finland moved north to seek work in the lumber camps. Some arrived as boys in their early teens, and nearly all were single. Many eventually married locally, and established small crofts on what was then Crown Land. Unlike the established peasantry, the crofters' rights of usufruct to the surrounding meadows and forests were extremely limited, and they continued to depend upon forestry work for a livelihood. During the slump of the early 1930s they were particularly hard hit, in contrast with the farming population whose relative self-sufficiency offered a measure of protection from market fluctuations. When the lands of each village were finally divided, crofts were converted into independent small-holdings, but to each was allotted only enough meadowland to support one or two cows, and enough forest to meet domestic needs. Though the intention of post-independence land reform was to enable smallholders to obtain parcels of land from the state large enough to realize economic self-sufficiency, further progress in this direction was halted by the Winter War of 1939–40, and subsequent hostilities.

In the aftermath of the war, a radical shift occurred in the distribution of forest land. First, those who had lost their homes on the Soviet side of the new border, comprising half the population of Salla, were given estates of equivalent size cut from state land in that part of the district that remained on the Finnish side. Second, former smallholders were enabled to obtain additional parcels of land to bring their estates to a size comparable with that of long-established landowners. Third, men who had spent the years of the war in active military service, many of them partial invalids, were given the chance to establish estates of their own (appropriately known as 'cold farms', as they were started from scratch). The result was a major transfer of land, most of it almost untouched forest, from the state into private hands. A premiss of government policy at that time was that national recovery could best be secured through agricultural growth, and, especially in the north, by promoting settlement along the margins of previously unproductive swamps which could be drained, cleared, and cultivated. Substantial grants were made available to this end. Nevertheless, farmers depended on a secondary income from forestry in order to secure a livelihood, as well as to cover their capital costs.

There are two ways of selling timber. One is to sell it 'standing' (*pystykauppa*), so that the company which buys it is also responsible for felling and extraction. The other is to sell it already cut and stacked (*hankintakauppa*), so that the company has only to arrange for its transport from the site. In this case the landowner himself carries out the work of extraction. The difference between the 'cut rate' and the 'standing rate' for timber (nowadays expressed per cubic metre) gives the rate at which the owner is remunerated for his labour, after deduction of instrumental costs. Prior to the final land division, all timber was necessarily sold standing from the provisional blocks of each village, as the boundaries of individual estates had still to be determined. The proceeds of felling from these blocks, which continued right up until the outbreak of war, were divided in proportion to the tax value of each estate. After the war, however, there followed a major switch towards selling timber 'cut and stacked'. Not only did the land division confer on every owner the undisputed right to harvest timber from a bounded plot, but also former smallholders who had previously earned a living by working for the timber companies, having obtained additional land from the state, were able to transfer to working in their own forest.

The *hankinta* method remained predominant until the mid-1960s.

But during this period, machines began to make their appearance in forestry work. The chainsaw, at first cumbersome, impractical, and extremely dangerous, had replaced the axe and hand-saw by the end of the 1950s. Then, during the 1960s, horses were rather rapidly displaced by tractors. Initially, ordinary agricultural tractors, which could be used, like horses, for farmwork in summer and forestry in winter, were adopted. But the trend of technological development was always towards heavier, more costly, and more specialized machines. At the same time, an ever greater proportion of timber came to be transported from the felling site by lorry rather than by flotation. The result of mechanization was both to cut labour costs and virtually to eliminate seasonal constraints on logging work. Heavy tractors and lorries could operate all year round in the forest. Most are owned not by timber companies but by private contractors, for whom the purchase price of each machine is nowadays around 800,000 Fmk (c. £100,000). Faced with costs of this magnitude, no contractor can afford to keep his machine idle for any length of time without risking bankruptcy.

The big companies had a direct interest in promoting the adoption of heavy machinery, since it helped secure an even flow of raw materials to the factories, as well as cutting the costs of extraction. The gap between the 'standing' price and the 'cut and stacked' price for timber consequently narrowed, until the point was reached where a man could expect to earn more under contract to a company, even felling in his own forest, than working on his own account. By 1970, about 60 per cent of all sales were of 'standing timber', and a decade later this figure had risen to over 90 per cent. Almost all felling is now carried out by a relatively small number of skilled forestry workers, who work all year round and are paid at piece-rate by the company to which they are contracted (apart from the state, which has its own organization for timber extraction, four companies are presently operating in Salla). Farmers had only to look on as the machines rolled in over their plots, leaving them and their sons, as well as their tractors, unemployed over the winter months. A son, lacking sufficient work on his father's farm, might either become a full-time forestry worker himself, or leave the area altogether to find a job elsewhere. Either way, the viability and continuity of the farm is threatened. Many farmers simply sold their entire estates to the forestry companies, sent their cattle to slaughter, boarded up their houses, and left. The rusting remains of antiquated logging machinery that litter the yards of many deserted houses serve as a poignant reminder of the social costs of technological development.

Opinions are sharply divided as to the merits of heavy machinery. Opponents claim that large forestry tractors cause considerable damage to immature trees and seedlings, and that workers hired by the companies take less care to avoid such damage than owners working on their own land. Some are so adamant in their objections that they refuse to sell 'standing timber' even if this means not selling at all. Others explain that they have been compelled to sell in this way, albeit reluctantly. It is commonly supposed that the basic reason for the drop in 'cut and stacked' sales is that owners are no longer adequately compensated for their labour. In practice, however, an owner is rarely presented with a choice between felling his forest on his own account, or working under contract to a company. More usually, the choice is between the former alternative, or no work at all. Under these conditions, it might be expected that owners would continue to sell 'cut and stacked' even though a full-time forestry worker could earn a lot more in a shorter period from felling a plot of equivalent size. The reason that most do not is that they lack sufficient hands at home to do the job. Few men of the older generation are still physically fit enough to carry out heavy work without assistance from their sons. Consequently, the only circumstances under which timber is still sold 'cut and stacked' are when an owner has both the necessary equipment and adult sons at home who are not themselves working under contract to a company. This normally presupposes that they can be employed in agricultural work during the summer months — in other words, that the family farm is still in operation. Ultimately, therefore, the 'compulsion' to sell timber 'standing' rather than 'cut and stacked' relates to the problem of finding a successor to the farm, a problem that I shall consider more fully in the next section.

THE FARM

Most of the homesteads constructed in Salla after the war follow a fairly standard pattern. The principal buildings, situated on two sides of a square-shaped yard, are the dwelling-house and cowshed. On the other side is a bath-house (*sauna*). The fourth side may include one or two more outbuildings, such as a woodshed, and possibly another shed for tools and machinery. Entering the dwelling through a small, double porch, a door on the right leads into a large L-shaped living room (*pirtti*), the inner corner of which is formed by a wood-fired baking oven and cooking stove. On the opposite wall are the kitchen cupboards, sink, and worktop. By one window is a table and benches, where people normally sit to eat and drink; around the remaining walls may be a variety of other bits and pieces of furniture. On the left-hand side of the house are two bedrooms (*kamarit*), and another furnished room is usually situated in the attic. These rooms constitute the 'private' area of the house, which visitors may only enter by invitation. The *pirtti,* by contrast, is open to all comers, and is the setting for all everyday, indoor activities and conversation. The cowshed, usually facing the dwelling across the yard, is a long, narrow building usually divided into three sections. At one end is storage space for fodder. The middle section contains stalls for the cattle, with room for anything between four and twelve animals, depending on the size of the shed. The other end section contains an entrance porch, a wash-house, and a small stable.

Surrounding the homestead are its dry fields, situated on relatively elevated sand- and gravel-based ground. These are quite small, usually around 1–3 hectares in extent. Initially, they were used for crops, principally potatoes and barley, the latter grown both for animal fodder and for domestic consumption. Today, although most households still maintain a small potato patch, very few grow any other crops. Barley, if grown at all, is fed to the animals as a partial substitute for commercial fodder. This change is connected with the general trend of specialization towards dairy production. Cattle which had previously pastured freely in nearby meadows and woodland over the summer months were put to graze on the much more nutritive grass grown in place of crops on the dry fields. A little farther from the homestead lie its hayfields, usually covering around 3–12 hectares. These fields were originally made by draining suitable areas of boggy ground, which could then be hoed and planted with timothy-grass. This method of hay cultivation began to replace the traditional practice of gathering hay from 'natural' meadows during the 1930s. After the war a formidable amount of effort was put into clearing new fields, most of it carried out by hand, as a result of which the old hay meadows fell into disuse. Today they are quite forgotten.

The dairy herd remains, as it always has done, the vital asset of the farm. Returning from evacuation, most households had, to start off with, only one or two cows, just enough to provide a domestic milk supply. As hay fields were cleared, so the herd could be increased. However, few households came to possess more than 10 milking cows, the most usual numbers remaining between 5 and 7. The regular collection of milk for sale began only in the late 1950s, with the establishment of a local dairy. Although the herds are relatively smaller than in pre-war days, their yield is considerably higher, as a result of more nutritious fodder and the importation of superior breeds. Sheep have virtually disappeared from Salla, though a few households have recently begun to specialize in sheep farming as an alternative to cattle. As nearly all clothing is bought, they are no longer required for their wool. Horses, too, have disappeared – to my knowledge, only two horses in Salla are still employed in agricultural work. Finally, though some households fattened one or two pigs every year for domestic consumption, none do today. It is cheaper to buy pork in the shops than to produce it at home.

Traditionally, work on the farm was governed by a strict division of labour in which by far the greater burden fell on the housewife (*emäntä*). Her places of work were in the *pirtti* of the dwelling and in the cowshed (*navetta*). In the former she was expected to mind the fire, look after the children, cook and serve the meals, bake the bread, mend the clothes, and perform countless other domestic chores. In the latter she had to feed and water the animals (which in the past included the preparation of a gruel of hay and wood-ash in boiled water), to milk the cows, and, in the days when butter was prepared at home, to churn the milk. All these tasks had to be performed day in, day out, every day of the year. The *emäntä* was usually first up, at around five o'clock in the morning, to light the fire and brew coffee, and she was most often the last to bed as well. From her point of view, the work she did in the *navetta* was as much a part of the domestic routine as her work in the *pirtti* – in one she would look after the animal component of the family, in the other she would look after its human component. Towards both, she would hold the same affection. Her husband to the contrary, though formally the master of the house (*isäntä*), had no business whatsoever in the *navetta*, his work lying in the fields and forest. Indeed it was normal for husbands to be away from home, especially over winter, for many months at a stretch; and during these periods the *emäntä* had no alternative but to manage the household on her own. A 'good' husband, before leaving for the forest to search for reindeer or to work on a lumber camp, would lay in stocks of firewood and hay to last over the period of his absence. If he did not, the *emäntä* had somehow to bring in the hay herself, as well as saw and chop the wood.

Today the position of the *emäntä* has altered radically. Although looking after cattle, like washing clothes or baking bread, is generally regarded as women's work, it is now common to see husband and wife working side by side in the cowshed, or even the husband at work on his own. There are a number of reasons for this change. The first lies in the increasing specialization of the farming household in dairy production and, related to this, the mechanization of timber extraction. The latter has entailed a substantial reduction in the demand for seasonal labour and so has virtually removed what had previously been an important source of secondary income, particularly for farmers whose holdings of fields and cattle fell at the lower end of the range. Such small farms are consequently no longer viable. Most have ceased production, and their owners, unless due to retire, have sold out and left to take industrial work in the south of Finland and in Sweden. To maintain the viability of the family farm under modern conditions requires major investment in land, livestock, and machinery. There is no doubt that the capitalization of dairy production has affected the definition of work in the cowshed, for the *emäntä* today is an equal partner with her husband in a joint commercial venture.

Another reason for the change, of perhaps even greater significance, lies in the dispersal of domestic groups. Until the early 1960s, most children in Salla were born into large families. For example, in one cluster of 4 houses, all built after the war by men of the same generation who had been in active military service, there were at one time no fewer than 38 children, of whom 23 were attending the local primary school. Today the school has closed for want of pupils, and the total population of those 4 houses is reduced from 46 to only 5: in one house a widow, in another a widow with her adult son, and a single bachelor in each of the remaining two. The children of the post-war generation, as fast as they have grown up, have left to find jobs elsewhere. Often enough, their parents have been left to face old age on their own, and as they die, or move into old people's accommodation, homesteads are left empty and gradually fall into decay. With age comes sickness. Many men, now accustomed to work in the cowshed, explain that their first experience of such work came when, for some reason or other, their wives or mothers were prevented by poor health from carrying on. Despite enormous advances in health care, illness today can have much more serious consequences for the management of a farm than in the past, since there is often no-one at home of the younger generation left or competent to help out. Indeed, this is the most common reason for giving up the cattle herd altogether.

Frequently, the first in the family to suffer ill-health is the *isäntä*. Men in middle age are particularly prone to heart disease which, if they survive, leaves them unfit for heavy work. Others are incapacitated by the back troubles that come from years of work in forestry. In addition, a remarkably high proportion of men in Salla sustained serious injuries during the war, the debilitating effects of which increase with age. Even in widowhood the *emäntä* may continue to keep cattle, without more than occasional assistance from her children. One widow explained to me that the death of her invalid husband had actually been a considerable relief. Despite losing the use of an arm in the war, he had built a homestead, cleared by hand 7 hectares of fields, and raised 12 children. For this, as for so many other veterans of the last war, the only reward was a framed certificate of his achievements to hang on the wall, a small pension, and rapidly deteriorating health. His wife had always taken the full burden of looking after the milking cows, and has continued to do so after his death, with at least one worry off her mind. But another worry remains – whether there will be anyone from among her children who will be prepared to take over when she can no longer manage.

The problem of finding a successor to the estate is recognized to be critical for the future of agricultural production, not only in Salla but throughout the 'marginal' regions of rural Finland that have suffered most from recent depopulation. In the early part of this century the problem had been quite the reverse: as a result of the division of estates between many heirs, they had often become too small to be viable. Today, even though the number of siblings frequently runs into double figures, it is difficult to find even a single successor. This is not simply due to lack of interest among the younger generation. The prospects for a son wishing to take over his parents' farm are indeed daunting. The parents, uncertain of the future, may have invested little or nothing in basic improvements. Perhaps the cowshed needs to be completely rebuilt, and more land needs to be bought or cleared so that the herd can be increased. On top of that, the successor has to pay off, in money, the equal shares of each of his siblings in his estate. He is therefore saddled, right from the start, with substantial bank loans at a time when the future profitability of the venture is far from certain. The demands of siblings for their share are often the cause of much resentment, particularly if they have benefited from further education – partly at their parents' expense – and then moved away to take jobs elsewhere, having done nothing for the farm. The son who stays at home receives none of these benefits, nor any recognition for the work he has put in. It is said that only in farming does a man have literally to 'buy' his job and his place of work. Added to this is a certain sense of shame, for the son who stays at home is considered a 'failure' in the eyes of those who can boast professional qualifications, a well-paid job, and a house in town.

If a son cannot be found to take over the farm, there may be the possibility of recruiting a son-in-law. However, most girls of the post-war generation have not the slightest inclination to become a farmer's wife, nor do they know much about what it involves. One man told me how his teenage daughter had once had to go to the cowshed on an errand. She returned round-eyed, confessing that she never realized her parents had all those cattle. As long as she could remember, she had never set foot in the cowshed before. Moreover, it is popularly well known that the smell of the cowshed 'sticks', and represents a stigma that few girls would gladly bear. Added to this is the understandable desire of daughters to get a better deal in life than their mothers. In Finland today it is accepted that every woman, unless on maternity leave or formally unemployed, should have a job. She normally plans to have around two children (three is already a big family by modern standards), who are from an early age put into day-nurseries so that their mother can go out to work. Whether or not this is a satisfactory arrangement, it is one to which most women currently aspire. It is, of course, quite contrary to the idea of staying at home to look after the family and the cattle, which is perceived to be equivalent to having no job at all.

Here, then, is yet another obstacle to the son who would consider succeeding to his parents' farm. It is difficult for him to find a wife. In some cases, farms have been taken over and successfully managed by bachelors working on their own, though their mothers may help with the milking. As one woman wryly remarked, in connection with the artificial insemination of cattle, the situation today is so topsy-turvy that men who know nothing of women are looking after cows who know nothing of bulls. And naturally, a bachelor can secure the continuity of the farm for only one more generation. But even though there are many single men who have proved as capable of looking after a dairy herd as their mothers before them, few have had to learn to milk by hand. In a number of cases, where milking machines have been installed, the junior *isäntä* uses the machine whilst the senior *emäntä* continues to hand-milk as long as she has the strength to do so.

More often, though, there is no-one to take over the farm. A common story runs as follows: children grow up, one by one they leave, some to local centres, others farther afield or even abroad. Maybe one or two sons stay at home, deriving an income from forestry work, though intermittently on the unemployment register. The parents age, the health of the *isäntä* begins to crack and he is put on a disability pension. The *emäntä* carries on, but already the herd has had to be reduced and some of the fields are out of use. Gradually her 'hands grow weak', until eventually she can no longer milk the cows. There is no point in installing a milking machine, since this would entail renovation of the entire cowshed. Even the possible marriage of one of the resident sons, bringing a young *emäntä* into the house, does not ease the situation, for it would require an impossibly large investment in buildings and machinery to return the farm to an operational condition. So the day comes when the cows are 'put on the lorry', and taken away to be slaughtered. For the old *emäntä*, it is a time of great distress, not unlike that which accompanies bereavement. She faces a kind of emptiness, a loss of purpose. The cattle had dictated a daily routine, from which it is difficult to escape. Long after the cattle are gone, she still rises at five o'clock in the morning, even though there is no milking to do. As for the hayfields, they are left to grow over, whilst the drainage ditches are filled with a luxuriant growth of willow scrub.

Today, on about two out of every three farms, all production has ceased, and about one in three homesteads are deserted – though some may still be neatly kept for summer residence. This naturally reduces the possibilities for co-operation between the working farms that remain. In the immediate post-war period, it was common for neighbouring farmers to combine in groups of around four or five for the purchase of tractors and threshing machines, whose use was shared between them. Much larger co-operatives were formed for the joint ownership of mills for grinding corn, circular saws for producing building material, and bulls for serving the cattle. Nearly all these organizations are now defunct, largely because of changes in productive techniques and practices. Crops are little grown, so that some threshing machines have fallen out of use altogether, and others are used only occasionally, rarely by more than one farm. As horses have disappeared, so every household has acquired a tractor of its own. Most saws are now in private hands, there is only one local mill, and cows are artificially inseminated. However, an important new field of potential co-operation has developed along with new methods for the production of green (or so-called 'AIV') fodder. Though every farm must have its own silo, other equipment for producing AIV may be obtained jointly, including the mowing machine and the special trailer into which the cut grass is projected. But however advantageous this may be in principle, it is difficult to share equipment when there are no other working farms in the immediate neighbourhood. The result, in some cases, is that farmers have had to put off plans for AIV production, lacking the funds to invest in their own. In other cases, the mower and trailer are shared between two, or at most three, partners.

In recent years, farmers have been under strong pressure to increase the area of their fields in order to support larger herds. The pressure derives in particular from the costs of artificial fodder, which have risen faster than the selling price of milk. From the balance between his regular 'milk credit' and his 'fodder bills' (to which must be added loan repayments on capital investment and a host of other recurrent expenses) the farmer derives his income, which is generally low in comparison with that of an industrial worker. As his income 'per litre' of milk falls, in real terms, so he must increase the productivity of the farm, simply in order to make a living from it. Paradoxically, whilst the majority of hayfields in Salla are abandoned and growing over, many farmers face insuperable problems in trying to secure the use of more land. This is not always so. I did record a number of instances in which disused fields had been placed at the free disposal of a neighbour who still kept cattle, particularly when that neighbour was also a close relative. One man explained to me that it is far more pleasant to look out over freshly mown, well-kept fields than it is to watch them falling into decay, so that the benefit is mutual. Others, less liberally inclined, insist on a rent – although there is a great deal of variation in the amount charged. But there are many more who refuse to part with their fields, or let others use them.

One of the reasons for this lies in the consequences of government policy directed towards reducing overproduction in the agricultural sector. Legislation introduced in 1969 enabled farmers to 'package' their fields, in return for an undertaking that every field thus 'packaged' would be withdrawn from production; the state was then prepared to provide substantial annual compensation. In other words, farmers were paid to stop farming. Although 'packaging' agreements were originally meant to last only for a limited period, they have been repeatedly extended, and most agreements are still in force. The policy did not bring about the intended results. The majority of those in Salla who 'packaged' their fields were about to cease production in any case, for reasons that I have already spelled out. Most active farmers would have nothing to do with the whole scheme, which they regarded as utterly misguided. The problem today, now that government policy is rather more favourably disposed towards the support of rural communities than a decade ago, is that fields urgently needed to improve the viability of working farms are 'locked up' by 'packaging' agreements. Naturally, the owners of these fields have a strong interest in keeping them 'packaged' for as long as possible, since it brings them a tidy income in the form of compensation payments, including a 'surface area bonus' to which they are additionally entitled. Besides these 'packaged' areas, a good deal of private land was sold to outside buyers, particularly in the early 1970s, a time of rampant speculation when highly paid businessmen and bureaucrats in Helsinki seemed prepared to pay almost any price to obtain a plot of land in Lapland. The state has since intervened to establish a prior right of purchase, buying land at the going rate and reselling it to local farmers.

Although in every village in Salla there are deserted homesteads, some have nevertheless suffered more heavily from depopulation than others. The worse hit are the resettlement 'colonies' pioneered after the war by those whose former homes were lost behind the new Soviet border, and the 'cold farms' established by war veterans. Local people, commenting on this fact, commonly attribute it to two major 'mistakes' of post-war settlement policy. The first was that rather than grouping houses into clusters, they were strung out along loop roads, leaving considerable distances between each. By all accounts this did much to destroy the relations of kinship and neighbourhood that traditionally obtained in the old villages where settlement was concentrated, usually on the banks of a lake or river. As a result, the sense of rootlessness that naturally followed resettlement was never fully overcome. Twenty years later, people still felt as though they had been stuck 'in the middle of nowhere' on the edges of dreary swamps. It was therefore not a particularly hard decision for anyone to pack up and leave.

The second supposed 'mistake' of settlement policy was that it overestimated the commitment to farming of smallholders who, before the war, had derived an income primarily from wage employment. This is a somewhat subjective judgement, undoubtedly coloured by long-standing political jealousies between former crofters and established landowners. The latter, who generally support the relatively right-wing agrarian party, now renamed the Centre Party, have always been quick to denigrate the efforts of ex-crofters, many of them well-known for their Communist sympathies. At times during the 1950s, they were even suspected of trying to sabotage the whole resettlement programme. Nevertheless, it is a fact that a sizeable proportion of men with a crofting background, who in pre-war days spent most of their time in forestry work, were less than enthusiastic about the farming life, and resented being tied down by the regular domestic routines it entailed. Often, their field-clearance was left half-done, their herds never rose above two or three milking cows, and consequently they remained heavily dependent on logging and other wage-work. Thus they were the first to suffer the effects of mechanization and the resulting reduction in manpower requirements for forestry. Since, before the war, the majority of crofters and cottagers lived in the central 'church village' of Salla, the problem of depopulation is most acute in the two colonies where the people of this village were resettled. In one of these, only a single working farm remains; a few houses are occupied by forestry workers and old people, but the rest are deserted. In the case of 'cold farms', the problem was compounded by the fact that many of the men who established them were partially disabled. Whatever their commitment to farming, they were physically unfit for the heavy work it demanded. In a number of cases the continuity of the farm depended on whether the *emäntä* was both prepared and well enough to take on virtually the entire burden of running the farm herself.

THE SIGNIFICANCE OF WORK

Pervading Finnish rural society is an austere and powerful work ethic. Bolstered by a strong tradition of evangelical Lutheranism, it insists that the only road to a good life is through unremitting physical and mental toil, for which the motivation must come from within the individual. In secular terms, this ethic is epitomized by the concept of *sisu* ('guts'), and is celebrated in the Finns' passionate craze for athletic sports, particularly those involving individual rather than team achievement. Olympic medallists (one of the most famous of whom has a summer cottage in Salla, courtesy of the local commune) are national heroes. The same ideal is enshrined in the system of piece-rate payment for forestry workers, which sets every man in competition with his fellows, and enables the company to pass off its exploitation of the worker as the latter's exploitation of himself. Whatever a person's political affiliations, and regardless of whether he derives his inspiration from the popularized doctrines of Karl Marx or Martin Luther, or a mixture of both, hard work constitutes the basis both of his own self-respect and of his rating in the community. A supporter of the Centre Party in Salla may well remark approvingly of his Communist neighbour that 'although a Communist, he has really worked hard'. A courageous record of wartime service is similarly a mark of esteem, and is recited at length in special anniversaries.

For the post-war generation, however, who have never experienced the real hardships faced by their parents and grandparents, work has come to acquire a quite different significance. It refers not to toil and exertion, but to having a 'job', that is, having paid employment outside the home. As a result of the occupational diversification that followed the expansion of administration and services into rural areas, a person's job has become a marker of his identity and position in the community. One's occupation serves on formal occasions as a title, and follows one's name in the telephone directory, which is not consulted just for numbers. The definition of work as a job is reinforced by rules governing the provision of benefits to those classed as 'unemployed', whilst the rating of a job is linked to the level of educational qualification it requires. Salla has long been a region of high unemployment, ranging between 10 and 20 per cent of the working population. Young people, as usual, are the worst affected. It is commonplace for people of the older generation to declare that other people's children, though not their own, are bone idle; that they do nothing but loiter in the bars, and do not accept work even when it is offered, preferring to live off unemployment benefit. Yet the personal problems experienced by young people in Salla, stemming from unemployment, seem to be largely a *result* of contradictions between the work ethic they have learnt from parents, and the occupational ranking which is the product of a vastly expanded educational system. To work one must first have work, that is, a job. In other words, a person's 'position' in the community is no longer the result of work, as it was for the pioneer farmer who hacked out a home from the forest, but is a precondition for work.

Consequently, the young person without a job experiences a doubled sense of shame, from which the only escape, often enough, is to move away. The younger generation of working age, as in so many European rural communities, is sadly conspicuous by its absence.

Note

1.   Fieldwork in Salla during 1979–80 was financed by a grant from the Social Science Research Council, whose support I gratefully acknowledge.

7 A Note on the Custom of 'Paying Off' on Family Farms in Poland

Lucjan Kocik

SOME CHARACTERISTIC FEATURES OF POLISH RURAL FAMILIES

The socio-economic system of Poland is founded on the public ownership of the basic means of production. The exception is agriculture. In Polish agriculture, individual farms, of which there are 3,100,000, cover nearly 80 per cent of the total area of arable land. Of approximately 8 million families, nearly 45 per cent presently live in the countryside, and of these 22.5 per cent are composed of at least 3 generations.

Members of the rural family normally form a single production unit. This is especially true for the larger farms where the demand for manual labour is very high due to the generally low level of mechanization. However, about 28 per cent of rural families, 1 million, own farms which provide only a secondary or additional source of support. These, as a rule, are not larger than about 2 hectares. The next category consists of rural families possessing farms which are a primary but not sufficient source of income. These make up about 20 per cent, 700,000, and own farms ranging from 2–5 hectares.

The members of these two latter categories of rural families are forced to seek non-agricultural sources of income, mainly in industry, and they gradually acquire aspirations towards the formation of more permanent connections with the city, especially for their children. According to the opinion of this group, work on the farm is increasingly seen in a negative light since 'only those who are strong and stupid want to remain behind'.

In this situation, where agriculture is combined with industrial work, villagers often adopt a consumer's attitude towards their farm, which is treated as a means of 'free subsistence'. Also, with growing frequency, the local status of rural families is determined by extra-rural criteria, rather than simply by prestige factors founded upon the possession of land.

THE CUSTOM OF 'PAYING OFF'

This chapter draws upon research conducted from 1976 to 1979 by the Institute of Sociology of the Jagiellonian University, Krakow, in six villages located in southern Poland. The villages were of various types, including traditional, peasant-worker and modern ones with distinct crop specializations. In all, 1,800 individual rural families were studied whose average farm size did not exceed 5 hectares.

The phenomenon of 'paying off' non-inheriting siblings is closely connected with the fact that all children have legal entitlement to the land and farm buildings of their parents. Within the 'traditional' Polish peasant family there was a complete identification of the family with the farm as the sole means of livelihood and as a measure of present social position and future perspectives. Land represented not only a material or commercial value but was also associated with sentiments of family continuity. Personal happiness, and even marriage, were often sacrificed for its acquisition. Those children who left the farm without obtaining a share of the land received a monetary payment equivalent to their share (i.e. they were 'paid off'). The entire farm represented extra-temporal value as the family's common possession and was protected by moral and customary sanctions.

At the present time, since farms below 8 hectares cannot legally be sub-divided, the custom of paying off has become the major form of regulating intra-familial obligations, despite the fact that the practice is actually legally forbidden. Formerly the paying off of siblings in Poland was fully justifiable as the only means of assuring them a part of the family wealth, in conditions in which there was a lack of non-agricultural employment. Yet, it has continued to persist up to the present day, despite radical changes in educational levels and increased opportunities for obtaining non-agricultural employment. Moreover, official prohibition has not significantly changed its method of functioning but rather led to its informal institutionalization. In this situation, it seems likely that we are dealing not only with obligations of a materialist nature, but also of an emotional, cultural and moral kind which arise from the 'traditional' patrimonial connection of the rural family with the farm. Membership in this 'patrimony' is determined by one's share in contributing to the family income, that is to say, to the farm. The feeling of one's right to such a share is still strong and continues to be upheld by social opinion. The denial of inheritance claims to the family farm, even in limited form, brings out feelings of resentment even among economically well-situated members of the family.

Explanation of this phenomenon solely in terms of the persistence of established custom is certainly insufficient, but, on the other hand, so is explanation cast merely in materialist terms. It is necessary to consider both aspects simultaneously.

Interestingly enough, neither the size of the farm, nor the types of farming practised, nor even important and pressing investment needs, play a significant role in determining attitudes concerning the obligation to pay off siblings. In all categories of peasant families and all the investigated villages, the custom of paying off was strongly supported (see *Table 1*). Over 76 per cent of those interviewed said they were in favour of paying off siblings in the strict sense. The remainder of interviewees came out in favour of some other form of compensation, not necessarily the exact equivalent of the value of the land share.

Table 1   General attitudes towards paying off

attitudes	%
land or paying off should be given	76.8
at least a richer dowry should be given	14.7
it depends on the family situation	6.0
ambivalent answers	2.5
	100.0

The situation in which a child has moved to the city is the one in which the attitudes towards paying off of the family farm became differentiated (see *Table 2*).

Table 2   Paying off when the child moves out of village

attitudes	%
paying off should be equal to other cases	32.5
the child should be helped only once (e.g. with furniture, flat, car, etc.)	23.0
something has to be given so that the child will remember	20.6
paying off should be lower than in case of those who stay on the farm	10.8
nothing has to be given	13.1
	100.0

Only in the event of one of the children moving to the city, and the parents securing its education, which enables it to take up a non-agricultural occupation, were attitudes substantially altered (see *Table 3*).

Table 3   Paying off when the parents have provided the child with education and a non-agricultural occupation

Attitudes	%
paying off because some kind of help is always necessary (rational motivations)	26.0
paying off because some kind of help is always necessary (emotional motivations)	32.4
it depends on the family agreement	11.5
nothing has to be given because education costs a lot	15.7
nothing has to be given because people in the city have better living conditions than those in the country	14.4
	100.0

Both positive and negative attitudes were expressed in terms of broad rational and emotional motivations. For example, to the former belong such statements as: 'One should pay off because, before the child received its education, it had worked at home'; 'In the country every child, as soon as it is capable, has its own duties to carry out, and therefore also has some rights as regards the farm.' Emotional motivations comprised such arguments as: 'This is their child, therefore they should help'; or 'Everybody wishes the child all the best.'

Analysis of empirical cases reveals that children are commonly given the right to a part of the value of the farm, and more often than not it is those who take over the farm who have to pay off siblings or relatives. This is not only evidence of family sharing of inheritance but also manifests sibling or family solidarity, which can sometimes work against the interests of the young wife or husband who marries into the farm. It is a reflection not only of material but also of the customary-moral attitudes towards patrimony; it gives to the family a sense of justice in relation to its children. Field data show that customary-moral or emotional reasons for paying off are given more weight than strictly material ones. For instance, it was said that: 'Money should be given, for there are children and they have to be aided'; 'The patrimony should be divided equally'; 'The parents have worked for all the children', irrespective of whether or not this threatens the viability of the farm. Interviewees who maintained that those who moved to non-agricultural occupations should not be paid off at all, expressed opinions such as the following: 'They were given money for their education'; 'The educated will manage by themselves'; 'It is not possible to give any more; it will cause troubles on the farm.'

The continued involvement of economically independent offspring in the parents' farm, by means of the system of paying off, points to an objective conflict between two main functions of the peasant family, namely, ensuring the welfare of the children and keeping the farm economically viable. According to tradition, those siblings who inherit the farm are supposed to pay off those who have moved to the city. However, although widely prevalent, this custom has begun to meet with increasing opposition, especially among young married couples inheriting a farm. We are dealing here with a conflict between two value systems.

On the basis of our study, it appears that this conflict of the traditional with the new is, to a significant degree, assuaged by the living conditions of today's families. Inheritance claims to the family farm no longer take such a sharp and openly bitter form as once was the case. On the contrary, they often possess a bonding function, not only of an economic, but also of an emotional, nature, serving to preserve the ties between non-inheriting siblings and the family farm. This is further demonstrated by the fact that payments are often not exacted in full by those living in the city, so that they do not lose all rights and ties joining them to the family farm. In the long run, this creates a certain form of dependency and integration between urban and rural families which often takes the form of mutual assistance. Urban families take advantage of farm products in exchange for providing seasonal labour. They also provide for the needs of their rural relatives when the latter visit them in town. These mutual services form an essential element in the integration of the family in its multi-environmental aspect. In the village setting, this leads to a restructuring of extended family relations.

The institution of paying off is slowly yielding to fundamental changes, leading to its possible disappearance. It is closely linked with wider transformations of the peasant family. Its complete demise, like that of other traditional customs associated with the functioning of the family farm, should theoretically take place when the land and the farm come to represent purely commercial and professional values. In Polish conditions, however, the wide range of aid given, on a regular as well as an intermittent basis, to inhabitants of the cities by their rural relatives, will most likely continue for a

Table 4   Forms of aid given to children living permanently in the city

forms of aid	No. of cases	%
financial aid for major purposes	758	50.8*
food supplies given on visits	941	63.0
food supplies for holidays	547	36.6
aid only on special occasions (e.g. birthdays and baptisms)	68	4.6
aid for special reasons	14	0.9
miscellaneous	96	6.4
not applicable (e.g. no children present in cities)	562	57.6

*Percentages do not add up to 100 because respondents often mentioned more than one form of aid.

long time. This was expressed by an appropriate saying which appeared in our interviews: 'In the city he will have plenty if his in-laws are from the country!' *Table 4* presents a classification of the various types of aid. The above forms of aid do not differ significantly with regard to farm size or type of farming practised. Nor does village origin seem to play a major role. These forms of aid appear to be universal for peasant families. The sphere of parental aid is relatively large and without doubt plays a significant part in inhibiting farm investments and the modernization of agriculture. However, one cannot overlook here what might be called the 'human factor' of the family, which in the face of difficult life-conditions in the city comes to the aid of its nearest kin.

8 Women's Work in Rural South-west England

Mary Bouquet

Compared with feminists and Marxists concerned with the productive and reproductive status of women's labour (Edholm, Harris,
and Young 1977), rural sociologists have made little use of these
concepts to analyse the changing nature of working relations on the
'family farm'.[1] This is surprising, in that many of the developments
that have taken place in the case of British family farming, have had
the effect of relieving women of farm work, thereby substantially
altering the notion of family labour which is characteristic of this
form of agriculture (Friedmann 1978b, 1981; Galeski 1971: 122). This
raises the problem of how precisely housework or domestic labour
on the farm is to be analysed and explained.

In this chapter I shall present a case in which productive and reproductive forms of domestic labour are to be distinguished. The
illustration concerns women's work on family farms in south-west
England. I shall describe women's work on the farm, given that they
no longer do farm work as such, and I shall relate this to the work
done by men. I argue that for this system of family farming to work,
two sets of conceptually distinct resources are involved, necessi-
tating two different labour processes within the family, and en-
gendering differences in the value systems of men and women.

SOCIAL REPRODUCTION: FAMILY,
STATE AND 'COMMUNITY' WELFARE

It has been argued that in most highly-industrialized areas where the
capitalist mode of production is dominant, the social reproduction of
labour is primarily achieved through the institution of the nuclear
family, and by the provision of state welfare (Littlewood 1981: 1). In
rural areas a relative sparsity of state welfare facilities means that a
greater burden of responsibility falls upon the family and, at another
level, upon the local 'community'.[2]

In rural areas where family farming is the principal form in the organization of agricultural production, the division of productive and reproductive labour between men and women is particularly sharp.[3] In seeking to explain the significance of unpaid labour within family and community in such areas, I suggest that there is a need to go beyond an explanation which assumes the profit motive on the part of a dominant class as the basic *raison d'être* (Servolin 1972: 41). My aim in this chapter is to demonstrate, through an examination of women's work both within the rural domestic group and in the wider social system of which it is a part, not only the crucial savings to be made in the sphere of production (i.e. specialized family farming), and that aspect of social reproduction not covered by state welfare, but also the expression of certain fundamental social values with which those concerned imbue their action.

In this sense, 'family' and 'community' represent ideals around which social action is organized and valued. At one level they indicate opposing tendencies in the directional flow of resources within the rural population: the tendency for an accretion of resources 'inwards' to the domestic group, idealized in terms of the 'family'; conversely, the tendency for their dispersal 'outwards' in order to meet the requirements of 'community'. I shall examine how women negotiate the balance between these values through their work, thus making an essential contribution to social reproduction. Consequently, although they may have been relieved of farm work as such, their labour on behalf of 'family' and 'community' is a *sine qua non* of modern family farming.

THE LOCATION OF RESEARCH

This paper is based on research carried out among 70 farm households in an Atlantic coastal parish on the south-west peninsula of England.[4] The population of the parish in 1971 was 1,300 persons, living in 430 households, of which 230 were in the main village of Hartland with the remaining 200 located in hamlets or as isolated settlements (see Hoskins and Finberg 1952).

Farm work (i.e. 'outside' work) in the area of south-west England from which the data are drawn is defined by the people themselves as a 'man's job'. This definition includes the work associated with bulk milk production, which is today one of their principal sources of regular income. While on the one hand it is possible to trace the steady exclusion of women from agricultural (nineteenth century) and dairy production (early twentieth century), on the other hand many have found it necessary or desirable to commercialize part of the domestic sphere by providing 'bed and breakfast' (or 'bed, breakfast and evening meal') for tourists (Bouquet 1981, 1982c).

Most of the farms are between 50 and 250 acres in size. The majority produce milk in quantities ranging from less than 200 litres to over 1,000 litres per day at peak. Some of those producing between 500 and 1,000 litres are specialists in dairying, with as many as 100 cows. Others keep fewer cows (30–80), combining the production of milk with that of other commodities: beef, sheep and some corn.

MILK PRODUCTION: THE 'SOCIOLOGY OF THE CROP'

Farmers frequently say that there has been a decline in the amount of co-operation among themselves over the years. In no area of farming is the alleged lack of co-operation more apparent than the actual process of milking dairy cows. The contractual requirements of the Milk Marketing Board mean that each farm must invest in a milking parlour, a bulk tank and an access road for the milk tanker to collect the milk, in addition to the dairy herd itself and all its 'reproductive' requisites ('productive consumption': Friedmann 1981). During the summer, when the cows are put out to grass, herds belonging to adjacent farms may be seen being driven in opposite directions twice each day at milking time. In the hamlets where the land is intermixed, the operation must be carefully timed to avoid meeting.

Yet even in the context of dairying there are occasions when co-operation is quite essential if the requirements of production are to be met. In winter, for example, the roads become blocked by snow-drifts, and farmers must then co-operate in clearing them with tractors and shovels so that the milk can be transported to the nearest collection point. This digging-out operation from the remote farms and hamlets can take several days, and thousands of litres of milk literally go down the drain. Faced with the common possibility of losing income, farmers have a mutual interest in co-operating.

The case of milk production illustrates the opposing tendencies within this farming system.[5] The accretion of resources 'inwards' is represented by the notion of 'going big', which means building up one's herd and technical equipment through the channels of credit open to those with sufficient land and who conform to the standards set by external capital. 'Going big' implies to a certain extent the cutting of locally-based forms of inter-household exchange, such as those which took place in the past, for example during winter threshing days; these were accompanied by an exchange of hospitality.[6] Tenurial and technological change, brought about by state intervention in the land market after 1909, and in agriculture from the 1930s onwards, changed the rationale and quality of such exchanges.[7] It created the need for specialized forms of co-operation at quite different points in the labour process, as illustrated in this particular case by the co-operative clearing of roads in order to get the product out.

There is quite clearly differentiation among farmers not only in the extent and quality of their land, but also in the degree to which they value 'going big'. There is thus variation in the level of risk at which they operate within the economy. The specialist producers, who tend not to divert their resources towards helping other people out (lending silage and machinery, lending a hand when somebody has calving problems), nevertheless, significantly, keep in contact with each other through their wives. I shall examine how this occurs in the main part of the chapter, which is concerned with women's work.

To conclude this section: although farmers claim that nowadays every man is out for himself and his immediate family, there are instances where it is clear that without co-operation this individualistic ideology and practice could not exist. The pattern of investment, particularly in dairying, has much to do with the isolation to which farmers refer. Yet when faced with circumstances beyond their control, they help each other because that is the only way out of the difficulty.

There is nevertheless a perception of equality among farmers despite the differentiation in terms of productive factors which demonstrably exists. It is precisely because each man must work for himself in relation to the market that, paradoxically, there is a recognition of the shared problems of modern farming in a world where national and international events can determine what is produced, how it is produced and the price offered.

I shall now turn to women's activities which, I shall argue, constitute a means of communication between modern family farms. This is a crucial part of social reproduction. While the links between their activities and those of the men are clear in terms of the use of the resources of the family farm (that is, farm and farmhouse), there are a number of ways in which their work and their evaluation of it differ quite sharply from the farmers'.

FEMALE ACTIVITIES

The final removal of women from agricultural production means that they are out of touch with that plane of reality within which the sense of equality, attributed above to farmers, is generated. For women this sense of equality is an abstraction, since they are not involved in the sustained practice of farm work, and cannot therefore assess the differentiation of their husbands in technical terms. The specialized knowledge which is necessary for present-day farming falls outside the experience of women precisely because of their own specialization, which is work within the domestic sphere — what Friedmann (1978b: 555) refers to as 'personal consumption'.

Women compete amongst themselves on their own terms through two sets of activities: the business of 'taking in visitors', and their participation in 'good causes' as defined for the community. For these activities, consumption goods are for women what technological equipment is for their husbands. It is through the elaboration of a system of values associated with women's reproductive activities, upon which farm work itself, in a sense, is dependent since none of these farms today is self-sufficient, that women have constructed their own hierarchically-modelled version of reality. The following discussion is of three fields within this dimension of reality in which women operate.

Reproduction

The reproductive activities discussed here comprise all those that are necessary to maintain the 'direct labourers' of the household. Nowadays these activities are specifically concerned with consumption functions, of which shopping is one of the most important.

Women consistently buy goods both in bulk, in order to economize, and in small quantities at the village store. The oscillation between the constraints of economy and those of belonging to a community, re-echoes the opposition between 'family' and 'community' as values. The coexistence of the same commodity at different prices within the action space of the majority of farmers' wives calls into question the logic of each pattern of behaviour. On the one hand, bulk buying and storage (often by freezing) represents the attempt of each individual 'family' to be competitive consumers. On the other hand, shopping in the village, though more expensive, represents a domain of public interaction complementary to, and balancing, the private domestic sphere to which the housewife is otherwise limited (cf. Brody 1973: 161). However residually it is used, the village shop furnishes a public space for the exchange of news between otherwise isolated domestic units.

The significance of consumption items within the domestic sphere arises out of an 'agreed' system of meanings, the generation and communiction of which depends upon the existence of an extra-domestic sphere. My suggestion is that the shop not only supplies the goods, but also provides a linkage area for gossip and discussion within which people imbue these items with meaning. The use of household items as signs and symbols in this language can be illus-trated by reference to the interior decoration of the farmhouse. An elaboration in the use of items such as carpets, curtains and wallpaper appears to be an index of status among the women. The carpeting of farmhouses begins with the stair-carpet and passages. Carpets and curtains are both important symbolic objects in the house, covering as they do such access areas as windows and passage-ways. They are less often renewed than wallpaper and paint which, particularly in the houses where visitors are taken in, are changed annually. These surface coverings create an impressive visual effect, and, in practical terms, they insulate rooms. As a further effect, the contrast between outdoors (farm) and indoors (house) has become pronounced. It is a measure of the extent to which the world of women is removed from that of their menfolk that, on the whole, the latter appear indifferent to the finer gradations of comfort indoors.

Yet when women visit each other's houses they are quick to notice the state of these furnishings. A woman is judged by her choice, which is taken as a statement about her knowledge of what is fashion-able or good quality according to the canons of taste of various groups, dependent to some extent on generation. The most expensive of these items, the carpet, carries the heaviest symbolic load. The carpet may have been a goal towards which a woman has worked by taking in visitors, sometimes for as many as twenty years.

The alterations and 'contributions' made by women to the farm-house are part of a logical system whereby women, otherwise separated by the nature of their reproductive work, are meshed into a hierarchy by the common values they share, which are partly expressed in the material goals towards which they work. Contributions such as these which occur over a period of time are considered dignified and proper. By contrast disapproval is expressed for the complete alteration of the farmhouse, made, for example, by one young wife upon moving in. Such action conflicts with the system of mother and daughter-in-law choosing together such items as carpets whereby such 'contributions' are expressive of a certain female solidarity between generations of women who marry into the family and the house.[8] Radical alteration to the house can be construed as a rejection of the contributions of the last occupant, who may well have been one's mother-in-law, and are seen in a sense as the identity of the person who made them.

A woman's prestige in the field of reproduction (i.e. as a housewife) would be impossible to assess locally without the additional activities that bring her into contact and competition with others. One activity which achieves this is the accommodating of visitors within the farmhouse.

Commercial Activities

The marginality of farmers' wives to agricultural production has been one of the forces which has encouraged them to take up the possibilities of tourism, becoming 'culture brokers' and thus turning their peripherality to economic advantage. The practice of taking visitors into the farmhouse over the past three or four generations has resulted in its integration within the developmental cycle of the domestic group, so that in this area it has become part of family socialization. This may lead a man on maturity to insist that his wife does *not* take visitors, precisely because his mother did so when he was a child and he no longer wants to be bothered with them. It is thus not only a question of resources (house space and time) but also a matter of the support or acquiescence of the husband/sons if visitors are to be taken. If the farmer's wife herself comes from a visitor-taking background it is much more likely that she will continue to do so. Where women do not have this background, as for example with those coming from an inland parish without the same tradition, they may experience more difficulty in integrating housework with commercial activities.

Almost without exception, the wives of farmers with medium-sized farms (50–250 acres) producing 'large' quantities of milk (over 1,000 litres per day at peak) take in visitors; the local 'big' producers' wives, without exception, either do so or have done so in the recent past. Neither of the two big non-local farmers' wives, one married to a milk producer and the other to a pig-breeder, takes visitors. This marks a sharp distinction between local and non-local practice and tradition. The wives of these non-local farmers consider it out of the question to take in visitors. They say that they look to their husbands to make the money and would consider the presence of 'paying guests' to be an invasion of privacy. As partners in the farm business they have access to money without any problems. Many local farmers' wives are also partners in the business, and some of their husbands are quite as 'big' as the newcomers. The distinction seems to lie at the level of the significance of the activity for those concerned.[9]

Taking in visitors necessitates a division of time and space within the farm household. In the first place the year can be divided into 'summer season' and winter: April to September, and October to March, respectively. During the summer season house time must be divided between the needs of the producers and the requirements of the visitors. Similarly, house space must be apportioned. In both cases, because time and space are valorized in relation to them, visitors' requisites may well take precedence: the family may, for example, sleep together in a single room, upstairs or downstairs, depending on availability. If an evening meal is provided, the dining room must be set aside, as must the sitting room and colour television for the evenings. The family makes heavy use of the kitchen during the summertime, and this is clearly one of the factors behind its enlargement, elaboration, and carpeting by the present generation of farmers' wives. If more than six visitors are taken at a time, fire regulations necessitate the installation of special fire doors, which makes the separation of family and visitors all the more apparent. In this spatial segregation it is possible to perceive an echo of the former divisions of the house, when the household comprised servants as well as parents and children (Bouquet 1982a). Today, the relation is reversed: family is confined to the back kitchen and back bedroom, while visitors are accommodated in the best rooms.

Although analytically it is important to distinguish between the time spent on reproductive tasks and that devoted to commercial activities, in practice much of the work overlaps. In the case of bed and breakfast, the bed linen can be washed with the family laundry, and the meal itself prepared with the family's. Bed, breakfast, and evening meal, which most farmers' wives in the area studied provide, involves a much greater time commitment. It might therefore be considered curious that women choose to spend their summers working up to eighteen hours a day at what is the busiest time of the year on the farm when, it has been argued, there is little or no profit to be made from the evening meal (Davies 1973). The women themselves say that they do so because they enjoy meeting so many people from different walks of life, and talking to them. They also concede that the money is useful: it gives women an independence from their husbands which they like, enabling them to buy not only 'long-term' household goods, such as carpets, but also to make immediate purchases for themselves, such as a jumper or a pair of shoes.

The concept of independence as it is used by women is closely associated with the expression of identity through the contributions made to the house, in particular, the surface coverings such as carpets and curtains, as already discussed. It is also expressed through the clothes they wear, to a far greater extent than is the case with men, chiefly because women's fashions seem to change with greater frequency than those of men.

Another aspect of women's enjoyment of taking in visitors is their appreciation of women's work, which family members are apt to take for granted. The isolation of the contemporary farmer's wife in the countryside makes such appreciation very welcome; this perhaps is one of the reasons why women continue to do bed, breakfast, and evening meal despite the allegedly narrow profit margin. The appreciation of visitors is important to a woman's standing within the hierarchy. Presents given by visitors to their hostess are of considerable symbolic importance in this respect, expressing as they do an extra, non-monetary plane to the interaction.

Precisely because taking in visitors places such heavy demands on women in terms of the management of time and space within the household, the capacity to do so is a measure of a woman's domestic competence. If the evening meal is not ready in time, for example, the competent farmer's wife will engage her visitors in conversation about their day's activities, serve the soup very slowly, and by that time the main course will usually be ready. Farmers' wives also find some of their visitors are ready to baby-sit for them during the evenings, which is when they want to go out and the visitors want to relax indoors after spending the day outside. The strategies employed by the farmer's wife can thus bring the visitors within the compass of her own plans and wishes. A certain degree of trust must exist between host and guest before this can happen, which is one of the reasons why such emphasis is placed on recruiting a 'good class of visitor'. This is only partly achieved through advertising in magazines such as *The Lady*. Most women rely on recommendation and word of mouth. In this way relationships are built up which can result in visitors returning year after year to the same farm for their holiday, with the result that they often become more like friends.

The position occupied by the farmer's wife in the local population is prestigious largely because of her mediating role with visitors. It is she who directs them to the local shops, beaches, and village events. Shopkeepers and innkeepers admit that without the extra trade brought by visitors they would have difficulty in making a living during the rest of the year. Unlike residents, visitors cannot buy on account at local shops and this is another reason for their popularity. Two of the items most often bought on account by farmers' wives are wallpapers and paints, purchased annually in February/March for redecorating rooms; they may not be paid for until August. This indicates how visitor money is anticipated, and ploughed back into village commerce *via* the farm household. Summer events organized in the village are important attractions for the visitors. When, in 1979, it seemed doubtful whether there was adequate support for the organization of the summer carnival, Women's Institute committee members (many of them farmers' or tradespeople's wives) expressed concern, because visitors are known to come especially for this event so that the whole community stood to lose by its cessation. Realizing this, enough people rallied round and the carnival was held as usual.

Visitors and their accommodation are thus a pivot for certain household and community activities for women, on the basis of which their hierarchy is constructed. Visitors are not only economically necessary to the population but have also been integrated into its symbolic system. This integration is not, however, without ambivalence; their presence is sometimes resented both by the menfolk on the farms and by other sections of the population, although they are not resented as much as other 'outsiders' who settle as second home owners or to retire.[10] Farmers themselves acknowledge, usually retrospectively, the contribution made by their wives to the household income through taking in visitors. It is no coincidence that taking in visitors became so important during the 1930s when the Depression afflicted this area so severely and farming did not pay. Visitor money was then seen as a 'box to which you could go in time of need'. Although the money is technically the woman's, it is in fact largely ploughed back into the household for consumption purposes.

The fact that taking in visitors has continued to the present day among farmers who have every appearance of affluence suggests that this is still the case. Of course, not all men are prepared to countenance this commercialization of the female domestic role or, one suspects, the external recognition it receives. Much depends upon the viability of the farm, or rather upon the way this is perceived by the different members of the household, depending to some extent on the role they have within it.

A third field of interaction which is significant for the social construction of female reality is represented by the term 'good cause'.

The 'Good Cause'

Good causes are distinguished by the events they generate, usually through voluntary association directed towards some 'community' goal. They may be taken up by already existing associations, or they may be external charities adopted by the community through the mediation of some local person with particular knowledge or experience, mobilizing them into action.

An example of the former is found in the Town Band's decision to raise money for new uniforms at a cost of over £1,000. Relatives and friends were galvanized into action for a series of events including an auction, a barbecue, and summer fête. An example of the second type of good cause is provided by the fund-raising work of a widow whose husband had been in hospital for over six years. In the course of her many visits to the hospital she had noted the absence of lifts; in 1965 she began her campaign, and by 1970 had succeeded in raising £4,000 which was used by the hospital to install two lifts and to furnish a sun-lounge.

These two examples illustrate the principal sorts of good cause: those internal and those external to the community. In the first case, resources are pooled towards objectives which will improve the quality of life as it is experienced by the local population. In the second case, those people who have dealings with external organizations or institutions and have found them wanting in some way, communicate their predicament to others in the community by transforming adversity into a positive cause.

The link between the third field of action and the first two is not immediately apparent, since good causes seem to be based on a pooling of resources which is opposed to the principle of their accretion to the household on which the other two are based. Although the tendency to pool resources seems to be opposed to their appropriation by each separate household, in fact, as the analysis has shown, individual endeavour towards certain ends within each household only has meaning in so far as it is part of an agreed system of values. This system depends on the incursion of the 'community' ideal in various ways within the interactional fields of reproduction and commercial activities. In the field of the good cause, interaction is based on the same classification of female competence, and the values implied by that concept, but this time the direction of the flow of resources is reversed and status is measured by contributions 'outwards', as opposed, for example, to contributions to the house.

There is a further dimension to the good cause, since there is room for manipulation by individuals at two junctures: the contribution stage and that of re-allocation. Those who cajole others into giving prizes or buying raffle tickets do so in the name of the good cause, but at the same time make an assertion of their personal power through that action. Similarly, those who invoke the good cause in the first place have power in the final allocation of resources once they have been amassed. So that, both in the events through which accumulation occurs, and in the overriding decision to take up this one, a small group of people, usually one person in particular, is at the same time enhancing her own personal standing within the hierarchy. Hence the reappearance of the opposite value at the very centre of the good cause.

The contributions themselves also have a bearing on the position achieved by women in the hierarchy. This is illustrated by the series of fund-raising events that were organized for the purchase of a 'community vehicle', at the instigation of the local General Practitioner, since Hartland is half an hour by road from the nearest ambulance depot in North Devon. The fund-raising events included coffee evenings and wine and cheese parties which were held in some of the large farmhouses by invitation of the farmer's wife. Refreshments were donated by committee members, their relatives and friends; home-made produce was sold on a stall. These contributions of refreshments and produce for sale are important in terms of a woman's standing in the hierarchy for two reasons. In the first place such items, which are made by the woman herself, represent her skill as a housewife in the domain of cooking, a skill essential to both reproductive and commercial activities. Secondly, there are few occasions when women have to decide among themselves the value of their own productions. On the one hand they want to make as much money as possible for the good cause, but on the other they must not price themselves out of the market. They also have to avoid giving offence to one another, since what is at stake is not just the domestic competence of a single woman, but, crucially, the negotiation of a balance between family and community.

CONCLUSION

Through an analysis of women's work based on the contemporary family farm in south-west England, then, it has been possible to demonstrate an oscillation between the values that I have designated 'family' on the one hand and 'community' on the other. The significance of this finding in the context of non-wage remuneration and informal co-operation in rural society can be summarized as follows.

In the first place I stress the analytical importance of consumption/reproduction activities for an understanding of the modern family farm, not just as a commodity-producing unit but also as part of a social system. Women's unpaid servicing role on behalf of the direct producers and other members of the family constitutes an essential circuit in the social reproduction of the modern family farm. Through their activities women help to maintain contact between those who have 'gone big' and the rest of the farming population. The use of farmhouses as a venue for fund-raising events was only one of the ways given in which this was done. What this illustration shows, however, is the relativity of 'going big' when it comes to the external welfare agencies, such as emergency health care, when the whole population may to some degree be vulnerable and, from this perception, define a 'community' need.

Women's fund-raising activities can be seen as an extension of their servicing role within the household: in the first place for those actively engaged in production and second, commercially, in the provision of accommodation for visitors. Their voluntary community service fills needs that are outside government welfare provision which, because of the geographical peripherality of the area, can assume the proportions of a social problem. At another level, however, it can be seen that those women with sufficient resources compete with each other for a position in the hierarchy which they have elaborated on the basis of wealth differential. This can be seen in their commercial activities and through the contributions they are able to make to fund-raising projects. The paucity of employment opportunities for women in the local labour market is such that if they cannot take in visitors there are few other possibilities open to them for making money and gaining prestige. The farmer's wife provides a model for emulation, to a much greater extent than do the wives of farmers who 'come from away' and do not participate in the field of commercial activities.

Female reality in this instance is defined by participation in three areas of action which have been described and analysed here. The difference between male and female versions of reality is that while the latter is initially dependent upon the former in material terms, the construction of the women's world becomes far more elaborate and 'visible' precisely because it is based upon consumption activities. The ambivalence of the social construction of relations within the contemporary farm household might become apparent if there should be a shift in policy which limits the current autonomy of the British dairy industry and thereby alters the role of the 'family' producer within it. This could conceivably change the logic of those alternative activities in which women engage.

The analysis has shown that women are the principal carriers of what might be termed a 'culture of capitalism', whereby the commodities with which they are concerned in their work are also the means of communication of information about status, identity, and so on. Thus women can be distinguished from men in terms of the resources that devolve to men as agricultural producers within the farm family. These resources, together with the labour and expertise of men, have been annexed for productive purposes by means of external capital invested in the enterprise. This annexation has only been possible through a sexual division of labour within the farm household, whereby women are responsible for reproducing the conditions necessary for men to engage in specialist production. The farm household as a unit of production and consumption under industrial capitalism provides a case through which to demonstrate the complexity of the levels of social reality which are somehow united therein.

In the case of men's productive activities, they are oriented by the price mechanism, while at the same time they are unable to alter the demand for products. External finance agencies are prepared to extend the capital necessary against the value of the land, with which to install those factors of production that reduce the requirements for hired labour, and bring into existence the specialized intensive form of labour characteristic of the family farm. These activities involve long hours in the maintenance of machinery and the fulfilment of other production requirements needed in order to meet standards set by external institutions with which exchange takes place. These also enable the farmer to continue and survive.

In the case of women, two forms of domestic labour are involved: one on behalf of the 'family' which is unpaid, and the other in relation to visitors which one might consider as 'paid'. Family sentiment prohibits direct payment for housework; yet the farm household could not function without it. Hence women are an essential link in the chain of production which begins on the farm, with the assistance of external capital, and ends in the factory. Family sentiment disguises this reality, just as the term 'farm family', in its commonsense usage, disguises the socially-constructed sexual division of labour within the farm household; both are essential to comply with the external standards upon which survival depends. These standards penetrate to the very heart of 'family life', through the division of time and space which occurs with the institution of taking in visitors, whereby women's domestic labour also has its price.

The analysis of women's work has therefore illuminated the essential division of labour necessary for family farming. It shows how facile is the view which separates life in the countryside from elsewhere in industrial society, except insofar as the provision of many welfare facilities taken for granted in urban areas are notably lacking in rural parts. The lack of facilities in many rural areas encourages the replication of domestic equipment, just as individual investment in each farm brings about the replication of the factors of production on each holding.

In the community sphere, which in turn affects the domestic one, there is a gap between state provision and the possibility of private provision, where the sheer amount of resources involved together with the expertise needed, are beyond the realization of the private proprietor. (This state of affairs is mirrored on the farm, where even milk producers on occasion find themselves in need of assistance.) Women are the principal organizers of events designed to raise money with which to overcome this shortfall. Voluntary work, like housework, disguises areas where crucial savings can be made by the state and commercial enterprise. In terms of the family farming system these events serve to maintain ties between households which, according to the logic of current patterns of investment and relations of production, ought to be separated, and indeed are often analysed as such. The perspective offered by an analysis of women's work clearly demonstrates that the logical opposition between 'family' and 'community', which underlies the action of both men and women, is expressed quite differently in each case. I have distinguished between the egalitarian ideal of the men and the hierarchical ideal of the women. The two orders of reality in which each category operates, while distinct, are nonetheless inter-dependent; and in their interdependency and opposition are clearly modelled upon the abstract values of 'family' and 'community' to which they relate.

Notes

1.   Research for this chapter was funded by the Social Science Research Council, 1977–80, and carried out through the Department of Social Anthropology, Cambridge. I wish to acknowledge helpful discussions of earlier drafts of this paper with Alison Bowes and Raoul Iturra, and my PhD supervisor, Alan Macfarlane.

2.   I am here using the term 'community' in its 'folk' sense, and in the sense that it has been enshrined in party political ideology by, for example, Mrs Thatcher, when she suggests that voluntary 'com-munity' service should play a much larger part in providing care and resources for those who need them.

In the present economic climate in Britain, where public spending on the social services has been drastically cut, it is obvious that 'family' and 'community' burdens will increase. It is sometimes less clear that the concentration of public resources in urban areas has meant that rural localities have been 'relatively deprived' for much longer.

The definitional, methodological and theoretical problems associ-ated with the use of the term 'community' have been discussed by Bell and Newby (1971), and Macfarlane *et al.* (1977).

3.   This has been noted by a number of authors, but its implications not fully considered. Arensberg and Kimball (1940) discuss the dichotomy of tasks assigned to the sexes in the farm family in Ireland as a division of labour which corresponds to the 'natural propensities of the two sexes'. But what is 'natural' among family farmers in Ireland does not necessarily obtain elsewhere: for example, Williams' description of Ashworthy, where 'farming is a man's job' (1963). This

would therefore seem to require explanation in terms of specific socio-economic conditions at different historical periods. Similarly, Littlejohn (1963) notes that the division of labour in rural society is probably more marked than in many areas of industrial society; this was not, in his view, for reasons other than the 'obvious' – lack of employment, transport and so on. 'After marriage men are gainfully employed while women work in the house and have children.' In my view the division of labour is not just a matter of commonsense but must be explained in a comparative perspective.

4.   I have discussed the farm household in greater detail elsewhere (Bouquet 1981, 1982a). My research involved eighteen months' participant obvservation combined with the use of archival sources in the parish of Hartland.

5.   See Box (1981) for a discussion of crop sociology in the Third World context. This approach might equally well be applied to commodity specialization among farmers in the so-called advanced societies.

6.   It has been necessary to omit, for reasons of space, much of the detailed ethnography of kinship and friendship networks among famers, as amongst their wives. I have dealt with this in Chapter 5 of my PhD thesis.

7.   See Erasmus (1956) for an analysis of reciprocal farm labour. Iturra's work on Galicia, north-west Spain, provides an interesting example of *axuda* groups which peasants form as part of their strategy to meet the conditions placed upon them by production for exchange (Iturra 1980).

8.   I discuss the structural position of the wife within the farm family in a recent manuscript (Bouquet 1982c). I take up one of the points made by Strathern (1982) concerning the nature of bilateral kinship where, because of the choice which exists in tracing kin ties, individuals can to a certain extent manipulate their identity. In the case of the farmer's wife, who 'marries in', the construction of her married or 'adult' identity can also be traced in her material contributions to 'family' and 'community'. These involve a manipulation of resources and of social values.

9.   This point relates to note 6, and the complexity of the female

networks of kinship, affinity and friendship. For reasons of space, it is also impossible to go into the question of gossip, which I believe also has a bearing upon the question of significance. For gossip is not only a sanction against those who differ in some way from what are considered to be normal standards of behaviour (Davis 1977: 178; Brody 1973: 151–4), but is also a measure of the impotence of those who engage in it and are themselves controlled by circumstances more powerful than they are. Where 'outsiders' are concerned, there is often a network of 'significant others' beyond the locally-based network.

10. It is interesting to compare the approaches of Newby (1979) and Strathern (1982) to the question of 'outsiders' in the context of rural England. The difference between the sociologist's and the anthropologist's conceptualization of the problem underlines the need for a synthesis in the current flowering of interest in rural social systems (Bouquet 1982b).

9   Domestic Work in Rural Iceland: An Historical Overview

Marie Johnson

In the last decade, as social scientists have begun to focus attention on the study of women, a number of issues have emerged as central areas of discussion.[1] In what became known as the Domestic Labour Debate an attempt was made to develop a theoretical framework for the analysis of women's household work, in particular its relationship to the market economy. This is not the place to detail the many contributions to this,[2] except to note that some of the later works criticized the debate as a whole for concentrating too narrowly on housework (Molyneux 1979: 21) and for employing a culturally and historically limited concept of domestic work.

> 'Why was the domestic labour debate set up in terms which led it into this cul-de-sac? One answer to this question is that our perspective, limited to the experience of housework within the capitalist West, and lacking an historical or international perspective on the phenomenon we were analysing, led us to equate or conflate certain phenomena which are in fact distinct. One example of this is that we held our concept "domestic" to be unproblematic, whereas in fact we were using the word in two analytically distinct senses: domestic work as work done within the home, and domestic work as a particular kind of work, such as child care, cooking and cleaning, servicing the members of a household. In our society, work which is domestic in the first sense is also generally domestic in the second sense, but this fact is specific to our society (that is, not universal) and it requires explanation.'

> (Mackintosh 1979: 175)

The need, then, is for a more detailed account of domestic work and greater scrutiny of the categories which we use. This chapter, which draws upon historical and fieldwork data from rural Iceland, demonstrates both how the composition of the household and the content of domestic work has changed over time.

THE LOCALITY

In the late 1970s Fróneyri was a small village of some fifty houses running for half a mile along the shore of a fjord. Six farms were worked further up the valley but for the majority of the people it was the sea which provided a livelihood. Some 150 years earlier the population was about the same size but its distribution was different and the type of work dissimilar. The availability of detailed census data in Iceland[3] makes it possible to extract some picture of this social and occupational organization.

It is not possible to speak of there having been a village in 1820, since the people of the parish[4] lived in farms scattered along the fjords. The total population of the parish was 234 (122 female, 112 male) and the number of named farms was 23. There was often more than one dwelling situated on a farm, identified as first or second abode, giving a total of 38 separate dwellings. Descriptions of such farms do not vary greatly from the sixteenth to nineteenth centuries (Gjerset 1925: 326–28; Henderson 1819: 87–8). The walls and roofs were made of turf, sometimes on a stone or timber framework. Although they did vary in size and comfort the farmhouses generally had a main room for living and sleeping, which was unheated, and a separate kitchen and outbuildings for animals and storage. Most accounts emphasize the small number of windows – a protection against the cold, and the dark, smoky, unhealthy atmosphere.

The majority (27) of houses in the parish at this time were headed by a man identified as the *húsbóndi* or master of the house. Only five women, all widows, were the head of their households. The other six houses had men as the householder, recorded as tenant (2), priest, widower, parish official, and former sheriff. In contrast with the contemporary situation only five houses contained a nuclear family of man, wife (*hans kona* in the census), and children. Four of the widows headed small households of themselves, their children, and foster-children, while one man lived with his son. The remaining twenty-eight farms had extended households consisting of the householder (a widow, in one case), his wife, children, foster-children, other relatives, servants, and parish paupers. As an example, the largest household of thirteen souls was made up of the man, wife, her two small children,[5] her brother, servants, two female and one male, a parish pauper aged 76, a male lodger and his wife, and a female lodger (a widow of 29) and her small daughter.

The people of Iceland derived their living from the land and sea. Some of their subsistence was directly obtained: fish, fish products, meat, dairy products, wool, berries, and peat for fuel. These farms were not, however, wholly self-sufficient. Fish, meat, hides, butter, wool, cloth, and eiderdown were bartered and sold for products they could not produce themselves, such as flour, wood, iron, rope, alcohol, coffee, and tobacco. While work was organized on a household basis, it was not only carried out by family members, because people were hired as paid servants (*hjú*). In the census 28 women and 16 men were described as servants.[6] From early periods in Icelandic history, the conditions of service, type of work, and remuneration of such workers were set down by law. For instance, the Farming Law of 1722 stated that a woman should rake hay during the summer; milk, weave, and provide dry footwear for one or two working men in the winter. It interestingly specifies that if she did men's work such as mowing hay, fishing, or peat-cutting, she should get a man's wage.

There was indeed a division of labour based upon gender at this time. Women not only did the domestic work in the sense we use it today: the bearing and raising of children, the maintenance of the household through cooking and cleaning, but also took part in the production of subsistence and exchange goods. During the summer months the most important work was harvesting the hay to feed those animals kept over winter. Men usually did the scything while women and children gathered and stacked the hay. In the early summer women cleared the hay fields of debris and spread them with manure, and men cut peat. Once the animals were turned out it was the women's task to milk them and make dairy products. Travelling was easier at this time of the year, so the men went to the trading stations to barter and trade. Later in the summer berries and *Lichen Islandicus* to make gruel were gathered, the wool collected from the sheep,[7] animals slaughtered and the meat preserved for the winter by drying, smoking, and salting. During the winter the women's main occupation was to clean, card, spin, knit, and weave wool, to make clothing for the household, and the cloth and knitted goods which were traded. As well as playing their part in the processing of the fish the female servants usually had to provide service for the male servants. The women served their food, made their clothing and ensured that they had dry clothes for the next day's fishing.

As the farming law quoted above indicates, the division of labour was not absolute. Women were known to do the male tasks of mowing hay and often had to care for the animals during the winter when the men were at sea. At this time it was not unknown for women to go fishing in the open rowing boats (Jónsson 1975: 3). Although wool work was mainly the occupation of women, mention is made of men doing tasks such as fulling (Henderson 1819: 282) and spinning, weaving, and knitting (Ólafsson and Pálsson 1975: 21).[8] Women's wages, in spite of the farming law, however, were lower than men's. Writing of conditions in 1752–57 Ólafsson and Pálsson (1975: 24) record that a woman received half the wages, in money and kind, of a man. A submission in the name of Iceland's poor to the Danish Royal Commission of 1770–71 mentioned the lower pay of women (*Íslands fátœklingar*, 1948: 73, 89) and this had not changed by the end of the nineteenth century, when Jónsson recorded that women's wages were half that of men's (Jónsson 1953: 67–68). It is clear that women were fully involved in the production of goods for consumption and exchange during this period. They also had the major role in the reproduction of the household, in the dual sense of bearing and raising children and carrying out cooking, cleaning, and other household duties. Their contribution was, however, undervalued, compared with that of men, as indicated by the difference in wages paid to female and male servants.[9]

As the century progressed, Iceland began to recover from the natural disasters and colonial oppression of the previous two centuries (Gjerset 1925: 317–67; Magnússon 1977: 121–27). In the parish being considered, the population increased steadily and the censuses indicate changes in the form of the household and patterns of employment. In 1850 some houses were specificed as being *þurrabúð*, literally a dry cottage without a cow, occupied by fishermen. By 1860 the majority of the male householders were recorded as being fishermen. New industries came to the parish in the form of a whaling station in the 1880s, and two more whaling stations and herring stations in the 1890s.

The census for 1890, when the population was 383, described 44 women as wife, 43 as *vinnukona* (working women) and 13 as *bústýra* (housekeepers). A *bústýra* or *ráðskona* was most commonly found in homes where there was no wife. She was usually a paid worker but, as the census shows, sometimes a relative (sister, daughter, foster-daughter) of the male householder or, as the presence of children shows, his consensual wife. The only other occupation shown for

women was wool worker, and three women were recorded as
lausakona, free workers, making their living this way. One woman
lived off her property, another on a pension and the others were
children, relatives and paupers. The data on the men shows the
continuation of the process, noted in 1860, of greater dependence on
fishing. Only 19 male heads of household were specified as being
farmers, while 28 gained a living from the sea; 37 men were called
workers. One man was a *ráðsmadur*, the male equivalent of the
housekeeper, running the farm for his widowed mother. A few men
specialized in land-based trades, as three carpenters, an artisan, a
smith and a builder are mentioned.

At this time there were 60 households in the parish, 21 of which
lived in *þurrabúð*. In these lived eight of the fishermen and their
nuclear families, two carpenters, the artisan and the builder, with
their families, a widow and her child, and a couple of daily paid
workers. The other households were three fishermen and their
wives, three with fishermen and housekeepers, and one nuclear
family and working man. There were another five homes which,
while not referred to as *þurrabúð*, had fishermen living in them. It
was in the homes where it was recorded that the householders made
their living from farming that the pattern of large extended households was retained. They had on average 10 members; the other 40
households had four.

The rapid expansion of the Icelandic economy at the turn of the
century, with the growth of commercial whaling, herring, and white
fish industries through the replacement of rowing boats with sailing
boats and eventually motor boats, is vividly demonstrated by the
increase in just eleven years of the population of the parish to 550 in
1901. The sea provided a living for the majority of men and greater
job differentiation is apparent. There were boat owners and out-
fitters, shipwrights, deckhands, helmsmen, whaleboat captains,
engineers, whale station supervisors, and workers, a total of 61 men
in all. Of the 18 farmers, 4 were recorded as also being fishermen
and one was also a merchant. Servants or workmen numbered 30,
and of these 6 were also fishermen. More specialist occupations on
land were mentioned: carpenter, housebuilder, ironsmith, tinsmith,
cobbler, carrier, teacher, hay-mower, and shepherd. It cannot be
assumed that the men were able to earn their living exclusively from
these occupations the year round, as some were clearly seasonal.
The man who was recorded as being a haymower, deckhand, and
carpenter is an example of someone engaged in multiple occupa-

tions. This, in all likelihood, happened more than the census in itself reveals. However, the trend is clear: men were tending to specialize as free workers in one trade which would have been part of their work as a tied worker in the previous century, and to move into the new jobs created in the expanding and technically advanced commercial fishing industry.

By contrast, the largest class of women, apart from wife, was servant/worker, a total of 52. Of these women, three were specified as cook, children's nurse, and winter girl (that is, a woman hired especially to provide maid service to the fishermen during the fishing season). Three more women, although not called servants, were winter girls and there were two midwives, a seamstress, another children's nurse, and a fishworker. Five women were housekeepers, two at least being consensual wives. Of the 58 women designated as wife, one worked as a housekeeper for her son, one was a weaver, and one a seamstress. Again, the census data does not reveal whether many of the women called wife and worker were in fact taking waged work in the fishing industry. I would suggest that many did this work; processing the herring and white fish when it was landed (see Verkakvennafélagið Framsókn *50 ára Afmælisrit 1914–64* (1964) for the history of the formation and effort to raise wages of the first working women's union). The census does show that, while a few women were able to specialize in their work, they were excluded from the fishing industry, except as processors.

By 1940 the population of the parish had fallen to 350 (181 female, 169 male) from its peak in the first decade of the century. During the intervening years the whaling and herring stations had closed, but salt fish was still produced. Eventually the freezing of fish superseded salting in importance. Electricity had reached the village in the late 1920s, supplied at first, as villagers recalled, by a rather unreliable generator for a couple of hours a day, twice a week. By 1940, 29 of the 60 homes had electric light, 34 had piped water, but the other families still had to fetch water from the streams or river. Nine houses had an inside toilet, but only three the luxury of a bath. This was before the age of central heating, so warmth was provided, if at all, by fires and stoves fuelled by peat from the hillside or coal brought in by boat. There were 71 households in the parish at this time, nearly all occupying a single house (*Table 5*).

Table 5   Households in Fróneyri, 1940

type	number
married couples and children	29
mixed	9
married couples, children + other kin	7
households with resident workers	6
mother + children (3 widows, 1 single mother)	4
married couples and lodger	3
married couples, children and pauper	3
elderly married couples	3
man and housekeeper	3
single people	3
brother and sister	1
total	71

Source: *Manntal á Íslandi 1940,* my classification

This classification of households demonstrates that the most common form was the nuclear family. Households were extended by the presence of one other person, a relative, pauper, lodger, or a maximum of two in the case of those households with resident workers. The mixed households were those that had 'extra' members who fell into more than one category. Six of these had resident workers as well as relatives and paupers, while the other three had a farmer, housekeeper, paupers, and relatives (two cases) and one a nuclear family, the householder's parents, brother, and a lodger.

As regards occupations this census is particularly informative since it lists both primary and secondary occupations. Fifty-four men got their living primarily from the sea, as deckhands, boat-owners, helmsmen, fish-workers, and by making nets and sails. Twelve of these are also recorded as being farmers or keeping sheep. Conversely, five of the twenty-three farmers had some connection with the sea. In addition, one farmer was also a carpenter, another a carrier, and a third recorded as a daily wage worker. Of the 11 workers, one was also a smith and one did fishwork. Of the three school-teachers, one did haymaking and another road construction during the summer. Other occupations held by men were shop-keeper, shepherd, artisan, daily wage worker, and fox hunter.

The majority (56) of adult women were classified as wife, but the additional information on the census shows that two did fishwork, one was a housekeeper, one knitted, and two worked on farms. Ten women were called workers and eleven housekeepers, while another ten were recorded as working inside the home or doing 'various farm work'. Four of these also did fishwork, one knitted, and one worked in a shop. There were also two kitchen girls, two fishworkers, two woolworkers, and one children's nurse. Just one new job is recorded for a woman, that of postmistress. As one of the older women said, speaking of this period, there was very little work for a woman apart from fishwork or domestic service. This was true even if they left the village, since of the eight women who were recorded in the census as working elsewhere in the country, six were domestic servants, one a worker and one worked in an office.

Although some houses had the amenities of electricity and running water, housework still involved a great deal of physical hard work. All clothes were washed by hand and fuel for cooking had to be carried in from outside. Many households kept a few sheep, which meant hay-making during the summer, smoking and salting the meat after the autumn slaughter and feeding the animals which were housed during the winter months. Chickens were raised, potatoes and other vegetables, and rhubarb grown. Most clothing, including shoes in the poorer families, was home-made. Large extended households had almost disappeared and families depended on wage-earners to support them. The food and clothing produced within the home was for consumption, to make a saving in the budget rather than being for exchange, and the major contribution to the household economy.

The working history of one village woman illustrates how women moved between paid and unpaid domestic work and fishwork. After leaving school as a teenager in the 1930s, she worked on a farm as a *kaupakona,*[10] doing both inside and outside work, for two years. Just before the war she left the village for a year to work at a herring station on the north coast. She was paid on a piece-work basis, so much per barrel of herring, and received no pay if there were no fish. Occasionally she and the other women worked as stevedores, loading the barrels of fish onto ships. In the winter when the herring season was over, she got employment as a housekeeper in the same place. After a term at a housewives' school improving her weaving, sewing, and cooking skills, she went to Reykjavík as a housekeeper. On returning to the village at the end of the war, she again worked as a housekeeper. After her marriage she worked in the fish factory until she had three small children in the 1950s. She then gave up paid work, but contributed to the family income by taking in fishermen as lodgers. When the children grew up she returned to the fish factory, working part-time.

THE CONTEMPORARY SITUATION

In 1978 when 219 people lived in Fróneyri, the majority (32) of the 56 households consisted of nuclear families. Other two-generation households were three mothers living with their children, and a brother and sister and her child. Thirteen households were of one generation: elderly single people and married couples, young couples with no children, a brother and sister sharing a house. Only seven households contained three generations, the additional person being an elderly parent or small grandchild. A point to note is that all households were composed of relatives, there being nobody living on parish charity, no resident domestic servants, housekeepers, or lodgers.[11]

These modern homes contrasted markedly with the farmhouses of 1820, and even the houses of 1940. All had piped water and sewage disposal, electricity, inside toilets, bathrooms, and central heating. From being the centre of work which provided subsistence and exchange goods, the Icelandic home has become the site of domestic work only in the restricted sense of child-raising and house-keeping; unpaid work was carried out by the housewife alone. As a consequence of the home no longer being the centre of production, there was nobody earning their living by doing domestic work: domestic servants no longer existed. The farms were somewhat different, since work was orientated around the home and carried out by family members. Farmers' wives who did the milking, lambing, hay-making, and accounts are distinguished linguistically by the term *bóndakona*, in place of housewife, *húsmóðir*. In 1975 two of the reasons given by the organizing committee for holding a general strike by women referred to farm women: that their work was undervalued because it was estimated to be worth only about £500 per annum and that they were not admitted as full members of the Farmers' Union. In Fróneyri, one woman made a little money by selling eggs, another provided meals in her home for men working in the village during the summer, and a third did sewing and upholstery. Four households in Fróneyri raised a few sheep, getting a little cash in return for the fleeces and a supply of meat for the winter. Most families grew potatoes and a few other vegetables, and some went berry-picking in the late summer. These activites were spoken of as hobbies, were of marginal importance to the household budget, and were certainly not as vital as they were in 1940. Women engaged in knitting, sewing, and dressmaking, but out of choice rather than necessity. The most popular sort of sewing was embroidery, for display rather than use.

The overall gender-related division of labour was that men were full-time wage earners while women had the dual role of wage-earner and housewife.

Table 6   Occupations in Fróneyri, 1978

occupation	female	male
children under 15	29	40
student 15+	12	10
retired	5	4
disabled	2	1
fish factory workers	32	28
full-time housewives	12	–
farming	6	9
shopwork	4	2
school-teaching	2	1
driver	1	–
post office	1	–
mechanic	–	2
fishing	–	16
total	106	113

Source: fieldwork

In *Table 6*, people are classified according to their main occupation or status.[12] There was movement between jobs, usually on a seasonal basis. The students and older schoolchildren worked in the fish factory during the summer, as did two of the schoolteachers. Four of the farmers' wives took fish factory jobs in the winter months when there was less to do on the farms and a fifth worked there part-time throughout the year. Two older men who kept a few sheep concentrated on them from May to October, returning to fish factory work during the winter. Young men who had not got a regular place on a fishing boat also worked in the fish factory.

Only a minority of women had paid full-time work. The factors determining women's participation in paid employment were their ages (itself related to the developmental cycle of the family), their husbands' occupation, and the nature of paid work available. Only eight women worked full-time in the fish factory all the year round. They were a mother and daughter who were the breadwinners for their family, a couple of teenagers saving money before going into further education the next year, two young unmarried women who lived with their parents, and two married women whose children had grown up. The last four did jobs other than the arduous and boring table work.[13] They were supervisors, an office secretary and a cook.

Part-time work in the fish factory, that is, a regular morning or afternoon shift, was the characteristic working pattern of married women with children. Significantly, these women had few children under school age, and with two exceptions, were married to men who worked on the land. In this they differed from the full-time housewives, nine of whom had children under school age and six who were married to fishermen. The other full-time housewives were two women aged over 60 and a woman bringing up a family of six (three wage-earners) in the absence of a husband. Fishing was on the whole a younger man's occupation and the fishermen's wives were young themselves and had small children. As fishing was the highest-paid work available there was also less economic pressure on these women to engage in wage labour. Table work in the fish factory was the only work available to these women. This was considered, by young women in particular, as extremely tedious, so in the absence of economic necessity they did not engage in it. Of those women who had jobs other than in the fish factory, two were single, two married but with no children, and one was an elderly woman whose family had grown up. The post office was located in the postmistress's home so she could keep an eye on her children, and so the driver could take her child along on trips. Only one, the shopworker, had to make arrangements for a child under school age.

Much of the sheer physical drudgery of housework had been eliminated by the advent of the services and utilities previously mentioned, and the whole range of household appliances. While the work was no longer so arduous, it is not really possible to argue that running a home took any less time than it did previously. Some of the work had disappeared almost entirely; an individual household did not have to get its food from the land or sea and process it from the raw state, clothing was not produced from homegrown wool, and shopping had replaced these activites. On the other hand, some aspects of housework were greatly elaborated. Meals were more varied, the house was cleaned at least weekly, the greater quantity of clothing was washed much more frequently than the once or twice a year of the past. Standards and expectations had risen.[14] It is doubtful, moreover, whether the longer full-time education for children lessened the burden of child-raising. In this rural area children did not start school until seven years of age and initially went only for half a day. No school meals were provided. During the winter months the snow and dark meant that children could not play outside, so women had to supervise them indoors.

As compared with the historical situation, all the responsibility and most of the work fell upon one woman. Men's contribution to housework and child-raising tended to be small. They might share the jobs of decorating and gardening but did little of the day-to-day running of the home. Men's contribution was to 'help out' by going along on the shopping expeditions (but not planning the menus or drawing up the shopping list); washing-up occasionally; taking out the rubbish, or hanging out the washing (but not doing the washing or ironing). They engaged in the more pleasurable parts of child care, such as bathing the children and reading a bed-time story. Even when men had a domestic skill such as cooking which they did as a paid job on board a fishing boat, they rarely practised it at home.[15]

Co-operation between women in the different households was on the whole limited to stepping in at times of crisis, such as when the housewife was sick, lending utensils and furniture and suggesting recipes when a party was being held, or offering to pick something up at the shops. A mother would also take some of the load off her daughter's shoulders when she was learning to cope with a new baby. It was with regard to child-raising that a degree of organized co-operation was shown. Older women, who had given up paid work, minded children for those who had waged work, or women worked alternate shifts in the fish factory and cared for each other's children when at home. During my time in Fróneyri, the women were discussing the setting up of a crèche in the village, since this sort of arrangement did not cater for all the women.

When I lived in Fróneyri I noticed that public notices were displayed in two places: the door of the fish factory and the window of the shop. I felt that this epitomized the modern situation, because money was earned in the factory and spent in the shop; they were the two places most people in the village would go to some time during the week.

CONCLUSION

In this chapter I have described the changes in the economy, occupational structure, and household composition in one Icelandic parish over 150 years. There has been particular emphasis on examining the category 'domestic work'. In the early nineteenth century, work to produce consumption and exchange goods was household-based; and therefore domestic work in the first sense specified by Mackintosh. In addition to the extended kin group the household consisted of paid servants, with the women being paid less for their work than the men. When the fishing industry expanded and diversified, new types of specialized sea- and land-based occupations opened up for men. A parallel process did not take place as regards job opportunities for women. Very rapidly, the household changed, becoming entirely composed of kin.

Today domestic work means the particular tasks of house-keeping and child-raising; these are carried out by a woman alone in the home, and she receives no wages. Historically 'women's work' was paid at about half the rate of 'men's work'; today it is is not paid for directly at all. In addition to having the responsibility of running a home, the women of Fróneyri participated in wage labour. I have sought to show that a full understanding of their situation can only be gained by consideration of the parameters set by the overall gender-based division of labour and types of employment available, as well as the demands of this dual role.

Notes

1.   The research on which this chapter is based was carried out while a PhD student in the Department of Anthropology, University of Durham. Thanks are due to the SSRC for financial support, the people of Fróneyri (a pseudonym) and Reykjavik for their friendship, and my colleagues at Durham, particularly Dr Judith Okely, for their constant support.

2.   The major contributions to the Debate are listed in Mackintosh 1979: 190–91, and reviews of the area of discussion are in Molyneux 1979: 3–27 and Kaluzynska 1980: 27–54.

3.   The first national census was taken in 1703. Census collection was irregular in the eighteenth century, resuming on a regular basis

between 1820–1960. Originals and printed copies of these censuses are kept in the Manuscript Museum in Reykjavík. For the years 1940, 1950 and 1960 I was able to use the forms filled in by the people of the village.

4.   The administrative area for the census was the parish which covered a number of fjords including the one in which I carried out fieldwork. By the 1970s this fjord was the centre of population, the others being depopulated.

5.   The census distinguishes 'her children', 'his children' and 'their children'.

6.   In some cases it is reasonable to assume that people with this description in the census are in fact related by kinship to the house-holders. This is deduced by examining the names.

7.   At this time the wool was pulled off the sheep rather than sheared.

8.   One of the men in Fróneyri, speaking of his natal home in the early years of this century, said it was his father who did the weaving.

9.   Such workers were tied to the farm where they took work for a year. After 1863 a licence could be bought enabling workers to negotiate their own terms of employment and pay. Initially such a *lausabréf* cost twice as much for a man as a women, in any event more than a year's wages. In 1894 the price was reduced to 15 *krónur* for a man and 5 for a woman aged over 22. The fact that the licence cost less for a woman can be seen as another indication that their work was less valued than men's.

10.   *Kaupakona* is distinguished from *ráðskona* in that the former does work outside on the farm (such as hay-making and milking) while the latter does cooking and cleaning inside the home.

11.   Apart, that is, from myself. It may be of interest that although I was a lodger I was sometimes referred to as the foster daughter!

12.   The women classified as retired were over the official retire-ment age of 67. Three of them and both the disabled women did

housework so could have been grouped with the full-time housewives. The disabled people themselves gave their handicaps as the
reason for their non-involvement in paid work and for this reason I
have classed them separately.

13.   My characterization of the work is based on experience since I
did this job. Table work involves cleaning the fish of bones, worms
and blood, weighing and packing it. It is paid on a complicated bonus
system which is related to speed and skill, meaning that the work is
not only tedious but stressful as well.

14.   A full account of contemporary domestic work is given in the
paper *From Housework to Holidays: Women's Domestic Role in
Iceland* presented to the symposium *Representations of Women* held
in Durham in March 1980. In this I discuss in particular the hidden
'invisible' aspects of housework and how the types of food served at
different celebratory occasions symbolize women's identification
with the home and family and men's with the public world (publication of this paper is being negotiated).

15.   In the case of fishermen who worked on trawlers and went to
sea for up to a fortnight at a time, absence precluded day-to-day
involvement in domestic work. During their time on shore between
trips, which could be as little as twenty-four hours during the main
winter fishing season, they were either resting, engaging in hectic
social activities or doing jobs around the house such as decorating
and gardening.

10 The Organization of Labour in an Israeli Kibbutz

Alison M. Bowes

Labour on the kibbutz is carried out in a clearly-defined period of about nine hours per day, six days a week, which the community itself designates work time: during it, people are engaged in specific, planned, collectively-organized tasks in the *meshek* (kibbutz economy), which further the community's economic enterprise (cf. Wallman 1979). Some of the decision-making processes through which the economic enterprise is planned take place outside work time, and others within it. The organization of labour in all kibbutzim shares certain structural regularities which result from the history of the kibbutz movement and the context in which it operates. At the same time, each kibbutz is an independently planned economic unit, and therefore generates its own regularly operated mechanisms for organizing labour. The kibbutz movement as a whole and kibbutz members themselves see the organization of labour as a problem on several levels. First, structurally generated and emically defined labour shortages have plagued the kibbutzim for decades: attempts to deal with them occur both at movement level and in each kibbutz. Second, the division of labour in kibbutzim is considered unsatisfactory, especially with regard to unwaged and waged workers, men's and women's work, and skilled and unskilled jobs: this problem too is faced by the movement and by each kibbutz. Third, within a kibbutz, individual social actors face their own labour problems, relating to the allocation of labour to various branches of the *meshek*, and movement between jobs.

To understand the organization of labour in a kibbutz, analysis must be directed at several levels, i.e. the kibbutz movement as a whole, the individual kibbutz, and social action within that kibbutz. I look first at the history of labour organization in the kibbutz movement as a whole, with particular reference to the Kibbutz Artzi Hashomer Hatzair (the most left-wing of the kibbutz federations).

Second, I focus on Kibbutz Goshen,[1] a member of the Kibbutz Artzi federation, and one of a category of kibbutzim which have experienced particularly severe economic and social difficulties. The case helps demonstrate the implications of structurally generated problems of labour organization for an individual kibbutz. Third, I examine social interactive aspects of labour organization in Goshen, and show how social interaction and socio-economic structure intermesh. Finally, I consider the wider implications of the kibbutz case for anthropological studies of labour organization.

HISTORICAL BACKGROUND

Kibbutzim are, and always have been, communes in which property is held and worked in common and rewards are shared. They also compete as units in the country-wide capitalist economy, and are subject to pressures from the federations to which they belong to be efficient and competitive, producing goods that will be sold on the open market. In the past, kibbutzim received considerable subsidies from government agencies, but more recently, such aid has decreased, raising the pressure for efficiency. Kibbutz economies have also been shaped by an internal orientation towards progress (E. Cohen 1966): one of the principal purposes of the kibbutzim has been to build a Jewish proletariat engaged in modern, mechanized, efficient production, a basis for the rebirth of the nation and the establishment and perpetuation of the state. Kibbutzim saw themselves as prototypes for the kind of society that would characterize the new state, communities with an irresistible attraction for Jews wishing to see their nation reborn.

Jewish men and women were to be the sole agents of national rebirth. Early kibbutzim adhered firmly to the principle of 'self labour', which meant that the Jews, previously employers and exploiters, would build their economy themselves. They refused for many years to hire workers, not to exclude others, but to avoid what they saw as the major evil of exploitation through employment. In fact, of course, the pre-state economy of Zionist settlement was firmly linked with the existing economic structure of Palestine, and the success of the 'Jewish economy' (Szereszewski 1968) depended on this already established structure. The beliefs of kibbutz pioneers that their settlements could be totally independent and non-exploitative were therefore somewhat naïve, as Zureik (1979) shows: nevertheless, the principle of self labour has been constantly re-examined over the history of the kibbutz movement, and, however naïve, cannot be ignored.

In the early days of kibbutz settlement, the principle of the equality of women was frequently stated: women were to achieve it by doing the same work as men, namely manual labour (Bowes 1978). Later on, women gradually moved out of such work into tasks like child care and jobs in the services such as cooking, laundry, and sewing. By the 1950s (and possibly earlier) most women were in service jobs classified as 'unproductive' and most men were in 'productive' jobs which accrued revenue for the community through the sale of produce (at first agricultural and later industrial). 'Productive' jobs were always accorded the highest ideological value (Baratz 1954; Katzenelson-Rubashow 1976), being the 'real work' of proletarians: this is still the case today, and consequently, women's work on the kibbutz tends to be regarded as less important than men's.

During the Yishuv (the pre-1948 Jewish settlement in Palestine), the kubbutzim expanded steadily. *Table 7* shows two peaks in the

Table 7   Foundation of kibbutzim, 1910–69

date	total kibbutzim founded	Kibbutz Artzi kibbutzim founded*
1910–14	3	–
1915–19	2	–
1920–24	17	3
1925–29	20	4
1930–34	26	3
1935–39	42	15
1940–44	14	5
1945–49	59	29
1950–54	17	8
1955–59	9	4
1960–64	2	0
1965–69	8	2
totals:	219	73

*The first was founded in 1922

Source: Compiled from Criden and Gelb (1974: 240–62). The table includes only those kibbutzim which survived until 1969.

process of kibbutz settlement, the late 1930s and the late 1940s. After the foundation of the state in 1948, there were fewer new kibbutzim, and the proportion of kibbutz dwellers in the Jewish population declined from a peak of 7.5 per cent in 1947 to a constant figure of about 3.4 per cent for the 1960s onwards (Shur 1972). Kibbutzim of the Kibbutz Artzi faithfully reflect the general trends. To some extent, the kibbutzim have succeeded in expanding: the number of settlements and the absolute population have grown (Shur 1972), although the rate of increase has slowed considerably in recent years. Economically also the kibbutzim have been remarkably successful (Kanovsky 1966), expanding and mechanizing their economies and gaining a marked advantage over other types of rural settlement, especially beneficial to them in the early years of the state. Kibbutz diaries in particular showed considerably above average productivity (Kanovsky 1966), and in the 1960s, kibbutzim proved especially efficient in the production of industrial crops such as cotton and sugar beet (Talmon-Garber and Cohen 1964). Their economic advantage was stimulated by a number of factors. First, their orientation towards efficiency in production and their commitment to economic success was undoubtedly crucial. Second, their experience of farming and their well established social arrangements gave them advantages over the moshavim[2] (family farm collectives) set up in large numbers in the early 1950s as the main form of rural settlement for Oriental immigrants (Weingrod 1966; Shokeid 1971). Many Oriental immigrants were 'reluctant pioneers' who had not farmed before (Weingrod 1966) and they found the moshav movement into which they had been summarily recruited difficult to comprehend (Shokeid 1971). The new moshavim took several years even to begin farming, and when they did, many continued to experience severe social and economic problems. Third, having had a head start over the new settlements, the kibbutzim could concentrate on those crops most suitable for their social relations of production: when agricultural over-production led to the imposition in the 1950s of government production quotas, the kibbutzim, as efficient and experienced producers, were able to claim large quotas at the expense of newer farmers (cf. Abarbanel 1975). Fourth, advantages accrued to the kibbutzim from their ability to introduce economies of scale (impossible in the family farms) and to train specialists (again in contrast to the moshav family farms).

The price of success for the kibbutzim was a constant shortage of labour. The movement did not grow fast enough to fulfil all the requirements of its developing economies. Mechanization only proved a partial solution, and from the 1950s (Don 1977), the development of kibbutz industrial enterprise exacerbated the labour shortages because the movement wanted the industrial branches to be large enough to be competitive in the wider economy (Stern 1965). In agriculture, the kibbutz economies became less diversified, as a result of the orientation towards efficiency; in the early years of the movement, mixed farms had been operated, to ensure even labour requirements over the year (R. Cohen 1972) but as some branches were dropped, especially labour intensive ones, such as vegetable-growing, annual labour requirements became less and less balanced.

'Efficiency' also meant the labour force became increasingly inflexible. Specialists were required, and as training was expensive, tended to remain in the jobs for which they had been trained for years at a time. The ideal of a permanent job and its accompanying skill and indispensability became important for those who wished to be well integrated into the community (Shepher 1972). In kibbutzim today, someone who 'cannot find a place', i.e. cannot get a permanent job, is referred to as a *pkak* (cork), a derogatory term implying failure as a member of the community, and indicating that the individual involved is a problem case for the kibbutz. Thus, people make every effort to acquire a permanent job and specialist skills, and once they have attained them, are very unwilling to move.

Kibbutzim tried to solve these labour shortages: attempts to increase recruitment failed because the former major source of members, European Jewry, was decimated during the Second World War, and its survivors were unwilling to join kibbutzim. After 1948, there was a flood of immigrants from North Africa but these people were considered by the settlement authorities and the kibbutz movements to be unsuitable for kibbutz settlement (Baldwin 1972). Spiro (1957) reports that young people in Kibbutz Kiryat Yedidim actually hated Oriental Jews and considered them to be savages. Despite these attitudes however, many kibbutzim employed Oriental Jews who were being settled in moshavim, before the moshav farms were started (Shatil 1966), justifying this by references to the national duty of the kibbutzim to participate in the absorption of new immigrants.[3] Thus, the precedent for hiring labour on kibbutzim was set, although discussions about its justifiability continue to this day, when hired labour is a common method of filling labour shortages.

Since the 1960s, many kibbutzim have taken on voluntary workers, ostensibly to fill the labour shortage, and these work on the kibbutz and in return receive their keep. The presence of volunteers, in fact, helps others (see below) achieve the goal of permanent jobs (Bowes 1980). They supply unskilled labour, doing jobs which are considered undesirable. The 'shortage' which the volunteers fill, like other 'shortages', is not absolute, but is primarily generated by the importance of permanent jobs in the community.

Thus labour shortages are built into the present-day kibbutz. Some are seasonal, occurring at peak periods in the agricultural cycle; others are routine, i.e. there are simply not enough people available for all the jobs in the *meshek*. Shortages have been generated by the ideological orientation towards progress, the pressure on kibbutzim to be reasonably competitive in the country-wide capitalist economy, the developing importance of permanent jobs and the relative collapse in recruitment in the post-1948 period. They could not be ultimately relieved without radical structural change in the communities and altered social relationships. In most kibbutzim today, there are two categories of worker, unwaged and waged, and these vary considerably in size from one kibbutz to another: there may be almost no wage labourers in one kibbutz, and as many as 50 per cent of the workforce may be waged in another (Davis 1977). The numbers of hired workers are particularly high in industrial branches (Don 1977; Leviatan 1973).

The unwaged category includes all formally enrolled members of the commune, all candidates for membership, various visitors (e.g. volunteer workers from abroad, soldiers carrying out part of their army service, youth groups from the world-wide Zionist organizations which are affiliated to the kibbutz movements), and children of the kibbutz, who spend some time working in the *meshek* from their earliest schooldays onwards (starting with tasks like tidying up in the children's house, and ending, in their last year at school, with one full day's work a week with adults in one of the branches). Some members work outside the kibbutz on a semi-permanent basis (e.g. in movement offices and enterprises or the army) or, less usually, in other paid employment (e.g. as university teachers). Their salaries are paid directly into the kibbutz account. Also, at any time, several male members will be away on army reserve duty: at the time of fieldwork, reserve duty was two months a year for most men aged between 21 and 56 years. Single women may be called up for reserve duty, but this very rarely happens (Hazleton 1977).

Waged workers are hired from outside the community: their collective employers are the members and candidates of the kibbutz, and decisions about how many and what type of worker to hire are reached by the General Assembly, the weekly meeting of all the members and candidates, which is the governing body of the kibbutz. Labourers may be hired temporarily, to do seasonal or specialist jobs, or more permanently in branches of the *meshek* which would be unviable without them.

Kibbutz economies are planned and managed by members and candidates, unwaged workers who have a constitutional right to be involved at this level in the whole of the enterprise. Hired labourers are employees who may have trade union representation, but otherwise no say in how the enterprise is run. Other workers (volunteers, youth groups, soldiers) have little or no formal representation and no formal rights to a say in matters of this kind.

It is important to note that members and candidates of the kibbutz (hereafter referred to as 'kibbutzniks') are a highly selected group, who have deliberately chosen the kibbutz as a way of life, and are aware of the principles of Socialist Zionism on which it rests. Before acceptance (or rejection)[4] as a member, at least a year's candidacy is required, during which one's suitability as a member is assessed. Even those born on a kibbutz do not automatically become members, but are required, usually after completing their army service, to make a formal decision whether or not they wish to do so. All kibbutzniks have a right and an obligation to work in the *meshek*, and a right to participate in community decision-making. They are entitled to receive housing, furniture, food, clothing, care and education of their children, access to all communal facilities and 'extras' such as higher education, holidays abroad and so on. There is a certain amount of bargaining over these material 'rewards' of being a kibbutznik: usually, basic necessities are provided on a strict seniority basis (e.g. long-standing members will have first choice of new housing), and 'extras' are given after negotiation in the General Assembly (cf. Talmon 1972). The standard of living of kibbutzniks generally is well above the Israeli national average (Don 1977).

All work in the kibbutz continues to be subject to an ideological overlay. Primacy is still accorded to agricultural labour, industrial labour coming second, and service work ('unproductive work') remaining of low value. Most women's work is therefore considered rather unimportant, and many kibbutznik women are dissatisfied with their position in the community (Tiger and Shepher 1975). The movement as a whole is concerned with 'the problem of the woman' (Leon 1964), and has tried repeatedly to raise the status of women's work by training specialists in kitchen management, child care, and so on. Permanent jobs too have an ideological component: their very existence, as I argued above, results from an ideological orientation towards economic progress, and today, they are commonly seen as a means of ensuring equality among kibbutzniks – if everyone has a permanent job, everyone is equally indispensable (Shepher 1972). The existence of hired labour in the kibbutzim is a constant topic of discussion, especially in the Kibbutz Artzi.

One of the most unpopular jobs in any kibbutz is that of the Labour Organizer, who allocates workers to the various branches of the *meshek* according to their need. When a branch reaches a peak period (such as harvest time), application is made to the Labour Organizer for extra labour. The unpopularity of the job derives mainly from the constant pressures to which the incumbent is subject, from the branches demanding labour, and from various categories of worker, either demanding new jobs or to remain in their present ones. Very frequently, the demands conflict, and not only must the Labour Organizer cope with the logistics of having the right number of workers in the right place at the right time, but s/he must also engage in personal bargaining to reconcile the varying demands of the parties concerned. The post of Labour Organizer is filled by a vote in the General Assembly, and is held for a short time (usually three months), before a new election is held. People who take on the post may do so during the slack season of the branch in which they normally work, or they may be in the process of re-evaluating their own position in the community, considering, for example, in which branch they may wish to work.

Despite the long-established importance of specialization, and the acquisition by many kibbutziks of permanent jobs, there is still much movement of labour between branches, and it is the organization of this which is the task of the Labour Organizer. Moveable labour can be divided into several categories, firstly kibbutz women of child-bearing age. Pregnancy and childbirth may remove women from their permanent jobs (if they have them) for as a much as a year: in the later stages of their pregnancies, many women move into less strenuous work, and after the child is born, work a short day for perhaps six months, gradually moving up to a full day's work. The second category consists of people not presently working in their permanent jobs, during the slack season of their branch; the third consists of movers, i.e. people in the process of looking for a permanent job or of changing one, and the fourth of volunteer workers from abroad, who are temporary workers in the kibbutz economy, although a permanent supply of labour (Bowes 1980) with other temporary workers, such as soldiers, kibbutznik students on vacation, etc.

CASE STUDY: KIBBUTZ GOSHEN

Goshen was founded in 1946 by a group of Egyptian Hashomer Hatzair members,[5] and set up on its present site in 1949. It belongs to a category of 'little kibbutzim' considered by the movement to be problematic because of their relatively slow numerical expansion. All the 'little kibbutzim' belong to the large group of communities founded in the late 1940s, around the time of the establishment of the state. Low numbers mean relatively slow economic progress, and Goshen is no exception to this. In 1975–76 it had only 139 members,[6] and very little sign of an industrial branch, usually seen as a mark of economic success (cf. Billis 1972). Its small size and comparative economic weakness, with the internal and external structural factors already outlined, influenced Goshen's particular approach to its labour problems, which it experienced in common with all other kibbutzim. Communities founded relatively late in the development of the movement followed precedents set by earlier ones, encountering the same problems as well as reaping some of the same advantages. They were variations on an already established theme, and there were few possibilities for radically different practices.

Structural Aspects of Labour Organization in Kibbutz Goshen

In planning its economy, Goshen followed the ideological precepts and organizational precedents of the Kibbutz Artzi federation. Goshen was established as a mixed farm aimed at increasing productivity and mechanization; the *meshek* became progressively less diversified; an industrial crop (cotton) was initiated in the 1960s; in the 1970s, two attempts were made to establish an industrial branch, the first of these failing completely, and the second just beginning in 1975–76.[7] The failure of a branch was not new to Goshen: some of the agricultural branches had failed in the past, and even the cotton growing, which was doing well in 1975–76, had already had one false start. Pear cultivation was being wound up in 1975–76, and the hot-house roses were soon to go: both these branches were thought to be too expensive to run (harvesting the pears was too expensive for the relatively low returns they brought, and the heating bills on the hot-houses were too high). Seasonal labour shortages occurred on Goshen at peak periods in the agricultural cycle: the cotton hoeing in the spring, the cotton pressing in the autumn, the hot-house rose season in the winter, the citrus harvest in early spring and the much smaller avocado and pear harvests in the late summer and autumn. Every three months too, extra labour was needed in the chicken houses to load chickens onto lorries to be taken to the abattoir. With the exception of the hot-house work, all these jobs were unskilled, and consequently somewhat unpopular with the kibbutzniks. Routine (i.e. permanent) labour shortage existed, though were not great in Goshen because of the lack of an industrial branch. Other labour problems were those of individuals moving between various branches of the *meshek*, young women, temporary workers, kibbutzniks looking for permanent jobs, and volunteers, who constituted at least 12 per cent of the workforce at all times (Bowes 1980).

In Goshen, the distinction between 'productive' and 'unproductive' work was drawn particularly sharply because of the community's relatively poor economic performance. Resources were concentrated in the agricultural and industrial spheres, with the idea that if the 'productive' sector became profitable, then the quality of the comforts provided by the services could be improved. With the partial exception of the children's services, the 'unproductive' sector suffered disproportionately from economic stringency. The agricultural and industrial branches had the most modern machinery: between 1974 and 76, brand new chicken houses and a brand new factory were built; the cotton branch was gradually acquiring new machines, and so on. By contrast, the kitchen workers had used the same small, old-fashioned, poorly-equipped kitchen since the early years of the kibbutz. Only in 1975 was work commenced on a new building, and the purchase of more modern equipment. The *communa*[8] had been partly mechanized, but half the work was still done in a row of old wooden huts of early 1950s vintage. The communal dining room too was a wooden hut; it was finally repainted in 1975, while plans to build a new one were shelved, not for the first time. The children's houses were quite well equipped, but in a poor state of decoration, and the workers often complained about this, to no avail. In 1975, some of the fences in the area of the children's houses were repainted: by this time, most of the old paint had come off, and the job was long overdue. Clearly, the urgency of economic progress dictated priorities in the allocation of resources. One result was that men's working conditions tended to be better than women's, adding to women's already general dissatisfaction with their jobs, and stimulating yet more attempts to move, especially from the kitchen, where working conditions were considered the worst of all.

Of all the kibbutz federations, the Kibbutz Artzi has most strongly resisted hiring labour, and the federation as a whole has the lowest proportion of hired labour in its kibbutzim (Davis 1977). Goshen had very few permanently employed labourers as it lacked an industrial branch in which, in other kibbutzim, hired labour is concentrated. In 1975–76, a nurse, an electrician and a kindergarten teacher were employed, and three regular workers came from nearby towns and villages to work in the hot-houses, the chicken sheds and the embryonic factory. Otherwise, teams of workers were occasionally taken on for specialist work (e.g. re-roofing the hot-houses, building, etc.) or in 'emergencies' (see below). Without exception, hired labour of any kind provoked discussion of matters of principle on Goshen: people would argue that the kibbutz must work for itself, and not 'exploit' people by paying them wages. The presence of the permanent employees was justified by referring to the needs of the kibbutz: the community, it was said, needed these people because no members could do the jobs. So in these cases, hiring was considered unavoidable. In fact, there were people on Goshen who had the requisite skills, but they were not available to do the jobs for other reasons (for one example, see Case 5).

In 'emergencies', ideological principles against hiring labour were submerged in the course of discussion by considerations of efficiency, also ideologically important. For example, in 1975, there was a crisis in the cotton fields: the workforce available simply could not keep up with the vital weeding. A motion was put to the General Assembly asking for a team of workers to be hired: this brought fierce objections outside the meeting, but the objectors did not attend, and the workers were hired. Only at later meetings was the general question of hired labour raised again, and the principle that hiring was ideologically unsound reiterated. Clearly, the question would be raised again the following year, when another cotton field was to be brought under cultivation; also, if the factory proved successful, it was more than likely that the labour shortage would be exacerbated. In 1975–76, the kibbutzniks of Goshen shelved the hired labour question: later, they would have to face it again, and reach some compromise between their principles of efficiency on the one hand and anti-exploitation on the other. There is little comparative data from other kibbutizim which would allow prediction of the compromise which would be reached, but the literature indicates (Stern 1965; Don 1977) that even in kibbutzim with a large, permanent, hired labour force, it is constantly stated to be a temporary measure, to be phased out when the kibbutznik workforce increases in size.[9]

The stated purpose of the volunteer workforce on Goshen was to alleviate uneven seasonal labour demands: in fact, as I indicated, volunteers were a major resource for kibbutzniks in their attempts to find permanent jobs. They did unskilled work, considered unsuitable for kibbutzniks, and were a major category of workers at the disposal of the Labour Organizer. The volunteers were not necessarily willing to do exactly as the Labour Organizer wished, and they too would engage in negotiations with him or her, very often putting forward demands similar to those of the members for less repetitive and more interesting work. Amongst the volunteers, particularly those who remained on Goshen beyond the average two or three months, a certain kudos surrounded anyone who managed to secure regular work in a branch, provided the work was reasonably skilled. This reflected the general kibbutz attitude, but volunteers did not have the same opportunities to become established in permanent jobs as kibbutzniks, mainly because they would only be on Goshen for a short time, but also because kibbutzniks were not keen for them to take such jobs (see Bowes 1980 for more details).

Case 1 is a particularly extreme example of a kibbutznik attempting to use a volunteer in his own struggle for status. It is a rare incident, because the confrontation of kibbutznik and volunteer was seldom made so explicit.

Case 1: The washing up

In 1974, all dishwashing in Goshen was done by hand: this was a hard, dirty and unpleasant job, made more so by the fact that there was not enough crockery to go round at mealtimes, and the dishwasher was constantly under pressure to keep up a supply of clean crockery as people arrived in the dining hall for their meals. One day in August 1974, V11,[10] a volunteer, was working in the dining room and M117, a student working in Goshen during his summer vacation, was washing up. The Labour Organizer came into the dining room and M117 demanded of him that he should change places with V11 who, as a volunteer, ought to be washing up. The Labour Organizer retorted that M117 could stay where he was, saying everyone, including members of the kibbutz, should take their turn at the dirty jobs, and referring to the ideology of equality. M117 went back to the washing up.

In this incident, M117 and the Labour Organizer were both arguing ideologically. M117 was demanding his 'right', as a member, to a more skilful job: although dining room work was not particularly skilful and not considered desirable as a permanent job, it was at least a step above washing up. The Labour Organizer appealed to the more general principle of equality. He won the argument not so much because of his skill in referring to a higher ideal than that chosen by M117, although this was certainly important, but rather because M117 had opened himself to accusations of being a bad kibbutznik, afraid to get his hands dirty. Of course, the Labour Organizer had some power over M117, in that he could, if M117 made trouble, continue to allocate him to the washing up for days afterwards: this measure was in fact suggested by some of the kitchen workers, in whose full hearing the argument was conducted.

One of the main categories of people moving from one job to another in Goshen consisted of young women in the process of having their families. Since most women worked in the 'unproductive' (service) sector of the economy, turnover of labour in the service sector generally was much greater than that in the 'productive' sector, and was concentrated in those areas of the service which involved less skill. The kitchen manager, the cook, the manager of the *communa* (clothing store), and the principal workers in the children's houses remained in their jobs for years at a time, acquiring, often through professional training as well as experience in the job, the skill and indispensability such permanent work brought with it. Less skilled jobs were considered less satisfying, so many women were constantly looking for a change of job. In the kibbutz literature, this kind of turnover and the disssatisfaction that goes with it has been well documented (e.g. by Tiger and Shepher 1975). One consequence is that it is much more difficult for women than men to achieve the goal of a permanent job, and that if they do succeed in acquiring one, they have to work harder at keeping it, as they may be absent from it during part of their pregnancies and their child's early infancy: this can demonstrate that they are not in fact 'indispensable', as a man in the same branch doing the same job might be.[11] These factors affected women's work relationships on Goshen: for example, in the hothouses, where roses were grown, the work was skilled, and women had opportunities to acquire permanent jobs. By comparison with the men working in the same branch, however, they were much more conscious of the importance of their skills, and demonstrated them in a more obvious way, especially to the other women, guarding their seniority jealously. They behaved thus because, as women, they simply could not become indispensable in the same way as the men could, even if there was no real likelihood of their having children (Bowes 1978).

Solutions to women's individual labour problems reflected the fact that women's work (even if it was the same as men's work) was considered less important.

Case 2: The care of the old

In the early summer of 1975, six weeks after the birth of her first child, C8 was allocated to the *communa,* to work the four-hour day customary for a nursing mother. After a few days and several rows with the *communa* manager, she went to the Labour Organizer to ask for a change of job. This request proved problematic, because there was no suitable job available, but the Labour Organizer, in consultation with other administrative officers of the kibbutz, manufactured one for her. She was to go and visit two bed-ridden old people in the community, take them their meals, see that they were comfortable, and give them some company. This had previously been done by the old people's female relatives, who had simply left their own jobs for an hour or two to do it. When C8 returned to full-time work, her 'job' reverted to being an informal family activity.

This sort of arrangement would never have been resorted to for a man looking for a job. And similarly, men would not have left their work to look after relatives. The case indicates a more general undervaluing of women's jobs: there were several other examples of the *ad hoc* creation and removal of jobs during the course of my fieldwork, all of which related to women's work. By contrast, men who could not find jobs, or who moved from one job to another were looked down upon, and blamed for what was seen as their own inability to find permanent work.

Case 3: A cork

M33 first went to Goshen as a hired worker in the late 1960s. On Goshen, he met a kibbutz member he wished to marry, and applied for membership himself. Once accepted for membership and married, M33 continued a lifestyle very similar to that of a hired worker for whom the kibbutz was an employer and nothing more. He saw the kibbutz as 'them', a group external to himself, consisting of people with whom he did not wish to interact, and who, in some cases, he actively disliked: thus he remained cut off from the community in terms of social interaction, and also declined to participate in kibbutz political life. His career as a hired worker had begun in the dairy, and once he was accepted as a member, he began to sample work in the agricultural branches of the *meshek* in rapid succession. In every branch, he complained that he could not get along with the other workers, and they complained that they could not get along with him. By 1975, he was working permanently in the dining room, where he was in charge of two or three other workers, usually volunteers, and thus isolated at work from other members of the kibbutz. M33 was defined by the rest of the community as a problem, and criticism focused on the facts (a) that he could not find a permanent job and (b) that a young, strong man such as he should not be working in the dining room, in unproductive, unskilled, service work. In the eyes of the community, his failure was two-fold: he had failed both as a worker and as a man. Although he had finally found a job in which he could keep away from his fellow members and in which they could keep away from him, the criticism continued.

There is a sharp contrast between Cases 2 and 3 arising from the sex of the individuals involved. Both had had problems in their relationships with their workmates, and were looking for new jobs. A 'job' was manufactured for C8, and disappeared when her work hours changed, whereas M33 had found a permanent job and was heavily criticized because it was thought unworthy of a man. By definition, then, women did less important work, but men did productive work, and, should they lower themselves into unproductive ('women's') work, they suffered criticism.

Interactional aspects of labour organization in Kibbutz Goshen

Social interactional factors relevant to the process of labour organization took a number of different, variable forms, including, for example, the relationships between workmates in a particular branch, individuals' reputed characteristics, and their strategies for finding jobs. If people were unable to interact satisfactorily with their workmates, they might go to the Labour Organizer and demand a move: this is what M33 (the cork) had done on several occasions. Sometimes one move would alleviate the problem, but repeated moves would eventually build up against the individual concerned; s/he would acquire a reputation for being difficult to get on with, and would find it more and more difficult to get a job: this had happened to M33, and he had finished up in the dining room, isolated and heavily criticized. Sometimes, branch workers would reject a new recruit on the basis of his or her reputation.

Case 4: Excluding a worker

In the winter of 1975–76, there was the usual annual shortage of labour in the hot-houses. By late December, the branch was working a ten- or eleven-hour day, and the workers started to complain to the branch manager[12] that they simply could not cope; another worker was needed, they argued, and justified, because their extra hours added up to at least one more day. Another worker would make them more efficient too, because the flowers could all be cut earlier in the day, and sorted more quickly, thus being less likely to wilt. The branch manager accepted their arguments, and went to the Labour Organizer to ask for at least one more worker. After some days, the Labour Organizer suggested that X5, a soldier doing part of her army service on Goshen, could work in the branch. When they heard this, the branch raised a storm of protest: they would not work with her, they said, because she was bossy and self-important. Some of them said that if she came, they would go. They succeeded in preventing the woman from working in the branch, and some volunteers were later on allocated.

X5's reputation had ensured that the workers would not accept her, despite the very real need for more labour. Their threat to walk out would probably not have materialized, but it was a way of indicating the strength of their feelings about X5.

In some cases, the community as a whole would be faced with a problem whose roots lay in social interaction.

Case 5: The gossiping nurse

Goshen's nurse in 1975–76 was a hired worker despite the fact that two kibbutzniks were trained nurses. One was rather elderly, and worked the shorter day usually allowed older people in the kibbutz: she helped the hired nurse, stood in for her on her days off, and did longer-term nursing jobs which would have taken the hired nurse away from her more general duties. The other trained nurse was much younger, but did no nursing work at all: in fact she did very little of any kind of work. Once she had been kibbutz nurse, but she was an inveterate gossip, and her patients had found the details of their complaints circulated round the gossip network. She was removed from the nursing job, and the hired nurse was brought in because there was in effect no nurse now available in the community.

One interesting aspect of this case is that, in itself, skill might not be a sufficient qualification for a job. Workers had also to meet certain social requirements which arose from the nature of the kibbutz as a face-to-face, closely-knit community. Had the woman worked in a hospital in a large community where her contact with her patients was brief and less personal, her interest in gossip might have been less problematic: in the kibbutz, where people were in contact with one another in all spheres of life, at work, in the school, in the communal facilities they shared, as neighbours, and as friends, it was a serious problem. Similarly in Case 5, X5 was not to be tolerated because she would not only have entered the work sphere, but also other spheres of the other workers' lives; in Case 4, M33 had to be isolated at work to reinforce his more general isolation (and perhaps vice versa). Thus social interactive factors were an especially important dimension of the approach to labour problems on Kibbutz Goshen because work relationships were firmly enmeshed with other relationships in the community. In general, this will be the case in every kibbutz, although the details of particular instances will of course vary.

Acquiring a permanent job involved face-to-face negotiation with the Labour Organizer, and support from other kibbutzniks, especially with those already in the branch the individual wished to join. Such support was derived from the personal social network of the individual concerned, and some types of network were more effective than others, as Case 6 shows.

Case 6: A job in the children's house

M65 had worked in one of the children's houses in Goshen for two years. She enjoyed the work, and hoped that she would be able to study to be a *metapelet* (a children's nurse, in charge of a house). In 1976, M65 got married, and after the wedding, left with her husband for a month's holiday in Europe. Whilst away, she would have to be replaced in the children's house. M82 had just left school, and was eager to work with the children, and she was also looking for a permanent job, because she was soon getting married and would therefore be exempted from army service. Her mother was a *metapelet* and was keen for her daughter to become similarly established. She campaigned on her daughter's behalf among her pioneer contemporaries who had power to influence such matters, and M65 returned from Europe to find M82 ensconced in what had formerly been her job. M65's own friends, her age group, had meanwhile complained bitterly about M82's 'taking their friend's job', as they saw it: M65, they argued, was senior to M82, she had experience of the work and she was good at it. But they were powerless to do anything about the situation: M82 had had powerful support from her mother and her mother's friends. Later, when M65 applied to the General Assembly of the kibbutz for study leave, to train as a *metapelet*, she was turned down, despite the efforts of her friends to recruit supporters for her. Her support, though reasonably widespread, was simply ineffective, in the face of M82's more powerful network. M65 had virtually no contacts among the older generation which effectively controlled formal decision-making on Goshen: her own parents had long since left the kibbutz, and so were not available to use their networks in their daughter's support.

Thus success (or lack of it) in finding a permanent job was tied up with the nature of the kibbutz as a social interactive group. In this case, social interactive factors operated in a slightly different way from the previous cases. Again, the multi-stranded interactions of the individual came into play, but qualitative distinctions between the interactive networks of different social actors can be made. Generally speaking, a wide network of contacts throughout the community could be a most effective tool in acquiring a permanent job, providing that the contacts included in it were in a position to exercise some influence over the Labour Organizer and the advising committees, as well as the General Assembly. Since the Labour Organizer and the members of the relevant committees on Goshen were, more often than not, members of the pioneer generation, then pioneer contacts were particularly important.

CONCLUSION

The organization of labour and the approach to labour problems in Kibbutz Goshen can be understood through an examination of both structural and interactional factors. Analysis of the place of the kibbutz movement in the Zionist movement and the state of Israel, and the place of the particular kibbutz under study in the kibbutz movement as a whole is vital. Early kibbutzim saw themselves as agents for the national rebirth of the Jewish people, a goal for which only Jewish men and women would work. They achieved numerical expansion, and economic success partly because of their own determination and abilities and partly because they gained an economic advantage over other rural settlements, especially after 1948. This success and the manner in which it was achieved generated labour shortages, for which various solutions were attempted, shaping the kibbutz labour force of more recent years, which is divided into non-waged and waged categories. Greater economic success, marked by mechanization, specialization and the development of industrial branches, has exacerbated labour shortages, and created heated ideological debate, especially in the Kibbutz Artzi. Specialization of work, resulting from an orientation towards efficiency, has altered the working lives of kibbutz men and some kibbutz women. Generally, kibbutz women are more likely to change their jobs than men are.

In the context of this general history, Kibbutz Goshen was characteristic of kibbutzim founded in the late 1940s–early 1950s: small, economically somewhat unsuccessful, and taking on very little hired labour. It experiences labour shortages as other kibbutzim do, because of the nature of movement history in which later kibbutzim followed organizational and ideological precedents set by earlier ones. As a relatively poor kibbutz, Goshen stressed the importance of 'productive' work particularly strongly, emphasizing and perhaps exacerbating the division of labour by sex. Ideological factors were very sharply brought into play when labour shortages were faced, especially in relation to hired labour and Case 1. Cases 2 and 3 showed how the division of labour was expressed in the attempts of a woman (Case 2) and a man (Case 3) to find jobs. Focusing on interactional factors, the discussions of Cases 4, 5 and 6 showed how social relations specific to Goshen both raised certain problems

(Case 5) and guaranteed particular solutions to them (Cases 4 and 6). In all these cases, structural aspects of labour organization also came into play: in Case 4, the structure of the branch, in Case 5, the question of hired labour, and in Case 6, the importance of well established support in the community for the acquisition of a permanent job.

Previous studies of the organization of labour in Israeli kibbutzim have treated the communities as models for other societies: for example, Macarov (1975) uses the fact that kibbutz members are unpaid workers as a basis for a study of motivation to work which offers lessons for other societies; Leviatan (1978) argues that rotation of managerial responsibility in kibbutz production makes it more efficient, proposing that it be used elsewhere; Wershow (1973) applauds the planning of jobs for old people in kibbutzim, suggesting that they can thereby lead happier lives. In making such recommendations, these observers fail to recognize the specificity of the kibbutz, merely lifting elements of kibbutz organization out of their context and proposing their transplant elsewhere. They follow a recent trend in the sociology of work, identified by Esland and Salaman (1975) of increasing academic specialization and fragmentation of interests[13] at the expense of the broader appreciation of work in society and the wide-ranging analysis which characterized the work of the pioneer sociologists, Durkheim, Marx and Weber. Social anthropologists have recently started to revive this broader view (Wallman 1979), and argue that the discipline of social anthropology is particularly well suited to the task, because of its traditional many-sided view of society.

In this chapter, I have taken a social anthropological view of the organization of labour in an Israeli kibbutz, and thus inevitably stressed the importance of its social context. The structural and interactional factors I have discussed are specific to the kibbutz, taking their particular form because of the historical forces which have shaped the kibbutz in the Zionist movement, in Israel and in each community. To follow the precedent set by other kibbutz researchers by attempting to derive prescriptions for other societies would be to deny the validity of the approach here employed, and to treat the kibbutz as a social experiment, a procedure which is, in my view, unscientific. This is not to deny that the study of labour organization in the kibbutz has wider implications: these are, however, theoretical ones for the study of labour organizations in other contexts, and not object lessons.

Throughout the discussion I have stressed the importance of ideological factors in labour organization. In the kibbutz, ideology is especially prominent because there is considerable ideological self-consciousness (cf. Evens 1980). Even so, ideology here, as elsewhere, is not always clearly defined, static or consistent: in the kibbutz, it has grown and developed with the community. Kibbutz movement ideology is constantly subject to reinterpretation, and hence to a kind of change, although it is not always easy to decide the degree or level of change which has occurred. Ideology and social action in the kibbutz stand in a dialectical relationship which must be taken into account when labour organization is examined. This has important implications for other studies: firstly, it is worth examining ideological aspects of labour organization generally, even though this may be more difficult in societies in which ideology is less prominent than it is in the kibbutz; secondly, the data emphasize the complexity of the relationship between ideology and social action even in a case where this perhaps appears on the surface to be relatively clear-cut (cf. Abercrombie and Turner 1978).

In the kibbutz case, the analytical bounding of the unit of study is also a complex matter. As Shepher (1980) argues, people in the kibbutz have several different ways of defining it, which are operated in an *ad hoc* fashion: when speaking of 'the kibbutz' (*hakibbutz*), they may, for example, be referring to the physical site, the economic enterprise, the community of members, candidates and their children, all those who work in the community or all those who live in the community. These notions are not coterminous, and the analyst must take particular care to clarify the analytical unit with which s/he is dealing. In my discussion of the organization of labour, I have focused on all those who work in the *meshek*, including members, candidates, children, mixed workers, volunteers and visitors (e.g. soldiers): all these categories of worker appear in the kibbutz economic records, and the analytical boundary of the study therefore matches one of the emic views of 'the kibbutz'. In other studies, the unit of study might not coincide with any emic perception, but its determination must still rest on prior investigation of community boundaries. At first sight, the kibbutz community appears to be quite simply defined: further investigation proves this not to be the case, and the question is, I think, worth raising in other contexts as well.

In many studies of work or labour in society, much women's work has been excluded. Oakley (1974) argues that sociologists have failed to see housework as 'real work', thus reflecting the values of their own society that work done by women is unimportant. Bythell (1978) says that outwork, an occupation of 'hundreds of thousands' of women in the nineteenth century is now 'virtually dead', but current estimates of the numbers of women who take in work in Britain give a figure of at least a quarter of a million (Mackie and Pattullo 1977), and Pahl (1980) suggests that outwork may be increasing, with the 'informal economy'. Women who work outside the home have also been ignored until very recently (Oakley 1974; Mackie and Pattullo 1977): Esland *et al* (1975) include no papers on women's work in their perhaps ironically titled *People and Work*. Social anthropologists, who are supposed to fight enthocentrism in all its forms do little better: though Schildkrout (1979) distinguishes clearly between housework and income-producing work in her study of 'Women's work and children's work' in Kano, Nigeria, she fails to emphasize the nature of housework and its place in society in any detail. She is the only contributor to the ASA symposium (Wallman 1979) to focus specifically on women's work.

In the kibbutz, it is much more difficult to ignore women's work, perhaps because it is done in the public domain, and is accorded significance in community accounts. As I have shown, women's work tends to be undervalued in the kibbutz, and as a result women tend to be unhappy in their work and change jobs, especially in their child-bearing years, far more frequently than men do. The analysis of the division of labour by sex has been a crucial element in the present discussion: it will be so, I suggest, in any context provided that the full significance of women's work, whether done in public or in private, is recognized, and aspects of it are not arbitrarily relegated to irrelevancy. We should not assume that work which brings no direct monetary return is to be discounted: at the same time, we should ask how the group under study values (or otherwise) such work, because, as in the kibbutz case, this is important for the organization of labour generally.

The argument in this chapter has operated at several analytical levels and I suggest that any successful study of the organization of labour must do so. In the kibbutz case, although each community is managed as a separate economic enterprise, structures of kibbutz labour organization can be understood only if each kibbutz is examined within the context of the state, the Zionist movement, and the kibbutz movement as a whole. Within the community, labour organization is a function both of wider structural features and of the history of the community. It is also, as I have shown, heavily influenced by social interactional factors.

Notes

1.   A fictitious name for a real kibbutz on which I carried out fieldwork in 1974 and 1975–76. I would like to thank its people for their hospitality, Dr Israel Shepher, Tel Aviv, for advice and support during fieldwork, the Social Science Research Council and the Anglo-Israel Association for finance, and Professor Norman Long, Wageningen, for continuing inspiration.

2.   The moshav movement began at about the same time as the kibbutz movement: moshavim founded before 1948 are usually referred to as 'veteran' moshavim to distinguish them from the 'immigrant' moshavim discussed here (see Baldwin 1972 for a detailed account).

3.   Some kibbutzim, it should be noted, refused on principle to take on hired labour, arguing that this was exploitation (Kanovsky 1966).

4.   Rejection is fairly rare. Usually, a candidate will leave the kibbutz before the point of rejection is reached, realizing that s/he is not welcome in the community.

5.   These Oriental Jews were markedly different from the Oriental immigrants of the immediate post-1948 period. They were Western-orientated, highly-educated, French-speaking and came from the upper strata of society. They had also been members of Hashomer Hatzair in Egypt, and were well prepared for kibbutz life.

6.   The Kibbutz Artzi federation regards all kibbutzim with less than two hundred members to be 'problem' communities.

7.   Even in 1980, it was still not certain that the industrial branch would be successful.

8.   Usually translated 'clothing store': ironing, pressing, mending and sorting of clean clothes and linen was carried out here, and some clothes and linen were made. The laundry was attached to the *communa,* and often treated as part of it: certainly, the laundry women and the *communa* women spent much of their working day together.

9.   Billis (1972) argues that this is unlikely to occur. He feels that the 'little kibbutzim' will remain small and dependent on agriculture, and that the veteran kibbutzim (founded before 1948) will continue to hire labour in their industrial branches.

10.   Social actors have been allocated random numbers and a letter prefix denoting their status. 'V' is a volunteer, 'M' a member, 'C' a candidate, 'X' an outsider working on Goshen (e.g. a soldier, hired worker, etc.).

11.   As I noted above, men might be absent from the kibbutz for two months every year in the reserves. This did not affect their permanence in their jobs. Thus we must accept that the dissatisfaction and turnover of women in jobs was due to a combination of absences and the general undervaluing of women's work.

12.   An elected and rotated position: the branch manager was the nominal head and representative of the branch, and had very little power.

13.   They list 'industrial sociology, occupational sociology, the sociology of the professions, itself fragmented into the sociology of medicine and education, and others (the sociology of industrial relations, or of class structures)' (Esland and Salaman 1975: 21).

References

Abarbanel, J. (1975) The Dilemma of Economic Competition in an Israeli Moshav. In S.F. Moore and B.G. Myerhoff (eds) *Symbol and Politics in Communal Ideology*. Ithaca and London: Cornell University Press.

Abdel-Fadil, M. (1975) *Development, Income Distribution and Social Change in Rural Egypt (1952–70)*. Cambridge: Cambridge University Press.

Abercrombie, N. and Turner, B.S. (1978) The Dominant Ideology Thesis, *British Journal of Sociology* 29, 2: 49–170.

Abrahams, R.G. (1981) *The Nyamwezi Today*. Cambridge: Cambridge University Press.

Aijmer, G. (n.d.) Some Reflexions on the Notion of 'Household'. Mimeo, Department of Social Anthropology, Gothenburg.

Akehurst, B.C. (1968) *Tobacco*. London: Longman Group Ltd.

Alavi, H. (1973) Peasant Classes and Primordial Loyalties, *Journal of Peasant Studies*, 1, 1: 22–62.

Alberti, G. and Mayer, E. (eds) (1974) *Reciprocidad e Intercambio en los Andes Peruanos*. Serie Peru Problema 12. Lima: Instituto de Estudios Peruanos.

Ammar, H. (1954) *Growing up in an Egyptian Village: Silwa, Province of Aswan*. London: Routledge and Kegan Paul.

Anderson, M. (1971) *Sociology of the Family*. Harmondsworth: Penguin.

Archetti, E. (1978) Una visión general de los estudios sobre el campesinado. *Estudios Rurales Latino-americanos* I, 1: 7–33.

Archetti, E.P. and Stølen, K.A. (1975) *Explotación familiar y acumulación de capital en el campo Argentino*. Buenos Aires: Siglo XXI.

Arensberg, C.M. and Kimball, S.T. (1940) The Small Farm Family in Rural Ireland. Reprinted in M. Anderson (1971) *Sociology of the Family*. Harmondsworth: Penguin Books.

Arrighi, G and Saul, J.S. (1973) *Essays on the Political Economy of Africa*. New York: Monthly Review Press.

Assadourian, C. (1973) Modos de Producción, capitalismo y subdesarollo en América Latina. *Modos de Producción en América Latina. Cuadernos de Pasado y Presente*. Cordoba, Argentina.

Ayrout, H. (1968) *The Egyptian Peasant*. (1st edn 1938) Boston: Beacon Press.

Baldwin, E. (1972) *Differentiation and Cooperation in an Israeli Veteran Moshav*. Manchester: Manchester University Press.

Banaji, J. (1976) Summary of Selected Parts of Kautsky's *The Agrarian Question. Economy and Society* 5, 1: 2–49.

Banaji, J. (1977) Capitalist Domination and the Small Peasantry: Deccan Districts in the Late Nineteenth Century. *Economic and Political Weekly*, special number, August: 1375–404.

Baratz, J. (1954) *A Village by the Jordan*. London: Harvill Press.

Barbour, K.M. (1972) *The Growth, Location, and Structure of Industry in Egypt*. New York, Washington, London: Praeger Publishers.

Bartra, R. (1974) *Estructura agraria y clases sociales en México*. Mexico: Serie Popular Era.

Bell, C. and Newby, H. (1971) *Community Studies*. London: George Allen and Unwin.

Bennett, J.W. (1968) Reciprocal Economic Exchanges among North American Agricultural Operators. *Southwestern Journal of Anthropology* 24: 276–309.

Bennett, J.W. (1969) *Northern Plainsmen: Adaptive Strategy and Agrarian Life*. Chicago: Aldine.

Bennett, J.W. (1982) *Of Time and Enterprise. North American Family Farm Management in a Context of Resource Marginality*. Minneapolis: University of Minneapolis Press.

Bennholdt-Thomsen, V. (1981) Subsistence Production and Extended Production. In K. Young, *et al.*, *Of Marriage and the Market*. London: CSE Books.

Bernstein, H. (1977) Notes on Capital and Peasantry. *Review of African Political Economy* 10: 60–73.

Bernstein, H. (1979) Concepts for the Analysis of Contemporary Peasantries. *The Journal of Peasant Studies* 6, 4: 421–44.

Berque, J. (1957) *Histoire Sociale d'un Village Egyptienne du XXeme Siecle*. Paris: Mouton.

Bettleheim, C. (1972) Appendix I: Theoretical Comments. In A.

Emmanuel, *Unequal Exchange,* New York: Monthly Review Press.

Billis, D. (1972) Membership Stability and Structural Developments in Israel's Collective Settlements in the Sixties. *International Review of Community Development* 27–8: 239–54.

Blumenfeld, E. and Mann, S. (1980) Domestic Labour and the Reproduction of Labour Power: Towards an Analysis of Women, Family and Class. In B. Fox (ed.), *Hidden in the Household: Women's Domestic Labour Under Capitalism.* Toronto: The Women's Press.

Bouquet, M. (1981) The Sexual Division of Labour: The Farm Household in a Devon Parish. Unpublished PhD thesis, Cambridge University.

Bouquet, M. (1982a) Production and Reproduction of Family Farms in South-West England. *Sociologia Ruralis* 22, 3/4: 227–39.

Bouquet, M. (1982b) Report to the SSRC on the Rural Society and Economy Spring Meeting: Anthropological Perspectives. Mimeo.

Bouquet, M. (1982c) Drawing the Line: the Domestic Organization of Farm Tourism. Unpublished manuscript.

Bourque, S.C. and Warren, K.B. (1981) *Patriarchy and Social Change in Two Peruvian Towns.* Ann Arbor: The University of Michigan Press.

Bowes, A.M. (1978) Women in the Kibbutz Movement. *Sociological Review* 26, 2: 237–62.

Bowes, A.M. (1980) Strangers in the Kibbutz: Volunteer Workers in an Israeli Community. *Man* 15, 4: 665–81.

Box, L. (1981) Cultivation and Adaptation: An Essay in the Sociology of Agriculture. *Sociologia Ruralis* 21, 2: 160–76.

Bradby, B. (1982) Resistance to Capitalism in the Peruvian Andes. In D. Lehmann (ed.) *Ecology and Exchange in the Andes.* Cambridge: Cambridge University Press.

Brading, D. (1977) *Hacienda* Profits and Tenant Farming in the Mexican Bajio, 1700–1860. In K. Duncan and I. Rutledge (eds) *Land and Labour in Latin America.* Cambridge: Cambridge University Press.

Briskin, L. (1980) Domestic Labour: A Methodological Discussion. In B. Fox (ed.) *Hidden in the Household: Women's Domestic Labour Under Capitalism.* Toronto: The Women's Press.

Brody, H. (1973) *Inishkillane: Change and Decline in the West of Ireland.* Harmondsworth: Penguin Books.

Brush, S. (1977) *Mountain, Field and Family: The Economy and*

Human Ecology of an Andean Valley. Philadelphia: University of Pennsylvania Press.

Bythell, D. (1978) *The Sweated Trades: Outwork in Nineteenth Century Britain.* London: Batsford Academic.

Cardoso, C. (1972) Sobre los modos de producción coloniales de América. *Modos de Producción en América Latina. Cuadernos de Parado y Presente.* Cordoba, Argentina.

Casalis, A.E. (1975) *Comparación de las estructuras tabacaleras de la Republica Argentina.* Universdad nacional de Buenos Aires.

Central Agency for Public Mobilization and Statistics (1971) *al-Hijra al-Dakhiliyya fi Jumhuriyyat Misr al-ᶜArabiyya (Internal Migration in the Arab Republic of Egypt).* Cairo: Government of Egypt.

Central Agency for Public Mobilization and Statistics (1977) *The General Population and Housing Census 1976: The Preliminary Results.* Cairo: Government of Egypt.

Central Agency for Public Mobilization and Statistics (1978) *Population and Development: A Study on the Population Increase and its Challenge to Development in Egypt.* Cairo: Government of Egypt.

Chayanov, A.V. (1925, 1966) *The Theory of Peasant Economy.* 1966 edition D. Thorner, R.E.F. Smith and B. Kerblay (eds) London: Irwin.

Cliffe, L. (1977) Rural Class Formation in East Africa *The Journal of Peasant Studies* 4: 195–224.

Cohen, A.P. (1979) The Whalsay Croft: Traditional Work and Customary Identity in Modern Times. In S. Wallman (ed.) *Social Anthropology of Work.* London: Academic Press.

Cohen, E. (1966) Progress and Communality: Value Dilemmas in the Collective Movement. *International Review of Community Development* 15–16: 3–18.

Cohen, R. (1972) *The Kibbutz Settlement.* Israel: Hakibbutz Hameuchad Publishing House.

Cook, S. (1977) Beyond the *Formen:* Towards a Revised Marxist Theory of Precapitalist Formations and the Transition to Capitalism. *Journal of Peasant Studies,* 4, 4: 360–89.

Criden, Y. and Gelb, S. (1974) *The Kibbutz Experience: Dialogue in Kfar Blum.* New York: Herzl Press.

Cuddihy, W. (1980) *Agricultural Price Management in Egypt,* World Bank Staff Working Paper 388. Washington: The World Bank.

Davies, E.T. (1973) Tourism on Devon Farms: A Physical and

Economic Appraisal. Report 188, Agricultural Economics Unit, University of Exeter.

Davis, J. (1977) *People of the Mediterranean.* London: Routledge and Kegan Paul.

Davis, J.E. (1980) 'Capitalist Agricultural Development and the Exploitation of the Propertied Labourer'. In F. Buttel and H. Newby (eds) *The Rural Sociology of the Advanced Societies: Critical perspectives.* Montclair, New Jersey: Allanheld, Osmun, and London: Croom Helm.

Davis, U. (1977) *Israel: Utopia Incorporated.* London: Zed Press.

Deere, C.D. and de Janvry, A. (1979) A Conceptual Framework for Empirical Analysis of Peasants. *American Journal of Agricultural Economics.* 61, 4: 601–11.

De Janvry, A. and Garramon, C. (1977) The Dynamics of Rural Poverty in Latin America. *The Journal of Peasant Studies* 4: 206–16.

DeWind, A.W. (1977) Peasants become Miners: the Evolution of Industrial Mining Systems in Peru. Unpublished PhD thesis, Columbia University.

Don, Y. (1977) Industrialization in Advanced Rural Communities: the Israeli Kibbutz. *Sociologia Ruralis* 17, 1–2: 59–74.

Dorfman, A. (1970) *Historia de la industria Argentina.* Buenos Aires.

Duus, S. (1978) *Tobakk og Politikk.* Bergen: Magister artium thesis.

Edholm, F., Harris, O. and Young, K. (1977) Conceptualizing women. *Critique of Anthropology* 3, 9: 101–30.

El Tabaco (1971) Que hay detras de un cigarrillo? Buenos Aires: *Collección problemas de la Liberación.*

Ennew, J., Hirst, P. and Tribe, K. (1977) Peasantry as an Economic Category. *Journal of Peasant Studies* 4, 4: 295–322.

Epstein, T.S. (1973) *South India: Yesterday, Today and Tomorrow.* London: Macmillan.

Erasmus, C.J. (1956) Culture, Structure and Process: the Occurrence and Disappearance of Reciprocal Farm Labour. *Southwestern Journal of Anthropology* 12, 4: 444–69.

Escobar, E. (1972) Fertilización en tabaco tipo 'Criollo Correntino' en relación con rendimiento, calidad y sanidad. IDIA, 294. Corrientes.

Escobar, G.H. (1975) *Principales Suelos del Area Tabacelera.* Corrientes.

Esland, G., Salaman, G. and Speakman, M.A. (1975) *People and Work.* Edinburgh: Holmes McDougall in Association with the Open University Press, Milton Keynes.

Esland, G. and Salaman, G. (1975) Towards a Sociology of Work. In Esland *et. al.*

Esteva, G. (1978) 'Y si los campesinos existen?', *Comercio Exterior* 28. Mexico City.

Evens, T.M.S. (1980) Stigma and Morality in a Kibbutz. In E. Marx (ed.) *A Composite Portrait of Israel.* London: Academic Press.

Figueroa, A. (1982) Production and Market Exchange in Peasant Economies: the Case of the Southern Highlands of Peru. In D. Lehmann (ed.) *Ecology and Exchange in the Andes.* Cambridge: Cambridge University Press.

Finch, J. (1983) *Married to the Job: Wives' Incorporation in Men's Work.* London: George Allen and Unwin.

Firth, R. (1979) Work and Value: Reflections on Ideas of Karl Marx. In S. Wallman (ed.) *Social Anthropology of Work.* London: Academic Press.

Foster, G.M. (1965) Peasant Society and the Image of the 'Limited Good'. *American Anthropologist* 67, 293–315.

Foster-Carter, A. (1978) The Modes of Production Controversy. *New Left Review* 107: 47–78.

Fortes, M. (1969) Introduction. In Jack Goody (ed.) *The Development Cycle in Domestic Groups.* Cambridge.

Franklin, H. (1969) *The European Peasantry – The final phase.* London: Methuen.

Friedmann, H. (1978a) Simple Commodity Production and Wage Labour in the American Plains. *The Journal of Peasant Studies* 6, 1: 71–100.

Friedmann, H. (1978b) World Market, State and Family Farm: Social Bases of Household Production in the Era of Wage Labour. In *Comparative Studies in Society and History* 20, 3: 545–86.

Friedmann, H. (1980) Household Production and the National Economy: Concepts for the Analysis of Agrarian Formations. *The Journal of Peasant Studies* 7, 2: 158–84.

Friedmann, H. (1981) The Family Farm in Advanced Capitalism: Outlines of a Theory of Simple Commodity Production in Agriculture. Paper presented to the Thematic Panel, *Rethinking Domestic Agriculture,* American Sociological Association, Toronto.

Gade, D.W. (1973) Environment and Disease in the Land Use and Settlement of Apurímac Department, Peru. *Geoforum* (Oxford) 16: 37–46.

Galeski, B. (1971) Social Organization and Rural Social Change. In

T. Shanin (ed.) *Peasants and Peasant Societies*. Harmondsworth: Penguin Books.

Galeski, B. (1972) *Basic Concepts of Rural Sociology*. Manchester: Manchester University Press.

Gasson, R. (1980) Roles of Farm Women in England. *Sociologia Ruralis* 20, 3: 163–80.

Giberti, H. (1970) *Historia economica de la ganaderia Argentina*. Buenos Aires: Ediciones Solar/Hachette.

Gjerset, K. (1925) *History of Iceland,* London: George Allen and Unwin.

Glavanis, K.R.G. (1981) Commoditisation and the Egyptian Peasant Household. Paper presented to the Rural Middle East Workshop, Centre for Middle Eastern and Islamic Studies, University of Durham, Durham, England.

Glavanis, K.R.G. (n.d.) Survival Strategies of the Small Peasant Household in an Egyptian Delta Village. Mimeo, unpublished.

Glavanis, K.R.G. and Glavanis, Pandelis M. (1983) *The Political Economy of the Rural Middle East. Current Sociology*. Trend Report 31, 2.

Goodman, D. and Reclift, M. (1981) *From Peasant to Proletarian: Capitalist Development and Agrarian Transitions*. Oxford: Basil Blackwell.

Harik, I. with Randolph, S. (1979) *Distribution of Land, Employment and Income in Rural Egypt,* Special Series on Landlessness and near-Landlessness 5, Ithaca, New York: Rural Development Committee, Cornell University Center for International Studies.

Harris, O. (1982) Labour and Produce in an Ethnic Economy: Northern Potosi, Bolivia. In David Lehmann (ed.) *Ecology and Exchange in the Andes*. Cambridge: Cambridge University Press.

Harrison, M. (1975) Chayanov and the Economics of the Russian Peasantry. *The Journal of Peasant Studies* 2, 4: 389–417.

Harrison, M. (1977) The Peasant Mode of Production in the Work of A.V. Chayanov. *The Journal of Peasant Studies* 4, 4: 323–36.

Harriss, J. (ed.) (1982) *Rural Development: Theories of Peasant Economy and Agrarian Change*. London: Hutchinson University Library.

Hazleton, L. (1977) *Israeli Women*. New York: Simon and Schuster.

Hedley, M.J. (1976) Independent Commodity Production and the Dynamics of Tradition. *Canadian Review of Sociology and Anthropology* 13, 4: 413–19.

Henderson, E. (1819) *Iceland*. Edinburgh: Waugh and Innes.

Hindess, B. and Hirst, P. (1975) *Pre-capitalist Modes of Production*. London: Routledge and Kegan Paul.

Hoskins, W.G. and Finberg, H. (1952) *Devonshire Studies*. London: Cape.

Humphries, J. (1980) Class Struggle and the Persistence of the Working-Class. In H. Amsden (ed.) *The Economics of Women and Work*. Harmondsworth: Penguin Books.

Hunt, D. (1979) Chayanov's Model of Peasant Household Resource Allocation. *The Journal of Peasant Studies* 6, 3: 248–85.

Ikram, K. (1980) *Egypt: Economic Management in a Period of Transition*. Report of a Mission sent to the Arab Republic of Egypt by the World Bank. Baltimore and London: The Johns Hopkins University Press for the World Bank.

Isbell, B.J. (1978) *To Defend Ourselves: Ecology and Ritual in an Andean Village*. Austin: University of Texas Press.

Íslands fátæklingar (1948) 'Verklýðsmál á Íslandi'. *Andvari*. 73 ár.

Iturra, R. (1980) Strategies of Production in a Rural Galician Parish. Unpublished PhD thesis, University of Cambridge.

Jimenez, E. (1983) En andahuaylas la tierra se queda sola: el largo 'exodo' de los campesinos. *El Diaro,* 22 January 1983: 11–12.

Jonsson, B. (1953) 'þættir um kjór verkafólks á sídara hluta 19. aldar'. *Andvari*. 78 ár.

Jonsson, B. (1975) *þurídur formaður,* Reykjavík: Helgafell.

Kaluzynska, E. (1980) 'Wiping the Floor with Theory – a Survey of Writings on Housework'. *Feminist Review* 6.

Kanovsky, E. (1966) *The Economy of the Israeli Kibbutz,* Cambridge, Mass.: Harvard University Press.

Katzenelson-Rubashow, R. (1976) *The Plough Women: Records of the Pioneer Women of Palestine*. (1st edn 1932) Westport Conn.: Hyperion Press.

Kautsky, K. (1899, 1974) *La cuestión agraria*. Paris: Ruedo Iberico.

Koning, N. (1983) Family Farms and Industrial Capitalism. *The Netherlands Journal of Sociology* 19, 1: 29–46.

Kroeber, A.I. (1948) *Anthropology*. New York: Harcourt, Brace and Co.

Laite, J. (1981) *Industrial Development ånd Migrant Labour*. Manchester: Manchester University Press.

Lambert, B. (1977) Bilaterality in the Andes. In Bolton, R. and Mayer, E. (eds) *Andean Kinship and Marriage*. Washington DC: American Anthropological Association.

Lehmann, D. (1982) Introduction: Andean Societies. In D. Lehmann (ed.) *Ecology and Exchange in the Andes*. Cambridge: Cambridge University Press.

Lenin, V.I. (1899) *The Development of Capitalism in Russia*. (revised edns 1908, 1977) Moscow: Progress Publishers.

Leon, D. (1964) *The Kibbutz: a Portrait from Within*. Tel Aviv: World Hashomer Hatzair.

Leviatan, U. (1973) The Industrial Process in Israeli Kibbutzim: Problems and Their Solutions. In M. Curtis and M.S. Chertoff (eds) *Israel: Social Structure and Change*. New Brunswick, NJ: Transaction Books.

Leviatan, U. (1978) Organizational Effects of Managerial Turnover in Kibbutz Production Branches. *Human Relations* 31, 11: 1001–18.

Littlejohn, J. (1963) *Westrigg: the Sociology of a Cheviot Parish*. London: Routledge and Kegan Paul.

Littlewood, P. (1981) Paternalism, Patronage and Clientelist Welfare in Southern Italy. Patrons or Bigshots? *Sociologica Ruralis* 21, 1: 1–18.

Long, N. and J. Dandler (1980) Diversified Household Enterprise and Labour Process in the Andes: a Research Proposal. Mimeo, University of Durham, England.

Long, N. and B.R. Roberts (eds) (1978a) *Peasant Cooperation and Capitalist Expansion in Central Peru*. Austin: University of Texas Press.

Long, N. and B.R. Roberts (1978b) Peasant Cooperation and Underdevelopment in Central Peru. In N. Long and B. Roberts (eds) *Peasant Cooperation and Capitalist Expansion in Central Peru*. Austin: University of Texas.

Long, N. and B.R. Roberts (1984) *Miners, Peasants and Entrepreneurs: Regional Development in the Central Highlands of Peru*. Cambridge: Cambridge University Press.

Luxemburg, R. (1913, 1951) *The Accumulation of Capital*. New York and London: Monthly Review Press.

Mabro, R. (1974) *The Egyptian Economy 1952–72*. Oxford: Clarendon Press.

Macarov, D. (1975) Work without Pay: Work Incentives and Patterns in a Salaryless Environment. *International Journal of Social Economics* 2, 2: 106–14.

Macfarlane, A., Harrisson, S., Jardin, C. (1977) *Reconstructing Historical Communities*. Cambridge: Cambridge University Press.

Mackie, L. and Pattullo, P. (1977) *Women at Work*. London: Tavistock.

Mackintosh, M. (1979) Domestic Labour and the Household. In S. Burman (ed.) *Fit Work for Women*. London: Croom Helm.

Mackintosh, M. (1981) Gender and Economics: the Sexual Division of Labour and the Subordination of Women. In K. Young, C. Wolkowitz and R. McCullogh (eds) *Of Marriage and the Market*. London: CSE Books.

Magnússon, A.A. (1977) *Northern Sphinx*, London: Hurst.

Mann, S. and Dickinson, J. (1978) Obstacles to the Development of a Capitalist Agriculture. *The Journal of Peasant Studies* 5, 4: 466–81.

Mantilla, M.F. (1972) *Cronica historia de la provincia de Corrientes*. Buenos Aires.

Marx, K. (1867, 1954, 1962, 1971) *Capital: A Critique of Political Economy*. Vols 1–3. London: Lawrence and Wishart.

Marx, K. (1971) *Capital*. Moscow: Progress Publishers.

Marx, K. (1972) *Kapitalen*. København: Rhodos.

Marx, K., English edition (1963) *Theories of Surplus value*. Part I. Moscow: Progress Publishers.

Marx, K., English edition (1964) *Pre-capitalist Economic Formations*. London: Lawrence and Wishart.

Mead, D.C. (1967) *Growth and Structural Change in the Egyptian Economy*. Homewood, Illinois: Richard D. Irwin, Inc.

Meillassoux, C. (1972) From Reproduction to Production. In *Economy and Society* 1, 1: 93–105.

Meillassoux, C. (1977) *Mujeres, Graneros y Capitales*. Mexico: Siglo XXI.

Melhuus, M. (1978) *Peasant, Surpluses and Appropriation: an Analysis of the Structural Integration of the Tabacco Growers of Corrientes*. Oslo: Magister artium thesis.

Melhuus, M. and Borchgrevink, T. (1982) Hvem er det som går og går og aldri. Husarbeid–kvinnelighet i praksis? Oslo: Universitetsforlaget.

Miller, J. (1970) A Reformulation of A.V. Chayanov's Theory of the Peasant Economy. *Economic Development and Cultural Change* 18, 2: 219–29.

Ministerio de Agricultura y Ganaderia de la Nación, Grupo de trabajo en sociología Rural (1970) *Investigación sociológica sobre el área tabacalera correntina*. Buenos Aires.

Ministerio de Agricultura y Ganaderia de la Nación, Dirección nacional de economia y sociológía Rural (1973) *Investigación sociológica del area tabacalera Correntina* (Resumen). Buenos Aires.

Mintz, S.W. (1974) The Rural Proletariat and the Problem of Rural Proletarian Consciousness. *The Journal of Peasant Studies* 1, 3: 291–325.

Mitwali, S.H. (1981) 'al-Amn al-Ghitha'i wa'l-Bunyan al-Zira'i al-Misri fi Dau' al-I'timad 'ala'l-Dhat' (Food Security and the Egyptian Agricultural Structure in Light of Self-Sufficiency). Paper presented to the Sixth Annual Conference of Egyptian Economists, Cairo.

Molyneux, M. (1979) Beyond the Domestic Labour Debate. *New Left Review* 116: 3–28.

Mooney, P.H. (1982) Labor Time, Production Time, and Capitalist Development in Agriculture: A Critique of the Mann-Dickinson Thesis. *Sociologia Ruralis* 22, 3/4: 379–92.

Morsy, S.A. (1978) *Gender, Power and Illness in an Egyptian Village*, Ph.D. Thesis, Michigan State University.

Murra, J.V. (1975) 'El control vertical de un máximo de pisos ecológicos en la economia de las sociedades andinas', in *Formaciones Económicas y Políticas del Mundo Andino*. Lima: Instituto de Estudios Peruanos.

Nash, M. (1968) The Social Context of Economic Choice in a Small Society. In E.E. Le Clair, Jr. and H.K. Schneider (eds) *Economic Anthropology*. New York: Holt, Rinehart and Winston.

Newby, H. (1979) *Green and Pleasant Land? Social Change in Rural England*. London: Hutchinson.

Nuñez del Prado Béjar, D. (1972) La reciprocidad como ethos de la cultura quechua. *Allpanchis Phuturinqa* 4: 135–54.

Oakley, A. (1974) *The Sociology of Housework*. Oxford: Martin Robertson.

Ólafsson, E. and Pálsson, B. (1975) *Travels in Iceland*. Reykjavík: Örn og Örlygur.

Ortiz, R.M. (1971) *Historia económica de la Argentina* Tomo I y II. Buenos Aires: PlusUltra.

Pahl, J. (1980) Patterns of Money Management within Marriage. *Journal of Social Policy* 9, 3: 313–35.

Pahl, R.E. (1980) Employment, Work and the Domestic Division of Labour. *International Journal of Urban and Regional Research* 4, 1: 1–19.

Papadakis, J.S. (1948) *Corrientes*. IDIA-numero Especial.

Paré, L. (1977) *El Proletariado agricola en Mexico*. Mexico: Siglo XXI.

Patnaik, U. (1979) Neo-populism and Marxism: the Chayanovian

View of the Agrarian Question and its Fundamental Fallacy. *The Journal of Peasant Studies* 6, 4: 375–420.

Perelman, M. (1979) Obstacles to the Development of a Capitalist Agriculture: A Comment on Mann and Dickinson. *The Journal of Peasant Studies,* 7, 1: 119–21.

Provincia de Corrientes, La secretaria de Planeamiento. (1974) *Corrientes.*

Ramos, M.P. (1972) *Etapas de acumulación y alianzas de clases en la Argentina (1930–70).* Buenos Aires: Siglo XXI.

Redfield, R. (1956) *The Little Community. Peasant Society and Culture.* Chicago: University of Chicago Press.

Richards, A. (1980) Egypt's Agriculture in Trouble. *MERIP Reports* 84. Washington D.C.: Middle East Research & Information Project, Inc.

Richards, A. (1981) Peasant Differentiation and Politics in Sadat's Egypt. Paper presented to the American Political Science Association meeting, New York City.

Richards, A. and Martin, P. (1981) Rural Social Structure and the Agricultural Labour Market: Sharqiyya Evidence and Policy Implications. Cairo Agricultural Development Systems Project, Arab Republic of Egypt Ministry of Agriculture – University of California.

Richards, A.I. and Robin, J. (1975) *Some Elmdon Families,* Elmdon.

Roberts, B. (1978) The Bases of Industrial Cooperation in Huancayo. In N. Long and B. Roberts (eds) *Peasant Cooperation and Capitalist Expansion in Central Peru.* Austin: University of Texas Press.

Roberts, P. (1984) The Sexual Politics of Labour in Western Nigeria and Hausa Niger in K. Young *et al.* (ed.) *Serving Two Masters.* London: Routledge and Kegan Paul.

Rofman, A.B. and Romero, A. (1973) *Sistema socioeconómico y estructura regional en la Argentina.* Buenos Aires: Amorrortu.

Roseberry, W. (1978) Peasants as Proletarians. *Critique of Anthropology* 3, 11: 3–18.

Sanchez, R. (1982) The Andean Economic System and Capitalism. In D. Lehmann (ed.), *Ecology and Exchange in the Andes.* Cambridge: Cambridge University Press.

Schildkrout, E. (1979) Women's Work and Children's Work: Variations among Moslems in Kano. In Wallman S. (ed) *The Social Anthropology of Work.* London: Academic Press.

Scott, C. (1976) Peasants, Proletarianization and the Articulation of

Modes of Production: the Case of Sugar-cane Cutters in Northern Peru, 1940–69. *The Journal of Peasant Studies* 3, 3: 321–42.

Servolin, C. (1972) L'absorption de l'agriculture dans le mode de production capitaliste. In C. Servolin *et al.* (eds) *L'Univers politique des paysans dans la France contemporaine.* Paris: Librairie Armand Colin and Fondation Nationale des Sciences Politiques.

Shanin, T. (1971) *Peasants and Peasant Societies.* Harmondsworth: Penguin Books.

Shanin, T. (1973) The Nature and Logic of the Peasant Economy. *The Journal of Peasant Studies* 1, 1 and 1, 2: 63–80 and 186–206.

Shanin, T. (ed.) (1984) *Marx and the Russian Road.* London: Routledge and Kegan Paul.

Shatil, J. (1966) The Economic Efficiency of the Kibbutz. *New Outlook* 9, 7: 33–9.

Shepher, I. (1972) *The Significance of Work Roles in the Social System of a Kibbutz.* PhD thesis, University of Manchester.

Shepher, I. (1980) Social Boundaries of a Kibbutz. In E. Marx (ed.) *A Composite Portrait of Israel.* London: Academic Press.

Shokeid, M. (1971) *The Dual Heritage.* Manchester: Manchester University Press.

Shur, S. (1972) *Hakibbutz Vehachevrat Israelit: Rekah Vebe'ayot* (The Kibbutz and Israeli Society: Background and Problems). Tel Aviv: Kibbutz Artzi.

Skar, H.O. (1982) *The Warm Valley People: Duality and Land Reform among Quechua Indians of Highland Peru.* Oslo–Bergen–Tromsø: Universitetsforlaget.

Skar, S.L. (1979) The Use of the Public/Private Framework in the Analysis of Egalitarian Societies: The Case of a Quechua Community in Highland Peru. *Women's Studies International Quarterly* 2: 449–60.

Skar, S.L. (1980) *Quechua Women and Agrarian Reform in the Pincos Valley: A Case from the Southern Highlands of Peru.* Thesis for the Institute of Social Anthropology, University of Oslo.

Slutzky, D. (1974) *Diagnostico de la estructura social de la Región Nordeste Argentina. Tenencia y distribución de la tierra en la región NEA.* Buenos Aires: CFI.

Smith, G.A. (1984) Confederations of Households: Extended Domestic Enterprises in City and Country, in N. Long and B. Roberts, *Miners, Peasants and Entrepreneurs.* Cambridge: Cambridge University Press.

Smith, P. (1969) *Politics and Beef in Argentina. Patterns of Conflict and Change.* New York: Columbia University Press.

Smith, P. (1978) Domestic Labour and Marx's Theory of Value. In A.M. Wolpe and A. Kohn (eds) *Feminism and Materialism.* London: Routledge and Kegan Paul.

Spiro, M.E. (1957) The Sabras and Zionism: a Study in Personality and Ideology. *Social Problems* 5, 2: 100–10.

Stauth, G. (1979) Dissolution and Peripheralization of the Small Peasantry: The Case of the Fellahs of the Nile Delta. Unpublished paper.

Stern, B. (1965) *The Kibbutz That Was.* Washington DC: Public Affairs Press.

Stølen, K.A. (1976) *Santa Cecilia. En analyse av bondeøkonomi og samfunn i Nord-Argentina.* Oslo: Magister artium thesis.

Strathern, M. (1982) *Kinship at the Core.* Cambridge: Cambridge University Press.

Szereszewski, R. (1968) *Essays on the Structure of the Jewish Economy in Palestine and Israel.* Jerusalem: The Maurice Falk Institute for Economic Research in Israel, and Israel Universities Press.

Szyliowicz, J.S. (1973) *Education and Modernization in the Middle East.* Ithaca and London: Cornell University Press.

Talmon-Garber, Y. and Cohen, E. (1964) Collective Settlements in the Negev. In J. Ben-David (ed) *Agricultural Planning and Village Community in Israel.* Paris: UNESCO.

Talmon, Y. (1972) Secular Asceticism: Patterns of Ideological Change. In her *Family and Community in the Kibbutz,* Cambridge, Mass.: Harvard University Press.

Taussig, M. (1978) Peasant Economics and the Development of Capitalist Agriculture in the Cauca Valley, Colombia. In *Latin American Perspectives* 18,5,3: 62–90.

Taussig, M.T. (1980) *The Devil and Commodity Fetishism in South America.* Chapel Hill: The University of North Carolina Press.

Taylor, J. (1979) *From Modernisation to Modes of Production,* London: Macmillan.

Tiger, L. and Shepher, J. (1975) *Women in the Kibbutz.* New York: Harcourt Brace Jovanovich.

Troll, C. (1968) The Cordilleras of the Tropical Americas. Aspects of Climatic, Phyto-geographical and Agrarian Ecology. In C. Troll (ed.), *Geo-ecology of the Mountainous Regions of the Tropical Americas.* Bonn: University of Bonn Geographical Institute.

Vergopoulos, K. (1978) Capitalism and Peasant Productivity. *The Journal of Peasant Studies* 5,4: 446–65.

Verkakvennafélagið Framsókn. 1964, *50 ára Afmælisrit 1914–64*, Rejkjavík.

Villaneuva, J. (1972) El origen de la industrialización Argentina. *Desarollo Economico*, 12, 47.

Wall, R. (ed.) (1983) *Family Forms in Historic Europe*. Cambridge: Cambridge University Press.

Wallman, S. (ed.) (1979a) *The Social Anthropology of Work* London: Academic Press.

Wallman, S. (1979b) Introduction. In *The Social Anthropology of Work*. London: Academic Press.

Webster, S. (1972) An Indigenous Quechua Community in Exploitation of Multiple Ecological Zones, *Actas y Memorias del XXXIX Congreso Internacional de Americanistas, Lima* Vol. 3: 174–83.

Weingrod, A. (1966) *Reluctant Pioneers*, Ithaca: Cornell University Press.

Wershow, H.J. (1973) Ageing in the Israeli Kibbutz: Growing Old in a Mini-Socialist Society. *Jewish Social Studies* 35, 2: 141–48.

West, J. (1980) A Political Economy of the Family in Capitalism: Women, Reproduction and Wage Labour. In T. Nichols (ed.) *Capital and Labour: A Marxist Primer*. Glasgow: Fontana Paperbacks.

Whitehead, A. (1981) I'm Hungry Mum: The Politics of Domestic Budgeting', in K. Young *et al. Of Marriage and the Market*. London: CSE Books.

Williams, W.M. (1963) *A West Country Village: Ashworthy*. London: Routledge and Kegan Paul.

Wolf, E.R. (1955) 'Types of Latin American Peasantry: a Preliminary Discussion. *American Anthropologist*, 57, 3: 452–71.

Wolf, E.R. (1966) *Peasants*. New Jersey: Prentice-Hall.

Wolpe, H. (1972) Capitalism and Cheap Labour-Power in South Africa: From Segregation to Apartheid. *Economy and Society* 1,4: 425–56.

Wolpe, H. (1975) The Theory of Internal Colonialism: The South African Case. In I. Oxaal, T. Barnett, and D. Booth (eds) *Beyond the Sociology of Development*. London: Routledge and Kegan Paul.

Wolpe, H. (1980) Introduction. In Wolpe (ed.) *The Articulation of Modes of Production*. London: Routledge and Kegan Paul.

Wood, C.H. (1981) 'Structural Changes and Household Strategies: A Conceptual Framework for the Study of Rural Migration'. *Human Organization* 40, 4: 338–43.

Zureik, E.T. (1979) *The Palestinians in Israel: a Study in Internal Colonialism.* London: Routledge and Kegan Paul.

Name Index

Subject Index